FRENCH PAINTING

TWENTIETH CENTURY
PAINTERS

Library of Congress Catalog Card Number 58-9163

© ÉDITIONS PIERRE TISNÉ, PARIS, 1958

PRINTED IN FRANCE

BERNARD DORIVAL

TWENTIETH CENTURY PAINTERS

PAINTERS

FROM CUBISM TO ABSTRACT ART

Translated by
ARNOLD ROSIN

UNIVERSE BOOKS, INC. - NEW YORK
ÉDITIONS PIERRE TISNÉ - PARIS

A pictorial revolution, without precedent in the Western world since the Renaissance, took place principally in France during the last years of the nineteenth and the first years of the twentieth century: non-realistic aesthetics were substituted for the realistic which had been honored for four centuries. For the first time in four hundred years a decorative and monumental conception of painting effected a counteroffensive against easel-picture painting which opened a window to the outside world; and at the same time that the human figure ceased to be the center of the painting, man, renouncing being the measure of all things in painting, gave himself a new image of Man in his pictorial creations where the old values of rational humanism had made way for new values—for lack of a better name we shall call them "ahumanist." In the face of such an overturning of values, what would be the reactions of those who came to art after the originators of this kind of painting? Would they refuse it or accept it? And, in this case, would it be to repeat it or continue it, to imitate it literally or push it further in the same direction? And to what measure, with what degree of opposition or adherence, would they pronounce themselves in favor of it or against it? These are the problems to which pictorial painting has given its answers after a period of almost half a century and of which a rapid survey will be the object of this work. In it we will bring to mind, each in turn, summarily, and even schematically for the sake of clarity, the different forms of the rather general reaction against avant-garde painting which developed from 1919 to about 1939, then its contemporary start again in a big way dating from the Occupation, and the consequences that it brought about since 1945: exasperation on the part of some people in regard to non-realistic painting, and the attitude of others who looked upon abstract painting with honor and placed its value very high.

5

The Advancement
of
Naïve Painting

F the outstanding fact in the history of painting between the two World Wars is the multiform and universal refusal of avant-garde searchings and, singularly, those of Cubism, the various methods of this opposition are of very different natures.
It is against the non-realistic painting of the Cubists that the artists faithful to the accepted traditions of figurative art, revolted and turned again to the imitation of visual reality. Thus a Neo-Realism came into being and prospered, cultivated successfully by two generations of artists. Other painters, on the contrary, accepting certain deformations or at least certain interpretations of Nature proposed by the Cubists, revolted, on the other hand, against their intellectualism and, calling for the aesthetics of the Fauves as well as for those of the first champions of Expressionism and their precursors, advocated an art of subjectivity, of irrationalism, of magic, less bothered by formal problems than animated by a conception of painting as a means of knowledge. There follows a new flowering of Expressionism whose champions will see their aims brought to fruition by those younger than themselves just before the war of 1939, an explosion of Surrealism prepared by such movements as the Dada or the "*onirique*" art of a Chirico or a Chagall, and continued by different successors. In all tendencies, however labelled or named, it was the same hostility in regard to pure painting and, in spite of appearances, the same reactionary attitude, belonging, if not spiritually, at least plastically, to that of the Neo-Realists.
But aside from these two forms of opposition to Cubism, there exists a third which cannot be placed on the same plane—namely, the art of certain people who have been sometimes dubbed as "Neo-Primitives," sometimes as "Sunday Painters," sometimes as "Popular Painters of Reality," sometimes as "Painters of Instinct," even, as I have called them myself "Painters of Instinct and of Heart," or, as they have been called in a much nicer way by Wilhelm Uhde, as "Painters of the Sacred Heart," when he wishes perhaps to call them simply other than the more banal "The Naïfs." Without pretending to name them all, nor even to enumerate as many as Anatole Jakovsky has in his book *Les Peintres Naïfs*, let us at least point out among them, in addition to the brilliant Henri Rousseau (1844-1910), André Bauchant, Camille Bombois, Dominique Peyronnet (1872-1943), Séraphine (1864-1942) and Louis Vivin (1861-1936), as well as, among those who later achieved fame, Aristide Caillaud, Louis Déchelette, Jean Eve, Jean Fous, Jules Lefranc, René Rimbert, Vivancos, etc.

That this expression of the anti-Cubist reaction occupies a very special place is proved by several facts: in the first place, these men who do not belong to the same generation and who are not known among themselves have never made up a group, nor even taken part in a common movement. They painted for their own pleasure, quite often without any thought of exhibiting their work, and it was not they who were grouped in any sort of way but rather it was their admirers, their critics and their historians who brought them together because of their fortuitous and spiritual affinities. On the other hand, they never entertained the slightest idea of opposing Cubism whose existence for the most part they did not even suspect. And finally, they are all part of a long tradition, of several centuries, of the painting of men like Braque, Picasso, Gris and as old perhaps as the art of painting itself: the tradition of a popular and naïve art which, in the face of scientific art, affirms itself from one age to another with the same irrefutable evidence. To limit ourselves merely to our own country France, and more so to the very province of Savoie, all those who have visited, at the foot of Mont Cenis, the chapels devoted to Saint Sebastian in the village of Lanslevillard and to Saint Anthony in that of Bessans, know that, in this place alone, naïve artists—local inhabitants or travelers en route for Italy, it really makes little difference which—at the end of the fifteenth century and at the beginning of the sixteenth, had created works of pleasant clumsiness in repeating awkwardly the formulas employed some hundred years before by the masters of transalpine or cisalpine art. And during the last lusters of the seventeenth and the first of the eighteenth century, how many admirable artisans have reinterpreted the indiscreet models of virtuosity of the scientific Baroque painting which they caught a glimpse of through the more or less faithful engravings, or knew through specimens as rare as they were mediocre which were imported from Italy or even from Austria. (1) Popular painting is a permanent fact, that of simple people who, working for others as simple as themselves, brought to their work deep feeling and affection and all their humility to make up for their lack of scientific knowledge thus translating in their own way the more skilful models.

The problem presented to us here is not to explain the existence of this naïve painting, permanent as scientific painting, whose exquisite and touching moonlit reflection it is; but rather to take into account its success at the eve and immediately after the war of 1914, or more exactly its advancement to the level of art— of a major art, an adult art, of an art equal in dignity, in quality, even in financial value, of a scientific art in a name which has always been held in scorn. This favor whose manifestations are innumerable since 1914, and even since 1908, the year Picasso and his friends, artists, critics, art lovers and art dealers held in the Bateau-Lavoir atelier a certain banquet in honor of Rousseau which has become famous.

In fact, since this date there has been much proof everywhere of naïve art. The year 1911 saw the retrospective exhibition of the work of Rousseau at the Salon des Indépendants and the publication by Wilhelm Uhde of his *Henri Rousseau, le Douanier*, published by Figuière, followed in 1913 by a special issue of *Les Soirées de Paris* devoted to Rousseau which echoed the success of the exhibition held at the Galerie Bernheim in 1912. Then, beginning in 1920, the number of books on him increased. Among their authors were experienced, wide-awake art lovers such as Roch Grey (1922), Hermann Kolle (1922), Philippe Soupault (1927), André Salmon (1927), Adolphe Basler (1927), Christian Zervos (1927). These masterpieces made their way into the most famous collections in Europe and America, and even into the museums, even that of the Louvre to which Jacques Doucet had bequeathed in 1936 *The Snake Charmer* by Henri Rousseau.

In his steps a pleiad of naïve painters, good or bad, set out on a path of ephemeral or lasting glory: the craze hardly lasts—about 1920 Boyer was sought after by the highest Parisian society; but Wilhelm Uhde, that untiring seeker, discovered

8

HENRI ROUSSEAU, LE DOUANIER – THE WEDDING – 1905 - (1,62;1,14)
MADAME WALTER COLLECTION, PARIS

Séraphine.   The Galerie des Quatre-Chemins held an exhibition of her work in 1927, and Uhde himself wrote an article on her in 1931 in the September issue of *Formes*. In February of the previous year Joseph Delteil introduced Bombois to his readers in the same revue; and already in 1927 Max Jacob had written the preface of the exhibition the Galerie Percier had organized at that time of the small exquisite pictures of René Rimbert, while the shrewdest collector that Paris probably had at that period, Roger Dutilleul, the "discoverer" (in the etymological sense of the word) of Picasso, Braque and Modigliani, acquired a rare ensemble of the canvases of Vivin and Bauchant.   Collective manifestations set the stamp favoring naïve painting, among them the ones held at the Galerie des Quatre-Chemins in 1928, at the Galerie Druet in 1929, at the Galerie Bernheim Jeune in 1932, at the Galerie des Beaux-Arts in 1933, at the Salle Royale in 1937, then at the Kunsthaus in Zurich, and finally at the Museum of Modern Art of New York in 1938.

Public enthusiasm in favor of this new art was not stopped by the war; the post-war period finally confirmed it.   In 1944 the Musée National d'Art Moderne

HENRI ROUSSEAU, LE DOUANIER – PUBLIC GARDEN – BUHRLE COLLECTION, ZURICH

organized an exhibition in homage to Rousseau in celebration of the centenary of his birth, while the Galerie Charpentier, one of the most traditional in Paris, dared to present an important collection of Bauchant's work in 1949 which was proof at last that the bourgeois French public had finally accepted naïve painting. New names were brought to attention. After Rousseau, Vivin (the object of a magnificent exhibition organized by the Gallery Bing in 1948), Séraphine (whose work was officially selected by France for the first São Paulo Biennale in 1951), Bauchant, Bombois, Peyronnet, Rimbert, Eve, Lefranc, art lovers and art critics alike discovered a whole generation of naïve painters: Caillaud, Déchelette, Jean Fous, Vivancos, etc. The continued popularity of this art was therefore not the effect of a something new which had suddenly become fashionable, but rather the expression of a permanent public need. And the question one may very well ask is: how does one account for the audience that this art attracted?

Several answers, all very different, may be given. More than a popular taste of a rather doubtful standard, one can cite, for example, this probing of the irrational in the creative art which simultaneously urges all our contemporaries to examine

11

paintings by children and insane people. Or still this taste for purity, for spontaneity, for a virginal quality which—siding them with Baudelaire's belief that *genius is childhood found again at will*—has turned their interest towards the work of these people who have remained children too long—people more often defined as rather simple-minded individuals. Or even this affinity (shared at that time by sociologists, ethnologists, historians of every kind and art collectors of folklore) with the collective expression of the "popular soul"; or finally this deep-felt need to return to the sources which the bearded fanatics in David's atelier, from pre-Phidian Greece to Gauguin and the Nabis, inspired in the successive generations of the nineteenth century—namely, a more and more demanding desire for archaic or exotic art reputed to be raw and direct, naïve, more authentic than that of advanced periods and peoples. What a godsend for this mania of primitive art in the full flower of the twentieth century, of primitives so primitive—or at least felt as such—as the artists of the Middle Ages or those of French Equatorial Africa whose productions of exquisite and touching beauty were discovered during these very same years. But if all these questions we have asked are legitimate, they do not, however, it seems to me, give the answer—the very answer I find elsewhere when I notice the fact that the "discoverers" of naïve painting have been quite rightly the champions of Cubism or analogous movements, as well as the first art lovers and critics. In fact, it was in Picasso's atelier of the Bateau-Lavoir, and nowhere else, that the legendary banquet in Rousseau's honor was held. It was Delaunay himself, passionately interested in the art of the master of Plaisance, who through his mother purchased the *Snake Charmer*. Then too, it was Guillaume Apollinaire who, to honor the loss of the great artist, wrote several poems of fervent admiration, a fair payment for the painting that Henri Rousseau had dedicated to him as well as to Marie Laurencin, called *Poet and his Muse*. It was Max Jacob who discovered René Rimbert, it was Wilhelm Uhde who during the same time that he posed for Picasso became fascinated by the paintings of Séraphine. It was the excellent painter Serge Férat who, while adhering to Cubism, collected, as did his cousin Grey, the finest of Rousseau's compositions. Was this their love of paradox, of non-conformity, of the undiscovered? Perhaps. But not only nor even essentially; for what attracted their interest in Rousseau's art and that of those around him was simply the fact that in it they found the legitimization and the antidote of Cubism.

That the painting of the "Naïfs" "authorises" the searchings of the Cubists and by its example firmly justifies their formulas is proved by the fact that Rousseau and his fellow artists practised simultaneously in their naïve candor, one would be tempted to say, certain processes that Braque, Picasso and their comrades had quite rightly elaborated. For example, let us take a look at the *View of Notre-Dame de Paris* painted by Vivin, offered by Mademoiselle Uhde to the Musée National d'Art Moderne in the name of her brother and reproduced here on page 14. What do we see first of all? On first glance it seems that Vivin has represented, one by one, all the stones which make up the wall of the quay bordering the Seine. Not that he had seen them; for if we were to stand on the quay and resting our elbows on the ledge of the wall, gaze at the opposite bank of the river we would see nothing but masonry— a stone masonry in which the stones themselves disappear; and Vivin has quite clearly seen nothing else. But he does not paint at all what he sees; he paints what

12

he knows, and he knows that this wall which he perceives opposite, on the other side of the Seine river, is constructed like any other wall—namely, by placing stones one on top of the other. He feels, therefore, no scruples in painting what his experience and his mind have taught him rather than what his senses reveal. Far from being sensorial his realism is intellectual and from this fact joins that of the Braques and the Picassos who themselves represented in their paintings the exterior world as they knew it. But here suddenly this truth is made manifest : their attitude is not, as this or that person claims, the result of some hypercultivated bourgeois Byzantinism intellectual to excess, but rather, quite the contrary, from Nature itself, spontaneous Nature, Nature as it is presented to us when it is not educated, not deformed by secular and accepted visual effects. The innate movement of plastic expression is not that of some academy seen in the light of ten generations of teachers, nor even that of the Impressionists who, like the Elstir of Proust, forces itself—at what cost of work!—to loosen this *aggregate of reasoning that we call "vision"* to arrive at pure vision, virginal vision, the raw visual sensation; but it is that of the Cubists because it is the same as that of simple-minded people and of children. (²)

And so here in his painting *View of Notre-Dame de Paris* Vivin proceeds in the same manner as the Cubists when he represents the cathedral from two entirely different angles. In the same way that Braque, Picasso and their comrades show in their paintings, for example, a figure represented full face and at the same time profile, so here Vivin has associated two representations of the building which he could not see simultaneously. He has looked at the nave, the transept and the choir from the Quai Saint-Michel, the façade from the parvis; and pivoting it in a ninety-degree angle so that it lines up with the nave, he has juxtaposed in his painting these two successive images. This, once for all, was to silence those who denounced the complex points of view dear to the Cubists as the height of artifice and the invention completely opposed to Nature. It was also to establish the purely conventional character of habit which, since the Renaissance, desired that everything represented in a painting be seen from the same angle by an immobile observer, and to give to painting this liberty of observation—or of representation—which had ruled supreme during the Middle Ages and also during the great periods of art.

But—and the fact is so obvious that it is hardly necessary here to insist—the methods used by the naïve painters in their works were neither because of the same reasons, nor as a result of the same searchings as the Cubists. If the multiplicity of the point of view is for them both a resource in searching for a total and objective representation and a means of respecting the two dimensions essential to the painting, far from being for them a manifestation of the horror the Cubists felt before traditional perspective, it is only the natural consequence of a lack of knowledge and an effort to conceal it. And yet in spite of this, if they represent the forms of the exterior world such as they know them, it is the fault of seeing and translating them as if they would have seen them. This lack of science, together with such clumsiness, is for them what the efforts to find something adequate to the pictorial ambitions of their métier is to the Cubists: each, in itself, is a definite role and consequently has definite results. Thus what is will, consciousness, reflection for the one is the exact opposite for the other—namely, the spontaneous application of pictorial means which they could not help using.

Not that their art is all ingenuous—far from it! It is not even certain that the decorative character which is frequently evident is involuntary; and one is no doubt

closer to the human truth of these artists when one considers that, for example, this allure of magnificently mural tapestry which is so striking in many "exotic" compositions of Rousseau was not something that the artist gave in spite of himself, nor was it a happy finish, but simply because he found beauty confusing and found genuine pleasure in bringing it into his work.

But it is no less true that the means he utilised in order to achieve what he did were employed instinctively because he had no others to turn to. An inextricable mixture of felt necessities and half-conscious inventions, an indissoluble combination of intentions and infused science, of spontaneity and tricks, naïve painting had about it an air of grace—one can almost say it is a quality of grace—that is unknown to Cubist painting. And so is it not astonishing that Cubist painting saw in itself not only proof of the justifications of experiments, but also and above all the realization of its dreams, resulting from spontaneity and inspiration of this ideal towards which from its manner of thinking, its lucidity and efforts, it spread a bridge of a sort of paradise regained which had never been lost and perhaps who knows? which had been promised. In this mirror of innocence it dared to contemplate its charac-

14

teristics which it had never even dared to imagine, and as a result, felt a nostalgia and a gratitude. Rousseau loved this painting for what it resembled in his own and for all that it differed so essentially. It was at the same time his encouragement, his despair, his reward and his peace. It was his conscience—good or bad; it stimulated and refreshed him. And because it played so many roles in regard to himself, it was dear to him and he made it dear to its art lovers—and thus it conquered a limited audience at first, then a greater one, and finally a much greater one than was seen by some as merely the opposite of Cubism which they had become tired of themselves and to which they had never ceased to be hostile. Thus it imposed itself on everyone and conquered in the modern contemporary world a special, natural and yet paradoxical place, but beneficial, sane and happy (and this in spite of the inevitable exploitation of false naïve painters and odious pretenders of clumsiness in art).

CAMILLE BOMBOIS — CHARTRES — (0,73; 0,60) PRIVATE COLLECTION, PARIS

ANDRÉ BAUCHANT – THE CREATION OF THE WORLD – (0,60; 0,92) PRIVATE COLLECTION, PARIS

There is no doubt that the reasons already given would have been insufficient to grant such a place to naïve painting if among its exponents there was not at least one man of genius—namely, Henri Rousseau, as well as others whose artistic sensitivity was equally as rare. If we place Séraphine among the naïve painters, it is merely as a matter of custom, for her art which is truly admirable belongs less to that of the popular naïve painters and more to that of simple-minded visionaries—in the end she fell victim to insanity and shared the same follies. There is no great relationship, in fact, between the perception and the métier of men like Vivin, Bombois, Bauchant, Peyronnet—and even Henri Rousseau—on the one hand, and those of Séraphine, this inspired creator of fantastic-shaped bouquets ending in plumed egrets and whose leaves are decorated in such a way that they are rich psychiatric symbols. Now, there is nothing clumsy in her painting, not even the thinness which so often characterizes naïve painting and which is no doubt the natural consequence of both their conscience and their application. Hers, on the contrary, is marked by a quality of wholesomeness and decision. Far from being translated into precious forms as is quite common in naïve painting with its precise

16

and rather soft touch, the tone is established by spots and heightened by little accents of different color. Thus the chromatic quality of her work brings out the vibrating contrast. Made up essentially of black and white, the colors give to the painting a sumptuous quality which fits extremely well with the decorative arrangement of the selected forms. Covering the entire painted surface and, at the same time, not leaving any empty space, Séraphine paints ornamental foliage and arabesques which fuse harmoniously. The hedges and wreaths bring out not only a strangely troubling and fantastic allure but have an extraordinary decorative power as well. A surprising fact: the ornamental luxury which we see in her paintings makes us immediately think of Oriental fabrics and of Chinese embroidery, though this humble housekeeper had never seen these things in such a place as Senlis. Moreover, the decoration is charged with magic which stamps the delirant imagination of such a person as Séraphine. On the petals of her flowers this expert painted stars of percussive and deep stare, like the lunula of butterflies.

This visionary magic is nothing strange to the art of Henri Rousseau of which, however, he merely defines one aspect. Much greater, in fact, than the rather monotonous work of Séraphine, the magical quality of Rousseau's art has its source in many inspirations. If he is scarcely interested in still life or flowers, he is interested, on the contrary, in portraits which he paints from the living model *(Portrait of Jarry, Self-Portrait)* or from imagination *(Portrait of Pierre Loti)*. Sometimes inclined to paint historical subjects *(The Centenary of Independence, War)* he has no less looked down upon *genre* painting and to celebrate popular customs of contemporary France he treated the subject with a poetical wholesomeness *(The Wedding, The Cart of Père Juniet, The Gunners)*. The same characteristic is noticed in his landscapes. Sometimes they are interpretations of real places seen in the Paris suburbs and painted in a meticulous way that does not exclude a definite freshness because he had deep love for his art. Sometimes they are purely imaginary and take on a symbolic and allegorical quality *(Summer)*. Thus there is not much separation between his inventive landscapes and his exotic works which perhaps make up the rarest irreplacable activity of the painter Rousseau.

Had he taken part in the unfortunate Mexican expedition which he liked to tell stories about? And if so did he come back with a nostalgia for the discovery of a faraway tropical world? One should not take him too seriously, all the more so since his virgin forests with their opulent plant life evoke the greenhouses of the Acclimatization Gardens rather than Mexican flora, or more accurately perhaps taken from the illustrations for the novels of Jules Verne published by Hetzel. This may have been the springboard for his imagination, but the inspiration for his *Snake Charmer* probably derives from the story of her recent trip to India which Delaunay's mother told him and which no doubt fascinated him. Whether transfigured memories or simply inventions of his mind, his exotic work has a quality almost of magical poetry. This is especially true when the introduction of an unwonted detail, often absurd—like the canopy on which the nude Yadwigha is sprawled out in *Yadwiga's Dream*—adds an unexpected, arbitrary and gratuitous note which merely increases this element of mystery. And, as in the case of Séraphine, both the magical and the decorative quality are one. Conceived in two dimensions only, these exotic compositions of trees, lianas, ferns, reeds, run and wind on the surface of the canvas with a measured and exact lavishness which calls to mind Romanesque image makers. Incorporated in a flat world, animals and people emphasize the decorative quality of the painting brought to such happy perfection. Standing before such masterpieces as the *Monkeys in the Forest, The Hungry Lion, The Promenade*, we are reminded of the famous frescoes in the Palace of the Popes in Avignon. Here clumsiness disappears with its meticulous brushwork; the quality of ignorance which so often characterizes Rousseau's métier is forgotten, blurred by the limitations of a rather myopic vision and a too analytical spirit which brings him round to the ordinary without, however, sacrificing any detail.

But whether visionary or realistic, decorative or exact, on a large or a small scale, Rousseau's entire work has essentially the same qualities: first of all honest drawing whose purity derives, as in Quattrocento painting, from the passion of understanding, of definition, of knowledge; exactness of local colors, always handsome, tasteful and generous—even when it is a question of blacks and whites; perfection of execution which again is result of loving care; enamel-like quality of the "*matière*" (painted surface) worked over for a long period of time, thickly painted yet subtle, without a flaw. It shows a wonderful compositional control in which a pleasing impression and a calm majesty result from a happy combination of large verticals and waving horizontals. And finally, it has the absolute sincerity of an art which is the constant creation and enterprise of a man's whole being—a man passionately devoted to his art, finding in painting a refuge from the drab mediocrity of his pitiful existence and a means of satisfying his dreams and even more a reason for living. Few works have a greater stamp of truth and necessity than his. Few works show such passion in the service of similar gifts. In spite of—or rather because of—his limitations, his insufficiencies, his intellectual and technical awkwardness, Rousseau's production, the supreme and unequalled expression of naïve painting, asserts itself with such qualities that no one is astonished to see his *Snake Charmer* in the center of one of the rooms of the Musée du Jeu de Paume filled with masterpieces by Cézanne, Gauguin, Seurat, van Gogh, Redon. Everyone will remember his *La Bohémienne Endormie* which was one of the finest paintings exhibited at the Orangerie des Tuileries in 1955 on the occasion of the exhibition of masterpieces from American public art collections. Those who mocked him no longer laughed: such confrontation was conclusive, and *le douanier* Rousseau, with his multiple work which nevertheless formed one impressive ensemble, takes front place today among the great creators of French paintings at the end of the nineteenth and at the beginning of the twentieth century.

Beside this master other exponents of naïve art necessarily become figures of lesser greatness, which nevertheless does not prevent them—quite the contrary—from representing even better than he and defining more completely a kind of painting which he, Rousseau, transcends. More than in his work, the limitations of Vivin and Bauchant are quite evident in their own: their thinness of drawing which is always rather dry, their awkwardness and insufficiencies. Insistence and reminders which are too obvious in their painting are merely the most apparent signs of a certain deficiency of vision and mind. But, on the contrary, what qualities in the color, in the treatment and in the composition! Aware only of the locality, they see it so correctly and render it so well that all at once they have translated the light itself. Fresh and pure air surrounds the monuments Vivin likes to paint in grays and yellows and in Bauchant's landscapes in which he situates his historical scenes or installs his

18

SÉRAPHINE LOUIS – THE
TREE OF PARADISE –
ABOUT 1929 – (1,95;
1,29) MUSÉE NATIONAL
D'ART MODERNE, PARIS

bouquets.   Solid and precise, these forms are enveloped everywhere with atmosphere and blend with the sky which, in order always to be inevitably blue, is of such a fine azure color and so transparent that one sometimes thinks of Fouquet's paintings and sometimes of Corot's made during his stay in Rome.   The economical but full-painted surface which incorporates and spreads this light, increases the light firmness of the form and already gives to these paintings a definitely decorative character—the same carefully finished quality that one finds in any furniture piece of a skilled and conscientious artisan.   It is this ornamental characteristic, heightened by other qualities, and above all the composition.   Placed in a very ordinary manner—and of necessity —front view or full profile, forms and figures are arranged in an honest way which harmonizes with the very simple, even schematic order which is made more obvious by the rather surplus lines of the drawing.   Thus Vivin's landscapes, Bauchant's bouquets have—like so many primitive paintings—a decorative allure which is in no way strange to the finest results of Bombois and Peyronnet.   Take for example Peyronnet's *Château de Reine Blanche* or Bombois's *Pont de Chablis*, both at the Musée National d'Art Moderne, as precise and as large as a page of the Limbourg brothers with their decorative display.

The qualities of this naïve art are as striking as their deficiencies remain evident; and thus appears even more manifestly the interest of a painting whose advancement (on condition that one does not make more of it than there is and that one firmly establishes the point of departure between authentic naïveté and that pretended by *genre* exploiters) is one of the most sympathetic signs of the evolution of contemporary taste.

The
Realistic Reaction
and its consequences

TAKING as his object the living, the ever-changing, the historian necessarily forgets the stagnant, the stationary—and as a result of this omission his perspective often becomes inexact or partial.   And so in retracing the history of the Nabis, the Fauves, the Cubists and their supporters, one runs the risk of shoving aside the fact that these conquerors of new artistic worlds were merely a handful of painters isolated in the mass of an immobile or reactionary majority.   Yet this active minority with its fruitful results has brought to light the production of a large number of contemporary painters irrevocably attached to the most academic traditions which honored the Salon of French artists known accordingly as the Salon des Artistes Français.   This sort of painting adhered to by such artists has no history, for it was a still-born art.   On the other hand, it may be considered more or less as a movement in reaction against avant-garde painting and because of this simple fact takes an equal place in the history of contemporary pictorial creation and can be qualified as Neo-Realist.

It differs widely from academism for several reasons. Upholders of academism held it scarcely less in horror than the avant-garde tendencies and with the same feeling towards Bonnards, Matisses, Rouaults, Braques and their equals, shut the doors of the Salon des Artistes Français, the Ecole des Beaux-Arts and the Institute to its exponents who, in turn, made no effort to force them open. Between the two World Wars they hung their paintings at the Salon d'Automne not too far from those of the Fauves and the Cubists. If they looked down upon avant-garde searchings, they did not ignore them and far from seeing in them, as the academicians did, an imposture or an aberration to be regarded merely with disdain, they took them seriously enough to feel the obvious opposition between them. Having nothing in common with the sleeping academism which placed its values beyond the present world, they naturally turned to other values in order to establish their counterattack against advanced painting and especially Cubism. [3] Full of contempt for the academic tradition of the nineteenth century and, quite the contrary, admirers of the Impressionists, Manet and Courbet, it was natural that they would turn to them. Rather than sickly academic idealism or photographic truth with its eclecticism full of every compromise, they preferred the frank realism of the Impressionists and the sincerity with which they individually studied Nature. Against the non-realism of the Cubists, they considered themselves the heirs of the independent masters of the third quarter of the nineteenth century with Courbet the chief master and spiritual leader of their movement.

Let us call this a movement, then, and not a group or a team. In fact, there was no confined relationship between the exponents of this reaction against the Cubists as existed among the inhabitants of the Bateau-Lavoir or of Puteaux. If a profound friendship united certain painters among them—for example, Dunoyer de Segonzac, Boussingault, Luc-Albert Moreau—they had for the most part neither subsequent contacts nor a common art dealer nor an explicit formulated doctrine. Nor for that matter could they have had any. Their very number made this mpossible. Much more numerous than the Cubists or the Fauves, they were not one or two dozen but a good hundred or less, and it would be useless to enumerate the aspiring geniuses who have gone down forgotten in history. We shall limit ourselves to list some of the better known painters. In addition to those already named—Dunoyer de Segonzac, Boussingault and Luc-Albert Moreau, we would like to bring to attention those of Dufresne, Waroquier, Gernez, Lotiron, Céria, Asselin, Bouche, Louise Hervieu, Loutreuil, etc. As a matter of fact, they have not deliberately adhered to this tendency but because of their common pictorial search we have arranged them in that order.

But the influence of Cézanne is the basis of their art as well as an understanding of Cubism. All of them, at one time or another, have heeded his lesson of discipline: Dufresne in his *Ondines de la Marne*, Luc-Albert Moreau in his *Après-Midi* of 1913, Boussingault who executed for the famous couturier Paul Poiret a decorative panel in which the solid figures are composed with ordered care, Dunoyer de Segonzac who in 1910 exhibited his *Buveurs* which is so closely related to Cézanne's *Card Players*, Waroquier who in his paintings of Italian and French cities and those of southern France found the getting rid of extraneous matter and the vigorous rhythm that characterize Cézanne's landscapes of his native countryside. From this school of painting they have all been filled with a horror of pictorial realism that aims at absolute truth. In regard to this, Waroquier seems to be the spokesman for them when he declared in 1917: "*We must lie in order to speak the truth better. We must lie against narrow reality... lie in order to satisfy intuitive truth, the truth of imagination, the truth that awaits discovery which is a thousand times more precious that what we believe to be acquired truth.*" They all learned to prefer the plastic to the exact, which allowed them to scorn the anecdote which from time immemorial has been the refuge and alibi of painters who sacrificed representation to the represented.

Armed by this Cézannism against the academic realism of the end of the nineteenth century, they were equally aware of certain Impressionist practices: irregularity of forms, excessive taste for spontaneity, the corollary of the rough sketch and the "window open to Nature" by a painter working without method or reflection. Elaborated over a long period of time and with the desire to achieve perfection, their canvases reach a blending of vigorous and synthetic forms in a thought-out ensemble. Most of them were completely indifferent, on the other hand, to translating the atmosphere of light, and rather than adhere to the fresh color scheme of the Impressionists with their *plein-air* approach to painting, they came to prefer the less brilliant palette of the Cubists: the earth colors, ochres, grays, leaning to black making up the basic color scheme, red, green and blue, less strong in intensity, automatically harmonized. They preferred the lustier pleasures of form—form constructed in such a way as to affirm permanence rather than movement, emphasizing universality by avoiding the usual—to the simple joys of color which mark so vividly the paintings of their Impressionist contemporaries. Simplification and synthesis reigned supreme masters of their art.

Life loses as a result but the style certainly gains. "*One of the essential elements in a work of art,*" stated Dunoyer de Segonzac in reference to this, "*is form. It is this which gives to a work of art its symmetry, its unity and its force. From form comes its rhythm, its harmony and that complete satisfaction which is felt from certain works of art.*" To recognize this ambition in their painting, one must take into account their debt to Cézanne and perhaps to Cubism whose atmosphere they could not avoid while at the same time they heartily detested and condemned it as decorative, doctrinaire, insincere and inhuman.

How many significant opinions they have voiced about this! "*If you truly love painting you will not demand that it be simply a wall decoration of the home but above all a substance for your inner life,*" stated Asselin who said elsewhere : "*No intellectual combination or theory can give birth to a work of art. Art springs from the wonder of life.*" Segonzac shares this anti-theoretical stand when he says: "*Aestheticism is the death of art,*" and cites with approbation the judgment of a peasant, one of his friends: "*it's strange how stupid the world becomes when it is too educated.*" Two other sayings, still more explicit of his anti-Cubism, touch on this school's affectation of modernity: "*In a period of aviation you can no longer paint from Nature,*" said a fellow artist. "*Delacroix and Corot recognized this in their introduction of locomotives which was the great novelty of the time,*" he said one day, and adding at another time: "*They wanted to join everything—false negro art, ethnological museums, the Dupuytren Museum, Hellenic art—to the taste of the day, aesthetically treated airplane motors, flat treatment, plastic synthesis, purified of art for art engineers. All this art is showing off and all its deformations dead.*" How would this affected and artifical Cubism penetrate the content of the Neo-Realists, the warm humanity born from the painters' feelings for things?   *"One day I said to a Cubist,"* Segonzac stated to Gaston Poulain, *"if you replace your circles by elements of emotion and life, you will have more force and intensity."*

Thus in their hostility to Cubism all these artists were led to seek what they had despised.   Less worshipers of still life than their exponents they used it willingly in order to introduce in their art not objects made by man but rather products of Nature: fruit, vegetables and flowers.   The human figure attracts them more either in their glorification of the nude or in their turning to the portrait with its so-called inner life.   But despite these recognizable facts their predilection is for landscape—the very landscape before which they modestly set their easels in an effort to represent it with sincerity.

And here we have the key to their art which they profess is the essence of all art: *"It is necessary to be absolutely sincere; interpretation should be in the domain of the unconscious; the day when the artist sees that he is interpreting all is lost,"* confessed Segonzac, who was the spokesman of his comrades inclined as he was to accuse as false the deformations and the interpretations of Nature.   Refusing this new pictorial language—the source of their deformations—there was but one step which they easily took.   Their métier is traditional.   The postulate of perspective has for them the force of a law.   They model their forms.   Chiaroscuro reigns in their paintings where everything is seen from the same angle.   Even anatomy is respected.   And conforming thus to traditional vision and métier, their works achieve the appearance of truth which appeases the public and, from this simple fact, automatically assures them a large audience which they, the innovators, believed to have been attracted by their humanity.   And without hesitation the spectator viewing their canvases receives a genuine pleasure which is felt even more by the quality of their technique.

All of them, in fact, are painters in love with their splendid métier, anxious to create exquisite works of art.   They all show extreme care of surface quality whether the paint is laid on thickly and generously or carefully in an enamel-like way but always of a quality of richness.   The desire is so great on the part of many of these painters to bring their canvases to such perfection that they finally take away all its vitality.   One is inclined to prefer a more hasty technique to such finished but lifeless form.   Segonzac has never achieved anything better perhaps than his water colors nor Dufresne his gouaches.

Without any other tie between these adherents than this very simple and unformulated common feeling of antipathy, tastes and convictions, the reactionary movement directed against Cubism in the name of fidelity to exterior appearances and to a traditional métier, is worth far more than any other for the quality of its talent.   Among the many exponents two names stand out : Dunoyer de Segonzac and Dufresne.   However great the talent of a sumptuous colorist like Boussingault with its careful refinement and poetically subtle treatment of contemporary elegant things like furry-coated fruit and downy flowers; however respectable the efforts of a painter like Waroquier towards rigorousness, force and pathetic grandeur; however rare or finely executed the small paintings of a man like Céria or Lotiron, the pastels of a Gernez, the canvases of a Luc-Albert Moreau, it is not doing injustice to their artistic worth to consider Segonzac and Dufresne as the two who most characterize the meaning of this pictorial movement and whose contribution we would now like briefly to define.

23

ANDRÉ DUNOYER DE SEGONZAC – BAIGNEUSE AU PARASOL – ABOUT 1927 – (0,63; 0,97) PRIVATE COLLECTION, PARIS

For Dunoyer de Segonzac it would be possible to qualify him as the contemporary Courbet if his water colors and especially his wash drawings and his pencil drawings did not reveal certain qualities stranger to the painter of Ornans and did not sometimes make one think of Poussin. From Courbet, as a matter of fact, he has the love and instinct of reality, of the most truthful reality that one can feel more than one can see. Moreover, this is proved by the subjects he has chosen: still life filled with dense objects which daily use makes more authentic *(La Soupière de Moustiers, Still Life with Bread and Wine, The Cutlet)*; robust and muscular male nudes *(Bacchus)*, a nude quality more sensual than voluptuous females *(Nude with Umbrella)*; landscapes, especially those of thick soil *(The Road from Couilly)*, hilly landscapes whose majestic range is established rigorously by the horizontality of the sea *(The Gulf of Saint-Tropez)*, landscapes with trees whose anatomy he likes to dissect, especially during the winter when the trees are almost bare. It is not so much the delicateness or sumptuousness, the pathetic or the poetic, but rather it is the concrete, the ever-present and real that interests Segonzac. One is not surprised

24

ANDRÉ DUNOYER DE SEGONZAC – THE ROAD FROM COUILLY – 1932 – (0,65; 1,00) MUSÉE NATIONAL D'ART MODERNE, PARIS

that he painted this reality as a realist anxious to respect tangible truth, without deforming it, without even proposing an excessive subjective interpretation. One is even less surprised to see this same passion for reality in a very special métier. If he enjoys piling up coats of paint, it is merely to heighten the effect of truth that he is striving to achieve. Working directly on the canvas, proceeding this way by successive approximations, each of his approximations is transformed into a surface coating which gives way to another and so on until finally the artist feels that he has at last equalled in his painting the visual truth that he has attempted to portray.

But as result of being animated by this realistic intention, Segonzac's work finally presents an aspect far removed from that of exterior appearances. His paint which is applied everywhere rather thickly gives everything—water, earth, trees, people—the same pulpous and heavy quality which he seeks for still other motifs. It is his love of paint quality for itself and for the beauty of the finished product, but there is also the feeling for construction with its desire for permanency and the universal, and finally the need for style and form.

25

Interested in heaviness, volume, density of forms, Segonzac for whom color plays a minor role (he is often satisfied with a few discreet tones) seeks to organize these ample and robust forms whose depth of structure is for him the essential quality. His main interest is the inmost eternal essence of things rather than their accidental manifestations in movement. The water, for instance, does not move; no wind blows through the trees; his nudes are portrayed at rest. He ignores the human figure because it is an expression, and any expression is something that changes: only the general, the timeless moves him to artistic expression through the medium of paint. If his quick sketches reveal his gift of catching things in the act of movement as a result of his acute observation—a special detail, an individual quality—his paintings, nevertheless, reveal his desire to eliminate these characteristics, which are so striking in other painters' work, in order to achieve a quality that we have defined as general and permanent. The reason for this is perhaps his taste for style, a style rather sharp because of the desired effect he has strived for, at least in his paintings which he achieves much more easily in his wash drawings and his water colors which in reality are nothing more than wash drawings heightened with a few tones of rather dark colors. Here his best qualities are revealed: a largeness and definiteness of drawing which retain, however, a peculiar lightness of touch, bathing the strong, definite forms in a shimmering light that comes from the sky. This reckless passion of Segonzac is a thought-out thing elaborated to appear spontaneous, it is a visional truth which wants to be objective but none the less achieves a certain poetical quality as a result of this happy marriage of the elementary and eternal things and forces of Nature and the permanence of a universal life that has always a special characteristic.

There is no evolution—or hardly any—in Segonzac's work as there was, for example, in that of Courbet and so many realists who evolved directly from themselves and persisted in their artistic endeavors with the assurance of a tranquil mind. In complete opposition to Segonzac, Dufresne has evolved a great deal. Formed early in life by French academism he leans towards a painting which had much in common with the Intimism of the Nabis. *(From the Hebrew world "Nabi" meaning "prophet" Tr.)* From 1906 to 1910 he sketched scenes of contemporary life, and this biting treatment of French manners drew him away from the contemplation of reality. And so it was not astonishing that he felt drawn to the Cubist movement—at any rate, to a La Fresnaye version of Cubism restricted to flat areas of color. About 1918 he executed a series of large compositions among the best he ever did, like *Les Ondines de la Marne, Le Beau Dimanche en Normandie,* revealing his taste for reconstructing natural forms in order to give them more unity and foundation, a more ample mass, simpler contours and a more evident style. The figures have a majesty in striking contrast to their common attitude revealing a touch of irony. These figures fill the canvas so well and so fully that no empty space is visible. Dufresne manifestly is looking for a decorative style which he seeks through the geometrical vigor of the composition on the one hand and the choking sumptuousness of his colors on the other *(The Tropical Forest).* But, in order to be interpreted in the sense of a rich and vigorous décor and constructed at the venture of daring interpretation, reality is no less present, recognizable *(Still Life with an Antique Torso)* and all the more familiar to the spectator since Dufresne has no reason to turn to the

26

novelties of the Cubist métier nor to those of avant-garde. In the same way that appearances are easy to define, he takes care to avoid breaking with tradition, satisfied to bring to the set forms and styles of painting certain measured license and a great deal of unconstraint.

This license—which sometimes brings to mind that of Dufy—and this unconstraint assert themselves even more when Dufresne, beginning in 1921 to break away from para-Cubism influenced by Cézanne, gives himself more to imagination to which a brief stay at the villa Abd-el-Tif in Algiers had acted as impetus as far back as 1911. But thwarted by the war, by the constructive discipline practised after the demobilization, this imagination did not begin to give its full measure till after 1920, leading the painter to an exotic fantasy *(The Hunt for Wild Beasts, The Slave Dealer)*, a dainty and capricious mythology *(Galatea, The Sacrifice of Iphigenia)*, historical

CHARLES DUFRESNE — THE PLASTER CAST — 1918 — (1,10; 1,10) PETIT PALAIS, PARIS

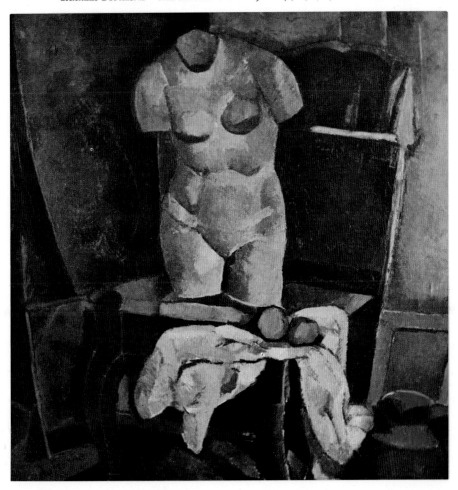

paintings *(The Rape of The Sabines, The Saga of Christopher Columbus)*, religious subjects *(The Crucifixion)*. The painter renews these traditional themes by the originality of a métier that associates the Baroque tradition, especially that of Tiepolo and Fragonard, with the hallmarks of contemporary non-realistic painting. Ellipses in the sinuous, nervous, unexpected contours; a high-toned and clear color, bathed in an unreal light in which lemon yellows, vermillions, emerald greens harmonize with the predominating electric blues; a thought-out, free treatment which breaks the tones, interposes them without any concern for the form of the objects; a painted surface that is both velvety and enamel-like with the strength and depth of laquer— these are the characteristics of Dufresne's métier, whose lyricism is in complete accord with the movement of the figures vibrating to a dance that seems to carry them off to the harmony of a graceful rhythm.

Sometimes, however, this vibration takes on a slower tempo when Dufresne devotes himself to a large decoration either in the form of tapestry drawings for Gobelins or Beauvais or in the form of paintings for the Palais de Chaillot and the Ecole de Pharmacie. Aware of the mural need for grandeur, he retains his elliptical drawing, his dream color, his nervous forms, immobilising and subduing them to the demands of a more forceful composition which recalls that of *Les Ondines de la Marne*. The designer, wide awake for a time to the message of Cubism, collaborates with the poet and the musician of so many rococo ballets.

Carried away by his fantasy towards the traditional escape worlds, he renewed hackneyed themes using a métier both submissive to old habits and sensitive to new examples. Intelligent enough to be aware of what was going on around him in modern painting and to consent to the limitations it imposed, he wanted to be nothing else but the *Delacroix de la Foire aux Croûtes* (⁴) as he jokingly referred to himself. But having accepted such a title he succeeded in being a little bit of a contemporary Delacroix. As the last inheritor of the long line of Baroque and Romantic painters, he belongs to a group that reacts to Cubism and modern painting with hostility; and yet he has often brushed aside contemporary non-realistic painting, proving therefore that all painting today, if it is sincere, cannot completely rid itself of the new aesthetics since it is essentially the expression of modern life and the necessary result of the genius of our time.

Favored by the First World War which had consecrated the bankruptcy of an intellectualism which Cubism revealed as well as by the loosening of French consciousness in the euphoria of victory, Neo-Realism flourished from 1920 to 1930; while the exponents of non-realism remained the object of passionate protestations, its outstanding painters benefited by a success whose most striking sign, internationally speaking, was the prize awarded to Dunoyer de Segonzac—the painting prize of the Venice Biennale of 1934—which is to say, awarded at a time when Fascist Italy recognized half-heartedly and with rather forced effort the artistic values of a France honored and regarded with jealousy. But if the prosperous years and the corollary taste for facility were profitable to this movement, those of the crisis which followed were not unfavorable to it. With clients daily deserting the steadily diminishing number of galleries, the art dealer tried to hold his customer who was becoming rarer by attracting his attention to a kind of painting less difficult than that of the Fauves and the Cubists: the Neo-Realistic art was there on the spot, all the more accessible

28

RAYMOND LEGUEULT – VAL SUZON – 1933 – (0,65; 0,92) MUSÉE NATIONAL D'ART MODERNE, PARIS

since the press praised it so highly. No longer liking—or not daring to like—the official painting of the Salon des Artistes Français, still rebellious against that of avant-garde, the critics revelled in this form of compromise, and celebrated those who were its leading exponents. In fact, there is nothing more eloquent in regard to this than the article in *L'Art Vivant*, whose collaborators made themselves the spokesmen for Neo-Realism. Under these conditions one is not astonished that Neo-Realist art found its native soil and that, taking over from its older adherents, a new generation inspired with the same spirit finally conquered the public's favor. This generation is that of Aujame, Brayer, Brianchon, Caillard, Cavaillès, Chapelin-Midy, Legueult, Le Molt, Lestrille, Limouse, Oudot, Planson, Poncelet, Sabouraud and Terechkovitch, to cite merely a few of these artists.

The war and its aftermath, to believe the statements of some of these artists, were the origin of their orientation towards a moderate painting. Witness what Poncelet had written in *L'Amour de l'Art* in 1935: *At the Front, where it was impossible to work, I had the chance to meditate. Understanding the frailty and the inconstancy of certain theories... I finally saw very clearly the road I had to follow. Moreover, the permanent*

29

MAURICE BRIANCHON – THE BOIS DE BOULOGNE –
1938 (0,92; 0,60) MUSÉE D'ART MODERNE, PARIS

*contact with humanity and Nature, the formidable brutality of this war were the cause
of a precocious maturity which certainly facilitated my orientation."* Now listen to the
words of Chapelain-Midy who, in the same revue, declared, the same year, in his name
and in all those of his age: *"In a way, we came when the party was over ([5])... No longer
is there any collective enthusiasm."* It merely agreed with the diagnosis that René
Huyghe stated four years earlier in the same revue where he had said: *"While the
partisans of the post-war generation were born with an excess of ardor and ambition,
those of our generation carry the heavy weight of being born tired."*

30

In fact, this disenchanted painting characteristic of the new generation of Neo-Realists has the mark above all of scepticism: painters no longer believe in the avant-garde adventure. Chapelain-Midy declared in 1935 that he had *"the presentiment that in this domain we have gone to the very end and moreover everything has been tried."* And all of them take up again the objections already formulated by Segonzac and like minds against this avant-garde experiment in general, and Cubism in particular; they find fault with the intellectual tendencies of avant-gardism, with its very content and with its methods that created new conditions in art. *"I never think about all that, I paint purely for pleasure, for myself... During the last thirty years there have been several pictorial movements important for their period. But today I think it is necessary to act again via technique. I have neither theories nor principles,"* confessed Roland Oudot, agreeing with Aujame, in condemning *"the aesthetic constructions of cold reason."*

Discredited by its doctrinal character—true or assumed—Cubism is discredited also for its partiality—that is to say, for this choice that it made of artistic means excluding the use of other resources. Less exclusive than its exponents, less inclined to brutal solutions, the young realists of 1930 were, on the contrary, prone to an art of compromise and to an eclecticism of synthesis: *"There is a need for things that are less extraordinary, less marked by genius, but more complex... Painting should be a sum of qualities of different structures, which synthesize and give to a work its necessary complexity,"* confided Oudot to the critic Nino.

Thus more subtle and less partial this kind of painting, thanks to its exponents, will not fall into one of the errors of avant-garde Cubist or Fauve painting that they liked to brand most: its "disdain for the human element," whose corollary is its inaccessibility to the large public. Chapelain-Midy, the lucid, frank spokesman of his supporters, proclaimed: *"Cubism in its abstract searchings has lost sight of the true aim and human significance of art. The spiritual values are in peril... The Cubists and the Fauves have found again the solid basis of painting, but they have limited themselves to the sole optic, material aspect which constitutes one of the essential truths of painting. It is for those who follow to bring to art the spiritual truths which are still lacking... Painting should not exist oblivious to exterior influences."*

The faults of Cubism thus denounced, it became easy for painters like Brianchon, Legueult, Oudot, Chapelain-Midy to take the opposite point of view and especially to return to this human, complex painting with the universal audience that it advocated. They merely had to adopt the métier which had been traditional since the Renaissance, to accept perspective, the unity of view point, the respect for anatomy, modeling, chiaroscuro, tones and values—in short, the centuries' old method of approaching painting from its initial step to the finished product. Resolutely moderate, they did not sacrifice form to light in the manner of the Impressionists, nor did they sacrifice drawing to color the way the Fauvist painters did, nor even, as in the case of Dunoyer de Segonzac, did they sacrifice objective truth to the beauty of pictorial painted surface. Drawing, form and value, these three acting as a sort of triumvirate, made up their *matière*, and this triumvirate won over color and even over the finished product with its characteristically enamel-like surface which had been so highly prized by those who had preceded them. In this respect their art is less modern than that of a Segonzac, which at least sees eye to eye with a Rouault or a Braque in its conviction of the "necessary richness" of the treatment.

Faithful to a traditional métier they apply themselves wholeheartedly to the imitation of Nature. *"The artist who forces himself to exteriorize the plastic feeling that he has in himself needs a support. This support is found in the objects and in the color-light which bathes the objects; and it is with the aid of these elements and by the means he uses to bring them together that he finally arrives at expressing himself,"* explained Limouse to Jacques de Laprade. This was entirely in agreement with Chapelain-Midy, who advocated *"a conscientious copy of Nature"* inspired by *"total realism,"* but a free realism which he defined in this way: *"I devote all my efforts to free myself of scholarly realism in order to try to bring into my painting more plastic imagination and freedom vis-à-vis Nature, in a word—true creation."* To look at Nature and to confine oneself to her but to interpret her—this is the fundamental position of all these painters; and these were the significant words uttered by one of them, Poncelet: *"The mission of art is not the unique goal of reproducing things but rather the free and personal interpretation of Nature and spiritual evasion."*

Interpretation, yes, but discreet interpretation: *"There is now a need for a great deal of humility, a little more modesty and sincerity."* This sentence written by Oudot in *L'Amour de l'Art* of 1935 would gladly have been countersigned by all his comrades who sought the right measure to the point of fearing all effect. Tempted to accuse research of imposture, they withdrew into a select group and preached the cult of good taste without realizing the affectation there was in avoiding being affected, as they tried to do; and without realizing the extreme they fell into, while insisting at the same time on the undesirability of being extremists.

Traditional in its métier as in its vision, this painting is still more so when it returns to the belief of the hierarchy of its subjects. If the exponents of this painting gladly turn to still life and landscape, they judge this form of expression inferior to those in which the human figure is of principal importance. To paint man is not only the means *par excellence* of *"approaching closer to man and life"* and to *"react against the lack of interior authenticity"* as Chapelain-Midy wrote, but it is also to take up the supreme problem of grandiose composition. In the painting grouping several figures, as the *Symphony of Summer* or *Suffering* by Chapelain-Midy, the greatest ambition of plastic composition, of balance, of perfect painting comes to grips with the problem of making everything "human" and of having it speak to all in a language which reaches out directly to them. Here only is achieved, in a supreme compromise, this eclectic search *"for complete works in which the spiritual is in perfect harmony with the material and where the eye and mind of the spectator each play their part,"* as thus stated by Chapelain-Midy in 1935.

Art of tradition and compromise, on a lower plane in relationship to that of Segonzac, Boussingault, Dufresne, this new expression of Neo-Realism, whose general characteristics we have just defined, presents itself to us with a unity which however does not exclude a certain diversity. Not only the diversity which results from the affirmation of individual personalities with their desire to be so discreet in this new attitude, but also the diversity which makes up the existence of diverging tendencies uniting all these artists by affinities of taste and common uneasiness. Thus this art presents a double image: that of painters inclined to gravity and those haunted by grace.

Here we meet principally Oudot, Chapelain-Midy, Planson, Poncelet, Caillard, all those who have come under the dangerous influence of Derain in his last phase, the pseudo-classic Derain of 1925. Sensitive to what they judged his general elimination of everything for the sake of grandeur and purity, they strike for a severe majesty.

32

To achieve this they gladly have recourse to vigorous drawing which imposes itself and unifies the design, to very constructed forms, immutably immobile, to a composition whose design is quite evident, to a clear grouping of few figures and of few objects, devoid of details, leaving in the canvas a large place for empty spaces. In these empty spaces Derain seeks to achieve an effect of restraint and force in order to obtain *the grandeur in simplicity* which Chapelain-Midy admired so rightly in the magnificent works of Piero della Francesca. Inversely, they gave up the seductions of color, being content with few tones and those generally discreet, refusing the facility of expressive execution with its thick, sensuous paint quality. But their ascetic taste does not, however, forbid them certain complaisant combinations, certain easy effects, all the more accusing since they wished to keep their work discreet, with their virtuosity expert in all its painting tricks, their insistent taste for finish, with all available means to give their work an almost artifical accent and an air of pretended purity. If Racine, that sublime French poet, succeeded after much difficulty in making his verse read easily, these painters, on the other hand, had a tendency to produce facile paintings which give the effect of difficulty, if not of severity, and of too much finery of restraint. The distance is less great than it would seem between their painting and that of men like Brianchon, Legueult, Cavaillès, between which that of a Brayer or a Caillard is a transition.

If these "Painters of Poetic Reality" cultivate grace and seduction, it is simply because they wish to achieve the same means of discretion, taste and facility. Less concerned with pure lines, neat forms, unequivocal composition, they, on the other hand, prefer color to drawing, the interpenetration of objects and figures to construction, the decorative quality to the clarity of order and the grouping of figures. Great admirers of Vuillard and Marquet, they delight in low tones, mouse gray, olive green, violet-tinted red, creamy whites, deep blacks, which they like for their close values and which they combine with taste. Even a Legueult who evolved as a result towards a higher toned palette, more varied in color, further away from Nature, closer to that of the Bonnard in his last years, began by singing these lullabies in a delicate seduction. With little affirmation or reticence, the forms fall apart one after another, all the more so since the subtle scientific passages facilitate the connection. Thus provided with a very coherent unity, the painting acquires a decorative grace which conforms with the serenity of the languid figures from which issues a distinguished music well made to please the ears of the bourgeoisie.

Painting of a happy medium, neither avant-garde nor academic, a measured painting of doses and compromises, sufficiently traditional to appease the conservative public but sufficiently beautified with modern fashions to appear new and fresh, the product of an excellent artisan of impeccable taste and of expert talent, a perfect Parisian article and an easy witness to its time, this art less authentic than that of the first generation of the adversaries of avant-garde and more reactionary, for this reason alone, represents none the less the most characteristic expression of this return to reality and to habitual values which, without confusing it with academic painting, animated a whole section of French painting from 1914 to 1939. It constitutes the most concise refusal that was made during the period, in its ensemble, of the brave searchings of the preceding age. But this refusal was clothed in other appearances which it is now our object to study: that of a second Expressionism and that of a fantastic art whose methods have been numerous from the painting of Chagall to Surrealism.

The Painters
of Anguish
and the
second expressionist growth

THE reaction against Cubism did not only take the form of a renewal of realism; it also favored a second growth of this Expressionism, still latent in modern painting since van Gogh and Toulouse-Lautrec. The years 1900-1910 saw the flowering of a first Expressionism which we studied in the first volume of this history of modern painting; a second Expressionism closely followed it whose different centers spring up mushroomlike here and there.

One of the most important was that which a renegade Cubist, Le Fauconnier, maintained at the Académie de la Palette. Taking part in the Salons where Cubism first made itself noticed, with a *Portrait of Pierre-Jean Jouve*, a very Cézannelike painting which he exhibited at the Salon d'Automne of 1909, Le Fauconnier refused the analytical form that this painting took and, in reaction, began to practise from 1912 onwards a brutally synthetic art which did not fall back before the deformations destined to simplify forms in order better to affirm their power and to explain more clearly their character as seen in his painting *Tree* dating from 1912. Revolting thus against the superstition with which his former comrades avoided the anecdote, he was not afraid to take on *genre* subjects and exhibited at the Salon d'Automne of 1912 his *Mountaineers Attacked by Bears*. This rehabilitation of subject matter and passion of character complemented their subjective interpretation; it is a specifically expressionist art that Le Fauconnier proposed to the pupils of the Académie de la Palette among whom were Yves Alix and Gromaire.

At la Ruche however—this strange edifice which housed the ateliers of Léger, Brancusi and Archipenko, and had been about 1906 one of the cradles of Cubism—Chaim Soutine, a young Jew recently arrived from Eastern Europe, installed himself about 1911. Soon friendly with Chagall and more so with Modigliani, who has left us an overwhelming effigy of him, Soutine is as sensitive to this expressionist manner adopted by his Italian co-religionist as he is by nature and religion marked by a certain uneasiness which is so evident in his painting. Soutine found a favorable soil in this milieu of uprooted and miserable foreigners who came in droves to Paris. Exile was therefore quite propitious to the development, in what was later considered "The School of Paris," of expressionist tendencies analagous to those which Soutine brought to their paroxysm.

An event which united all Frenchmen was soon to convince some of these people uprooted from their country and filled with despair—namely, the war. It brought them face to face with the vanity of intellectual constructions, with the powerlessness of reason and with the misery of man before his destiny. And this painful consciousness of the utter hopelessness of life remained with many of them at the end of hostilities, either because the proof was strong enough to have left its mark forever on their souls, either because the spectacle of post-war France filled them with indignation, fear and anxiety for the nourishment of an intellectual life. Thus Expressionism found recruits among whom were names like La Patellière, Goerg, even Fautrier—the Fautrier of such paintings as *Christ on the Cross* and *The Wild Boar*, both in the Paris Musée National d'Art Moderne. At the same time that Expressionism developed in Holland and in Belgium (which owes more to the role of Le Fauconnier than is recognized, since he established himself in the Low Countries during the First World War), and in the Germany of 1929 which was the chosen land of Expressionism, the same tendency prospered in France and paralleling Neo-Realism saw the triumph of a state of mind and of pictorial realizations in complete opposition to that of Cubism.

We have used the word "tendency," for it is not a question here any more than it is in the case of Neo-Realism of a cohort of friends all preoccupied with the ardent pursuit of their common experiment. No doubt this or that painter whom we list—more than they themselves do—in the family of Expressionists had at certain given moments friendly relations and artistic contacts—Gromaire and Goerg, for example. But more often than not they hardly saw each other. Each of them followed his own path, and the analogies that can be noticed in their artistic productions can be explained essentially by the "climate" of the period which acted directly on their close sensitivity, the political, social, spiritual, human "climate" as well as the more especially pictorial one.

There is therefore, from this moment on, nothing astonishing in the fact that they share with the Neo-Realists the same hostility in regard to Cubism, in which La Patellière saw nothing more *"than a museum lesson, a technique in itself, a fruit detached from the tree."* He had for it the same reproaches of intellectualism and of inhumanity: *"We know only too well today,"* declared Goerg, for example *"that a painting has its laws at the expense of emotion, that it is a plane surface, a combination of volumes... but I say that this is not sufficient."* And indicating the remedy at the same time as the evil, Goerg proclaims that *"what I like in art is Man."*

From all this there results in the Expressionists as in the Neo-Realists a return to subjects in which man occupies a principal place—subjects which are capable of affecting man—as well as the desire to obtain a large audience by a more accessible painting. As opposed to still life painting (artists like La Patellière and Soutine turn to it with biting humor) and even landscapes (in which the two artists have excelled just as Gromaire has), they all prefer the human figure, either the nude chosen principally by Gromaire and carried out with complete mastery, or portraits, but above all paintings of men, women and children, alone or in groups, engaged in some sort of action or not, where they are able to express their bitterness and suffering of life better than anywhere else. Here, above all, is their chief means of expression: Soutine with his *Grooms*, his *Choir Boys*, his *First Communion* or his *Old Actress*; Gromaire with his *Flemish Reaper*, his *Traveling Lottery*, his *Sunday in the Suburbs*; Goerg and his *Monsieur and Madame Goujon Bouchon* and his *Maître de Moissons*;

EDOUARD GOERG – THE THREE RELIGIONS · (0,72; 0,91) PRIVATE COLLECTION, PARIS

Le Fauconnier and his *Chamber Music;* and finally La Patellière evoking with tenderness the peasants of his native Britanny in his *The Rest in the Storeroom, La Vachère, The Siesta at Bois-Benoît.*

But it is not enough to speak of man; it is necessary to portray him in such a way that everyone may understand him. Thus the Expressionists eschewed the innovations of the Cubists and the Fauves which the public found disconcerting.

More timid than those who had preceded them (the exponents of the first Expressionism) they adopt a rather traditional métier which is founded in particular on perspective and modeling with their tonal values resulting from light and shade.

But here we must be careful, for this métier is not that of the Neo-Realists. It is a freer one, more inventive, borrowing a great deal from the novelties of avantgarde painting. Light and shade is not utilised to figurative ends as it was in the painting of Ribera, Courbet and Segonzac; but to model the form, to bring out—as in the case of the three painters mentioned—the volumes and to "people" the space of light. It serves above all as a function—as it does in Rouault's paintings—to

AMÉDÉE DE LA PATELLIÈRE – THE END OF THE WORLD – ABOUT 1929 – (0,73; 0,92) MUSÉE NATIONAL D'ART MODERNE, PARIS

create the spiritual "climate" of the work, to bring out the mystery or the drama that a La Patellière or a Soutine feels in his subjects and wishes us, the spectators, to feel as well. Thus it is used in itself. Moreover, there is no preoccupation of having it agree with physical truth; the light comes from any source, often emanating from the figures themselves, rising rather than descending, falling on the objects from right and left simultaneously. A poetic treatment of light and shade for dramatic effects replaces thus its traditional use. All the same, the figures are not exempt from destined deformations, as is quite evident in Rouault's work with its profound character that we feel as an intense experience. Meeting a railway worker on the road, Gromaire was struck by the hardiness of the man, his very strength; and he was not afraid of giving to his painting this same striking image—*The Vagabond* at the Musée National d'Art Moderne—not only in transforming this being of perishable flesh and blood into a decay-resisting wooden statue, capable of withstanding the elements and the centuries, but he made a knife edge of his mouth, nails out of his nose and chin, barbed wire out of the folds of his shirt.

37

Soutine's same love of exaggeration which verges on caricature decisively chisels the drawn faces of underfed children, prematurely aged, lengthens their necks, their noses, their skulls, makes their eyes goggle, draws back their lips in a hideous grimace, bares their teeth, makes their bony hands hang, strips their bodies of all healthy flesh, and makes us realize through the living subject he paints that this human being is already claimed by death, whose odor is already in the painter's nostrils, and which he makes us unmistakably identify as the terrible odor of putrefaction. The execution also finally allows the Expressionist to communicate his conception of the world to us. Mainly ignorant at least in their beginnings, the most expressionist phase of their whole activity, of those researchs into matter which the Neo-Realists pursue; less anxious to create a beautiful object than an emotional one, the painters of the tendency which we are now considering—above all Soutine—love large and violent brushwork; the pathetic way in which it scrapes the surface, the very abundance of this surface, all affirms, cries, proclaims the joyful creative fever, whose *matière* bursts forth like volcanic lava. And this is not only a means for Soutine to exorcise his personal demons but it is also an effort, a despairing effort, to transcend the world of painting into the secret realm of reality—that of people and objects, closed to all but those possessing the artistic vision. He wishes to merge utterly with this reality both to possess it and to find in it an escape from himself, to kill it and to kill himself in it, to create it and create himself in it.

Treatment, painted surface, deformation, light and shade are therefore the fundamental equipment of the Expressionist painter: drawing is not so important for him and even less important is color whose richness and precious quality do not appeal to him. Like the universe of the Neo-Realist painters, his is also dark and gray—completely different from that of Rouault. Perhaps the reason is that Cubism has just passed through this phase, bringing back dark-toned colors into fashion. In vain does Soutine allow his reds to bleed in his canvases and to highlight with some pleasure the rare and complex color effects which he has noticed flowering on a rotting carcass —these rich diverse colors bury themselves, if one may use the expression, in those of his somber backgrounds, thus achieving an immediate and successful unity. And more than his night blues, his dark greens, his blacks, it is his chromatic quality as an Expressionist painter that is defined by the ochres of Gromaire, the smoky grays of Goerg, the blackish browns of Le Fauconnier, the earthy colors of La Patellière, all proofs of the influence on these painters of the Cubism which they had renounced, but from which they could not but draw certain aspects when these suited the expression of their own pictorial experiments and their human message.

What in fact is this human message? What do they feel towards man, society, Nature, and destiny? Horror, terror, pity, malaise, according to the individual painter. Horror is the domain of Goerg whose satirical painting expresses utter scorn of humanity and an indignation made all the more corrosive by the fact that it is never indignant (what a difference from the fury of Rouault!). On the other hand, it leers, it is full of biting irony, it is all sarcasm and denunciation. We think of certain German Expressionists like Grosz when we consider the bourgeois society which Goerg flays, which is nothing but a sewer where cupidity, sensuality, hypocrisy, pride and cruelty abound. If Alix meets Goerg when he condemns, judges and holds up the absurdities of the contemporary age to ridicule, and if his very judgment masks itself under the apparent impassiveness of Gromaire's painting, it is because the animator of Soutine's fervent art is that great generator of pity: love. Doubtless

MARCEL GROMAIRE – WAR – 1925 – (1,30; 0,965) **PETIT PALAIS, PARIS**

CHAIM SOUTINE – GROTESQUE – (0,81;
0,43) PETIT PALAIS, PARIS

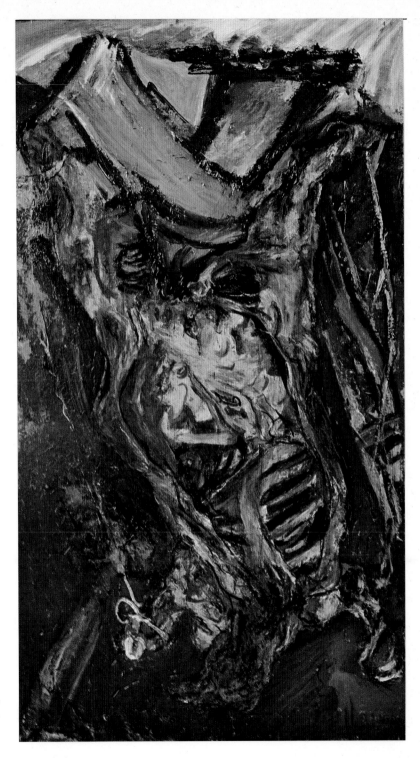

CHAIM SOUTINE – THE CARCASS OF
BEEF – 1926 – (2,02 ; 1,14) MUSEUM,
GRENOBLE

in his landscapes Soutine expresses an apocalyptic vision, a tragic world, a prey to the destructive effects of the unleashed elements. Painter of man and particularly of childhood, he is all tenderness, a virile and tortured tenderness when he thinks of suffering and death, the inescapable fact of the human condition. This destiny, that he feels as a drama, La Patellière experiences as something as unknown and as mysterious as the universe, but whose mystery can be deciphered in the confused mirror that objects present : *"All form, "he said," is the realization of a spiritual virtue... a figuration of the spirit."* Thus, alone among these painters of anguish, he asserts himself on occasion as the poet of the fantastic, touching here and there in his work on a Surrealism which he passes, thanks to the force of the pictorial incarnation of his visionary apprehensions *(The End of the World, The Temptation of Saint Anthony)*.

By the expression of these human experiences, entirely by the means of their experiments, the French Expressionists are very closely related to those who, especially in Belgium but also in Holland, Germany, Switzerland, the Scandinavian countries, even in Spain and in Spanish-Portuguese South America, worked in the same period or a few years after them. Special characteristics singled out their painting: the most remarkable is the great importance given by the French—that is, painters born in France or, like Soutine and Chagall, painters who had adopted France as their mother country—to the purely pictorial problem in painting. If a painting for the Germans, for example, was merely an effusion—and this to a point where a work of Max Beckmann is abominably badly painted—the French painters and those of the School of Paris, on the contrary, thought that their message would be nothing if they did not strive together for plastic form in works that aimed at plastic expression. *"A lyricism without unity cannot attract us for very long,"* professed quite rightly La Patellière, speaking of his compatriots; for—and this is quite evident in his own work—he preferred the epic theme: the epic to which he tends, as Millet did, in his evocations of peasant life and to which Gromaire frequently has access *(The Boatwoman, The Secondhand Dealer, War.)* In fact, the rigor of their construction transforms and magnifies the personage represented, and the deformations imposed by the painter himself serve not only to express the given character, as well as the emotion felt by the artist in his presence, but also to bring it alive plastically, to give it a monumental life and a life that is hieratic in form. These painters modify this process of transformation in a highly significant way; for they can never completely forget the truth which avant-garde painting has driven home again and again for fifty years—namely, that a painting is an entity, an independent reality, living its own life and subject to special laws which govern its sculptural function. Try as they might to accept and practise perspective, a deaf distrust, whether they are conscious of it or not, leads them quite often to give up the whole thing for the emptiness of a near background from which a figure stands out better: the infinity of the sea or of the Flemish countryside so dear to Permeke is repugnant to Gromaire, who prefers to cut up his figures against a flat sky; and Soutine himself placed his figures against a wall with its opaque shadows.

The figures are monumental and plastic all the more so since they become part of well arranged compositions. Gromaire, for example, arranges his compositions against geometrical schemes of an agressive visibility, while Goerg, Alix, La Patellière are less ostentatious; but their compositions lose none of their strength. And with Soutine, the rhythmic instinct is so strong that all the forms, and the details that make up these forms, take on a quality of unity and strength, with an underlying structure which is almost sculptural. This characteristic, which is one of the chief forces of the beauty of Soutine's canvases, is best seen in his views of Céret and of Cagnes.

Organized and thought out pictorially, the works of the French Expressionists are thus marked by more deliberation than those of painters abroad; they are also more discreet and point to a keener desire for form. The painter who wants to pour out everything does it as completely as he can: thus the German or Mexican Expressionists do not speak; they shout, brawl, yell. The French, on the contrary, seek not so much to find a high tone but to find the *right* tone—and in certain instances and according to the message the individual artist wishes to communicate, this can be a whisper (La Patellière), a soft tone (Gromaire) or a corrosive note (Goerg). And, preferring this to shouting and quantity, they finally substitute style to this artistic disorder. Even in the case of an extremist like Soutine, effusion never reaches the stages of formlessness dear to men like Max Beckmann, Siqueiros, sometimes even to Permeke as he was during his time in Munich. Nervous or majestic, trembling or hieratic, the French Expressionist painting betrays a constant search for style which is often nothing but the corollary of the painter's specific and essentially plastic conscience.

And it is not astonishing, from this time onwards, that these painters—at least, for the most part—followed their own paths, diverging from their initial Expressionism, having all of them come face to face with the decorative problem or, at any rate, with that of pure painting. The discovery of the landscape of southern France, and the commission to paint one of the walls of Paul Beaudouin's dining room, reveals the direction of La Patellière's art between 1928 and 1932, the year of his premature death. Gromaire's turning to the art of tapestry—and his role, in its determined renewal as a medium of art expression, was as great as Lurçat's—and his execution of a large decorative frieze for the Sèvres Pavillion of the International Exposition of 1937, brought him into direct contact with an art more concerned with rigorous composition, majestic plasticity—in short, the essential qualities that distinguish mural painting from easel-picture painting. Goerg, however, less sensitive to the decorative quality, did not get too far away from the Expressionism that he practised until about 1940, the day when—like Rouault in his last years—he fell in love with the richness of paint quality and wanted to translate into concrete form his peaceful visions—translate them into the enamel-like surface of a thickly painted canvas almost phosphorescent in its effect. But of all these cases the most significant is that of Soutine: never controlling his emotional unrestraint, his vehemence comes to a standstill, as we can see from the series of magnificent landscapes which he painted sucessively at Céret (1919-1922), at Cagnes (1925), then, beginning in 1929, at the chateau of Lèves, on the outskirts of Chartres. Nature, which he regards with less frenzy but which seems to be on the point of a volcanic upheaval and of dislocating itself in blocks, then coming together in all sorts of ways, is for Soutine merely the insubstantial kingdom of the winds which blow him in a definite direction and strengthen the cohesion of his form. Always in some mad frenzy of execution, it has become calmer, and if it is not so much a feeling of peace that seems to penetrate into his work, at least we find it marked by a sadness which softens his tragic melancholy and grants him finally a measure of peace.

While the representatives of this second Expressionism stand somewhat apart from it, far from suffering from their infidelity, they made several recruits: the fact remains that it was the necessary expression—*one* of the necessary expressions—of the plastic and spiritual state of the time. From the period of 1930 to the war, it gathered in this way new champions among two generations of painters, attracting sucessively Walch and Desnoyer, then the promoters of the movement called "Forces Nouvelles" and their comrades Gruber and Marchand.

Scarcely younger than La Patellière (1890), Gromaire (1892), Goerg (1893) and Soutine (1894), but ripening more slowly, Desnoyer (1894) and Walch (1898), who did not achieve the complete affirmation of their personality till several years later than the others (about 1930), these painters without doubt are above all independent. Their personalities—they are among the strongest of those painters who were born to fame between the two World Wars—fit with difficulty into the category of a school or even of a movement. But Expressionism is so flexible and responds so well to the aspirations of most of the painters between 1920 and 1930 that it is not at all arbitrary to group them among the painters of this tendency. Not only are they brought closer to pure painting, more inclined not to dig into the painted surface and moreover not to despise the licenses and conquests of avant-garde art, Fauve or Cubist; but above all they affirm themselves, one after the other, as colorists, the only advocates about 1930 of a resource generally discredited by those of their own generation. Beyond Cubism, they look to the Fauves and to Bonnard in particular; their painting takes on the aspect of fireworks with a richly colored palette with its new symbolism of joy of life. This dynamism and movement reign supreme in their paintings in perfect harmony with a blaze of reds, blues, yellows, greens, which is more evident in Desnoyer's work, whose verve and fecundity find their vehicle of expression in popular street scenes and holiday festivities; while in Walch's work this desire for color and expression is not so exuberant, though both these artists express something quite different from the ardent fever of certain Expressionists. And each, in his own way, expresses a joy of life, whether peasant or plebian, a love of life overflowing with optimism which is, as we see, quite contrary to the despair of the Expressionists.

But if there is, however, a similarity in their art, it is first of all because of the passionate nature of their character and of the decidedly *subjective* character that they give. Walch, for example, takes a fruit or a flower and by treating it his way makes it larger than a human figure. He does this purely to affirm its splendor which has absolutely no relationship with the beauty of human beings. And if Desnoyer himself constructs his figures by means of a strong design and by simplified volumes, it is not only evidence of the influence Cubism has had on his work, but also a means of expressing in full visible measure the hidden and specific structure of the forms. As with the Expressionists, painting for them takes on the form of passionate caricature which enables them to obtain the secret of things and, once they have obtained this secret, to pass it on to us.

Thrilled to the quick by flowers, fruit, animals, objects, as well as by the sight of natural beauty (they both excel in still life and in landscape painting, observed in

44

the case of Desnoyer, imagined in that of Walch), their sensitivity is above all affected by man: a trait which separates them from the Expressionists. Reconciled to his troubles and to his melancholy and to his peaceful family life some time after, Walch is above all the smiling titular deity of a small, fantastic provincial world composed of women, children, domestic animals, flowers with a rich life—all objects accompanying by their silent life, the life and dreams of men; Segonzac, who was, more than any other painter of his generation attracted by the portrait, is with his unimpeachable generosity the poet of physical and popular sports, carnivals and games. He feels the rather healthy vulgarity with such compassion that it becomes —as in the case of Suzanne Valadon—a form of painted poetry.

After this it makes very little difference whether their evolution—ended quite suddenly by the premature death of one of them—brought them both further away

FRANÇOIS DESNOYER – LA FOIRE DU TRÔNE – 1936 – (1,29; 1,62) MUSÉE NATIONAL D'ART MODERNE, PARIS

from Expressionism to a form of painting that is more concerned with construction, color, and purely pictorial research; their relationship with this tendency which is so characteristic of the milieu of their formative years remains none the less of capital importance: in the elaboration of their art it assumed the same determining role as that of the painting of the movement referred to as Forces Nouvelles.

"Let's be young again! Painting is not dead.   Its course has not stopped.   Forces Nouvelles is born."   So raved the critic Waldemar George on the occasion of the second exhibition that the Galerie Billet-Worms held March 14-26, in 1936, of the works of a group of young painters who, the preceding year, had already exhibited under the name of Forces Nouvelles: Humblot, Jannot, Rohner and Héraut.   Greeted with almost general enthusiasm, praised not only by the famous Spanish aesthetician Eugenio d'Ors but also by the French critic Waldemar George, and drawing painters of their own age into their orbit, like Tailleux, Civet, Claude Venard, the movement, brushed aside by two solitary painters, independent of each other, Francis Gruber and Balthus, enjoyed just before the outbreak of war in 1939 a prosperity that it owed to the fact that it responded to the two most common and most specific tendencies of the moment: the Neo-Realist and the Expressionist movements.

Following in the footsteps of their leaders who are unanimous on this point, the supporters of Forces Nouvelles have not one good word to say for Cubism, and furthermore for the whole field of modern painting, Impressionism included.

Nobody over a period of seventy-five years finds grace in the eyes of Héraut, the theorist of the movement and the man who writes the preface of its second manifesto.   Passing beyond all the modern painters, even beyond those from whom they derive inspiration, like Oudot, Chapelain-Midy, Derain, Vallotton, these young artists direct their attention to the masters of the past, at least to those among them who have practised the most sober art: Piero della Francesca, Mantegna (whose *Dead Christ* Rohner interprets in his *Drowned Man*), Caravaggio, Zurbaran, and above all Georges de la Tour whom the public had recently discovered in 1934, thanks to the exhibition entitled "Realist French Painters of the Seventeenth Century."

What they admire in these painters is their realism, their style and their poetry. Consequently, they accept their métier—that traditional métier to which they give their unswerving loyalty far more deliberately than do the Neo-Realists.   They make no concession to the innovations of modern painters.   Perspective, modeling, light and shade are everywhere in their painting, which does not even draw the line at illusions.   Thus they acquit themselves of what Eugenio d'Ors called *"their duty"* which was according to him *"to re-establish piece by piece, title by title the richness of their ancient patrimony."*   With them and through them the anti-Cubist reaction finishes in a peculiar paroxysm and in a general way the tendency to react against all modern painting which had made great strides since 1914.   The break with seventy-five years of contemporary art is irrevocable, and the return to the past triumphs.

The time of anarchy is over, they proclaim, it is necessary to return to order of the severest kind.   Enemies, in this respect, of the facile elegance of certain Neo-Realists, cherishing the research that others had made of discipline and severity, it is an art of tension and of asceticism that they advocate.   They want nothing to do with color, painted surface or execution!   Their universe is monochromatic, consisting

46

of earth colors and grays; economic in their use of paint to a point of parsimony, they use it in the most impersonal way. On the other hand, they profess a cult of drawing —an insistent drawing, vigorous, implacable. Held in by the contour that encircles it, the form is the object of their solicitude as well. In their ardent desire to achieve this, they are not at all afraid to surround their art with an atmosphere that tends to tone it down and thus makes it less decisive. In order to render the objects and figures in a harder way, these impenitent realists are not afraid of being unfaithful to truth! The drawing with its sculptural impersonal coldness and the modeling of forms and figures in the same tone transform everything into wooden statues, pieces of quartz and steel.

The corollary of this construction, which at times is brought to extremes, is the static quality that triumphs in their paintings. What force, we ask ourselves, could possibly move these heavy forms? And in this emptiness how could they possibly

ANDRÉ MARCHAND – LES INCONNUS – ABOUT 1938 – (1,70; 2,22) MUSÉE NATIONAL D'ART MODERNE, PARIS

move themselves? A tragic silence is the only tone, among these petrified figures set in total immobility, to strike some sort of note in this mineral universe.

And here this quality is confronted by another which arises from the stark nakedness of the forms and the backgrounds. Removed of all extraneous details, or—if there are any—details of the severest kind, these forms and backgrounds are silhouetted against the immense emptiness of the others. And from these vast denuded surfaces we are confronted with a desolation made even more desolate since these surfaces flow into each other with greater vigor: a tight composition gives consummate expression to this concept of pathos.

The art of this movement derives this tendency from Expressionism, whose subtractive version it constitutes. It expresses also the feeling of despair; but it

48

says it, however, through a form of mutism. The means are entirely opposite if the objects are analagous: to create a feeling of the human quality and of pain, to translate this feeling of horror and fright that the young painters of 1936 felt still more legitimate than their elders who had preceded them. Nourished in some by the memory of tragedy, it existed in others through fear, certainty and fright of being incapable of blocking its progress.

The sincere dramatic accent of their art is incontestable, all the more so since we cannot deny the youthful frankness of their effort which is marked by noble sentiment. The danger that menaced their movement was not here but in the impossibility, on the one hand, of going beyond this paroxysm of intellectual fever and, on the other, in the facile usage of the difficulty. The exponents of Forces Nouvelles hardly knew how to escape from one of these dangers; and they arrived at a point in their work where they took up the role of refusing virtuosity and became the Sybarites of pictorial ascetism, and if they avoided the other it was a leaning to a more agreeable painting which more than anyone else they knew how to control by remaining objective. Time will tell whether their movement was of short duration and, consequently, whether the only ones to have realized their ambitions were two men whose aims and tastes were closely linked: André Marchand and Francis Gruber.

Before achieving a form and style of painting which in its elegance and refinement makes us think of Chinese art, André Marchand began painting very much like Jannot, Humbolt and Rohner. Reacting as they did against Cubism and the flat treatment of planes, he followed them in appealing to a traditional métier and placed his well modeled forms in a perspective space illuminated by light and shade. He preferred among the Old Masters, just as they did, those painters who through discipline and an almost ascetic quality of restraint achieved by getting rid of all extraneous detail the highest quality of style: Piero della Francesca, Paolo Uccello, these were his gods in 1935. Following their example he prefers drawing to color, form to atmosphere, composition to execution. Precise contour, deliberately void of unnecessary details, surrounds these almost colorless forms painted in a harmony that goes from gray to blue with a slight touch here and there of a few mauves, reds and blacks. These shiny forms, without any striking characteristics or details, remind us of antique marble with the same immobile quality. André Marchand had been greatly impressed by a brief stay in the Sahara; and the dry desert atmosphere is found again in his work, where the light—as in certain paintings by Louis le Nain—takes all the color from the objects and gives them a modeling which is almost sculptural in its three dimensional relief. Against a gray of parallel verticals, cutting numerous horizontals at right angles, these canvases—where there is no sign of oblique lines or ellipses—bring out an architectural strength emphasized by the desired simplicity of the paint quality and the systematic impersonality of going about it.

But of this ascetism there results a wild allure which is enough already to give a tragic character to his compositions. Other elements are used to affirm this more intensely. First of all, the quality of emptiness—this emptiness of skies and backgrounds which seems to weigh on the figures like some unseen menace. To this we add the unusual proximity that Marchand establishes between this or that figure and object, and we thus understand the reason for the strong dramatic sense which

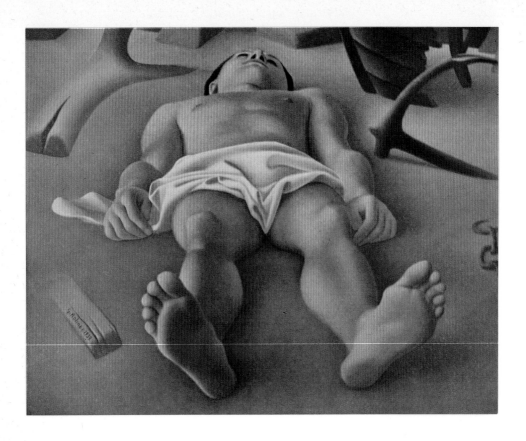

emanates from his work and closely relates it not only to that of Rohner, Jannot and Humblot but still more to that of the Expressionists.

But André Marchand's Expressionism is not a concession to fashion, nor is it even the fruit of circumstances favoring the development of an intimate uneasiness. Rather it is one of the characteristics of his nature which has established the evolution of his painting. Leaving the period in which he belonged to the painters of the Forces Nouvelles group, he turned to a second form of artistic expression which is best evident in the works he did just before the Liberation, *The Hostage*, for example, or *Christ on the Cross*. Broken-line drawing, contrasting form, full of deliberate hardness, high tones, unreal colors of invented and brutal contrasts, vibrating execution, search for character, extreme expressions, a pathetic quality achieved by less sober means—the artist's new manner reveals him no less concerned with translating a message of sorrow and making it "Expressionist." Moreover, it makes no difference if as a result he finally found peace and turned his attention to the problems of pure painting; his adventure, in this domain, is analogous to that of a great many Expressionists who, either because they felt the impossibility of remaining always in this line of art, or because this transmutation of their deep anguish burnt it forever out of their heart, have turned to another path which, however, would not have been what it was if they had not first poured out their anguish in the *folge* of Expressionism.

No one can say where Francis Gruber would have gone in his painting if a premature death had not cut off his career; in any case, he remains the most Expressionist of all the painters of his age. Closely related to the exponents of Forces Nouvelles (of the generation to which he was markedly related), he was drawn to them not only through his hostility for contemporary painting and his corollary

FRANCIS GRUBER – THE COMING OF WINTER – 1935 – (2,06; 2,06) MUSEUM, ARRAS

cult for the traditions of the Old Masters, but also because, like them, he sought for a means of expressing the same quality of tragedy in a style that had rid itself of all extraneous matter and thus sought to affect the spectator (as do the masterpieces of Piero della Francesca and Paolo Uccello) rather than appease his sense of splendor and sensuality. Using as they did perspective, modeling, light and shade, Gruber, too, shows a predilection for expressive tortured forms, drawing out disproportionately the limbs of his subjects, whose ankles he makes excessively slender, drawing out more than reason tells us their meagre necks, swelling out their bony foreheads in a way that Nature would abhor. More Expressionist than these painters because of the liberties he takes, he insists more than they do on draftsmanship and design; literally finely etched his brushwork reminds us of that of the German painter-engravers of the fifteenth and sixteenth centuries. In an incisive way, he imprisons, defines and makes vibrant in a masterly way his form which he embodies in a jagged contour. Extremely sensitive and constructed of many small planes and of huge contrasting volumes, this form possesses at the same time the simple truth of a pathetic subject drawn from life, and the sculptural and monumental soaring of a Gothic wooden statue of the fifteenth century. Gruber is a far too subtle painter to situate his form in the void; his canvases are filled with airy spaces, a sharp and humid air, which seems to make this vibrant world shiver with cold. He is extremely economical with colors; tones of vinous red sometimes of seething dullness illuminate his gray. Often apple greens and lemon yellows mingle their strident colors with this overall color effect; sometimes the entire canvas is composed of biting, luminous harmonies which, towards the end of his life, will become softer, more pearly, more lapped in the lavender and mother-of-pearl quality of light, as in his series of landscapes of the forest of Fontainebleau. His treatment is as important as his sense of color. His brushwork which is stroke and drawing all in one serves as a means of expression, as does his richer paint surface which in his final years becomes more enamel-like in quality. His style is, however, just as proud as before. Less tense but more condensed, less obvious but more necessary, it corresponds perfectly to his creative fever which is often visionary *(The Coming of Winter, Homage to Callot)* and which less uniform and sometimes filled with humor and tenderness becomes alternatively sarcastic, morbid, tranquil, objective, and haunts the sick painter whose constitution is underminded by asthma and alcoholism, a sick man already doomed to die. If his last, more serene paintings (those of youthful nudes in the woods) are the paradoxical swan song of the man himself and of his artistic logic, they constitute as well the total of all his experiments and the success by which expressing himself in a pure, essential Expressionism, he outstrips and consecrates it. Thus he succeeds in realizing in his work this tendency whose successive and different expressions take up a preponderant part of French pictorial activity during the period 1914 to 1939.

PAINTERS OF THE
FANTASTIC
from Chagall to Surrealism

THE Expressionists had sung of anguish. At the same time, other painters sang the fantastic. These participated like their fellow artists in the rebellion of irrational forces against the excessive intellectual tendencies of Cubism, and gave whole hearted support to the conception of a fluid style of painting as against that of an exclusively plastic mode. The analogies are close between these two tendencies: in both we find the same rejection of pure painting, the same return of the majority of the painters to the traditional idea of métier, the same exaltation of direct communication by painting in which the artist expresses himself and by which he frees himself; the same attempt to insist on the value of vague emotion; the same conviction that it is only by this emotion and through this emotion that we can enter into contact with the deepest truth of being. None the less, this conception marks a difference between Expressionism and the style of painting whose modifications we intend to study: with very few exceptions the Expressionist painter, *a voyant* of the concrete, does not leave the realm of Nature to soar into that of the supernatural; whereas it is the realm of the fantastic, the *sur*real which constitutes the world of Chagall, Chirico, the Surrealists and their followers whose experiments we will study in this chapter.

Having received an academic training at the Society for the Protection of the Arts at St. Petersburg, Chagall came to France in 1910 and settled at La Ruche. Immediately he comes under the influence of both Cubism and Orphism. After the first impact of these new ideas, he begins to paint more orginal pictures towards 1912, and these are already the ancestors of Surrealist painting. In such canvases as *The Village and Me* or *Self-Portrait with Seven Fingers*, although his intense colors are obviously inspired by those of Delaunay and although the sharp construction of his form as well as the clear-cut organization of the painting all betray the influence of the painters of Puteaux, ([6]) the Expressionist conception of the communicative value of painting and his own shining lyricism already mark him out as a creative genius of the first order. The most original aspect, however, of Chagall's work is the rich strain of fantasy with which he transforms the objects and subjects which come tumbling from his memory and introduces them into his own personal world—a world that is impossible, illogical and unreal. Obsessed by the memories of his Russian childhood with its people and countryside, its customs and costumes, haunted by the stories of his childhood which spring from Jewish rather than from Slavonic folklore, finally burning with anguish when confronted by the world in which he lives, he uses as subjects for his painting his own face which he visualizes as a seven-branched candelabrum, the cattle which his uncle Neuch used to sell as well

MARC CHAGALL – THE VIOLINIST – 1912-1913 – (1,88; 1,57) STEDELIJK MUSEUM, AMSTERDAM

as the isbas of the snowy steppes, the greatcoats of the moujiks as well as the unrolled Torah, and all these memories enrich his imagination which finds artistic expression in canvases full of splendid fantasy. And so in his composition entitled *To Russia, Donkeys and Others*, a pink cow grazes in a dark sky, while peasant women seem to dance a frenzied sarabande in the rest of the composition under the ironic onlooking stars. We are transported into the realm of pure fantasy which from now on we will never leave.

In spite of Chagall's efforts, which now follow, to modify his technique, to change even his paint quality, he will never forsake those enchanted worlds where the most fantastic dream becomes reality, where a man walks upon the waters, flies out through an open window, where animals play music, where objects no longer have contour nor thickness nor weight, but become polychromatic and dazzling, like butterfly wings, diaphanous and featherweight, which exist in the fantasy-ridden world of an imaginative child.

Now begins a more Expressionist period (1922-1927); and then coming down from the heights of his empyrean to the commonplace things of daily human existence—his world, rather the world of his experiences *(The Rabbi)* which he is incapable of evoking without bathing it in fantasy *(Double Portrait of a Wine Glass),* is orientated later (1927-1935) towards the evocation of a gracious universe whose inhabitants are flowers and lovely young girls *(The Acrobat),* but whose details make it as unorthodox as a dream *(The Lovers in the Flowers).* Haunted later by the warning signs of the impending catastrophe, he paints gloomy war scenes—scenes of persecution and death which become more numerous during his exile in the United States and especially after the death of his beloved wife (1944). Dream and horrible reality mingle in these paintings *(War, The Soul of the Town).* Filled with a new

MARC CHAGALL – THE HEN (GOUACHE) – ABOUT 1920 – (0,49; 0,65) MARCEL MABILLE COLLECTION, BRUSSELS

GIORGIO DI CHIRICO – MYSTERY AND MELANCHOLY OF A STREET – 1914 – (0,87; 0,71)
STANLEY R. RESOR COLLECTION, NEW YORK

joyful inspiration on his return to France which is responsible for his landscapes of Paris, he again mingles the imaginary with the real. And this we may say in general, from one end of his career to another and whatever type of painting he does—still life, landscape, portrait, social painting, religious painting—Chagall's inspiration will just not soar without the impetus of this very decided imaginative element. The objects and beings which inspire him and which he untiringly reintroduces into all his paintings and which, without doubt, are of absorbing interest to those psychiatrists interested in his inner life—clocks, chandeliers, violins, animals, reindeers, youthful nudes, angels he makes them all winged and soars with them into an ethereal world where everything whirls, mingles and rises ever higher. His treatment of form, which is slender, light, drawn out as in certain works of El Greco's last period, adds to this impression of fantasy, less however than does his color. His colors are arbitrary—this pig is green, this face red—but above all it is so rich, so iridescent, so seductive, that it becomes very obvious that such color simply does not exist in our poor workaday world. Lively or somber, rich in this almost musical attractiveness, it receives an added strength from the paint quality, especially when Chagall uses gouache, whose dullness he transforms with a mastery hand into a disquieting phosphorescence. And so this art of a wonderstruck child flowers for the whole length of a varied career, and so completely is he obsessed by his dreams that he obstinately refuses to renounce these childhood wonders. Thus an exuberant style of painting developed in a way that we have just shown, and this style is born about 1912 not of the pathetic reality of the Expressionists but rather of the most whimsical fantasy. The fantastic at last gained a foothold in Western painting which had practically ceased to cultivate it since the end of the Middle Ages—with very rare exceptions of which the most glorious example is Goya—but from Chagall on seems to feel a deep need to express an urgent vision in this *genre* which we shall shortly see assuming greatness in the art of Georgio di Chirico.

At the same time as Apollinaire was becoming enamoured with the multicolored and riotous dreams of Chagall, he found among the paintings exhibited at the Salon d'Automne of 1911 and at the Salon des Indépendants of 1912 strange canvases which evoked his admiring attention, canvases in which he saw dead cities dear to d'Annunzio's artifice whose only inhabitants are the shades of invisible people and in which streets stretched out in long perspective under the emptiness of a lonely, hopeless sky. The painter, in fact, was an Italian born in Greece and who after having lived in Munich, Turin and Florence, finally settled in Paris in 1911—this, of course, was Georgio di Chirico.

What was attractive and stimulating in these works to the "discoverer" of the Cubists, the godfather of Orphism, the art lover who was sensitive to avant-garde research? Perspective took a place of supreme inportance, the forms were modeled according to the most traditional rules while those of light and shade were applied with an implacable rigor; even the *trompe l'œil* (deceptive appearance through painted illusion) was not distasteful to the artist. Reactionary in this respect, they were even more so in their obstinacy to sacrifice to a tyrannical drawing a color which had merely local tones, to paint in the most applied manner, to give to the painted surface the most conventional aspect of porcelain and to the painting itself a quality of finish capable of delighting the public of the Salon des Artistes Français.

Was Apollinaire, who had preached a kind of painting without subject, sensitive to the themes of these canvases? They were decidedly literary—literary and heavy in the worst sense of the word, filled with everything that is falsely poetic— those compositions of Arnold Böcklin which Chirico had seen in Munich and had not admired in vain. In Böcklin, one of the most unhappy currents of nineteenth-century art that of the narrative painting of Nazareens, Feuerbach and Marées, makes its reappearance.

As academic in their inspiration as in their execution, academic to the point of realizing, twenty years ahead of time, the evolution of their author who far from abstaining from contributing to this movement like Derain or Utrillo succeeded in making himself the noisy spokesman of the most worn-out traditions, it would be inexplicable that they might have fascinated Apollinaire without a half-inspired, half-applied strangeness and capable, in any case, of producing a change. Sometimes favored by true premonitions (as, for instance, his portrait, in 1912 of Apollinaire with a bullet hole in his temple,) and gifted with a typically Italian science of *"combinazione,"* excelling in mingling, mixing, fusing objects in a magical way to bring out the extraordinary, Chirico transformed with majesty the Italian equivalent of Böcklin and of the nineteenth-century Germans into a vision of the universe. In these inspired, systematic images "of the country of orange groves," the academic was metamorphosed into a fantastic world, an open prey to the hunger of poetry which tortured the animators of the movement after the drunkenness of Cubism. This explains the enthusiastic reception given by so many *littérateurs*—and even poets—to these dream illustrations which led up to Chirico's metaphysical period (from about 1915 to 1925) an entirely Italian period which becomes the principal object of this study.

That this need to react against the exclusively plastic orientation of Cubism and of the Section d'Or ([7]) is a general phenomenon just before the outbreak of the First World War, is proved not only by Apollinaire's enthusiasm for Chirico and Chagall, but also by the about-face of two painters: Marcel Duchamp and Picabia.

Always changing, restless—and perhaps sceptic—to a point of never being able to stay in some sort of formula; capable—more than Picasso—of renewing and rearranging which he feels with compelling need, Picabia had in turn practised Impressionism, an early abstract style (1908-1910), Cubism (1910-1911), a second abstract style marked by masterpieces like *Undine* (1912-1913), to arrive finally after so many experiences to the conclusive evidence of their vanity. There was therefore nothing for him to do but to denounce this vanity whose ridiculous character was brought to his full attention through the advent of the war.

Similarly, Marcel Duchamp, indifferent to his Cubism of 1911 *(The Chess Players)* and to his research in dynamism which brought him in 1911 to create the Salon de la Section d'Or *(Nude Descending the Staircase)*, Marcel Duchamp also finally realized the emptiness of his pictorial preoccupations and felt the urgent need to renounce falsity—the falsity of all art.

A brief stay in New York in 1915 brought these two painters for a short time in close contact with each other; they devoted themselves to overthrow the art idol and to practise, through ridicule, what we can call the "anti-art." Staring open-mouthed, Americans saw Marcel Duchamp exhibit (under the name of R. Mutt), as though it were a question of a piece of sculpture carved with a pair of scissors, a urinal product, the first-born of a "ready-made" series destined to show the absurdity

58

FRANCIS PICABIA — LA FEMME AUX ALLUMETTES — 1920 — (0,92; 0,73)
PRIVATE COLLECTION, PARIS

of artistic creation. In painting pseudo-machines, Picabia killed two birds with one stone: he took to the American cult of machines and to the superstition of all art. Surrounded by artists and art lovers who were all disgusted with plastic, sceptic and anarchic problems, the two of them—Duchamp and Picabia—brought new life to the revue 291 which Picabia transplanted in 1917 to that city of anarchy which was Barcelona.

An analogous movement, however, was begun in Zurich, in that strange country of Switzerland whose neutrality transformed it into a haven for all the pacifists, for all the rebels, for all the intellectuals who, according to one of them, Ribemont-Dessaignes, aimed at nothing less than *the destruction of all human values.* Convinced by the spectacle of universal butchery of the world-wide stupidity of modern Western civilization, as well as that of the absurdity of human life, poets and artists suggested that they confront their contemporaries with their sarcasm and their criticism. Two rebellious German writers, Hugo Ball and Richard Hülsenbeck, a Rumanian poet, Tristan Tzara, an Alsacian painter and sculptor, Hans Arp founders at Zurich of the cabaret Voltaire (whose name alone explains the program), created at precisely six o'clock on the night of February 8, 1916—if we can believe the witness of one of them—the Dada movement, whose name was found purely by chance by Tristan Tzara himself on merely opening to a page in the Larousse dictionary. Coming across this name, they accepted it because, as the historiograph of the movement tells us, *it signifies nothing and wishes to signify nothing.* And soon it was in Switzerland the affirmation of this spirit of negation, of doubt and of a need of renewal. On March 30th 1916, Dada gave a concert followed by lectures on Paul Klee and Lao-Tse; a Galerie Dada exhibited the works of artists more or less advanced, the only ones really spiritually granted were Hans Arp and Max Ernst. And above all, more concerned with ideas than with forms, more curious about literature than about art, Dada published several revues: beginning in June 1915, *The Cabaret Voltaire*, in July 1917 *Dada I, recueil d'art et de littérature*, and in December of the same year *Dada II; Dada III* came to light a year later. The program was listed with verve: "Dada," we read in the July 26, 1916 issue, *"is the art without nonsense or parallels, which is for and against unity, and decidedly against the future."* And in *Dada III, revue d'art et de littérature*, comes forth the following creed: *"Dada, abolition of logic; dance of the impotences of the creation, Dada; of all hierarchy and social equation, installed for thieves by our valets, Dada; each object, all objects, the feelings and the obscenities, the apparitions and the precise shock of parallel lines are the means of combat, Dada; abolition of memory, Dada; abolition of the future, Dada; abolition of archeology, Dada; abolition of the prophets, Dada; abolition of the future, Dada."* And, if all these words are not sufficient to convince certain intelligences, which no doubt are hardly intuitive, the testimony of a man like Ribemont-Dessaignes will make Dada's ambition clearer to us *"a permanent revolt of the individual against art, against morals, against society... and we can see that it liberates the individual from the mind itself since it places genius on the same level as the idiot."*

Peace finally enabled Dada to transport itself to Paris where, during the long war years, an analogous spirit had given birth to several revues such as *Sic* (1916) or *Nord-Sud*, the organ of André Breton, Philippe Soupault and Louis Aragon. Spread by Picabia who from 1918, in Switzerland, joined the Dada movement, it enjoyed its most active years: Matinée at the Palais des Fêtes, Rue Saint-Martin, manifestation at the Université Populaire du Faubourg Saint-Antoine, at the Salle Berlioz (May 27, 1920), *Mise en accusation de Barrès par Dada* (March 13, 1921), participation in the Salon des Indépendants of 1929, organization two years later of a Salon Dada which sounds the death knell of the movement: Picabia quarrels with his former comrades; André Breton and Tristan Tzara quarrel with each other, and there was nothing left for Dada to do but to imitate the example of one of its members, Jacques Vaché, who committed suicide in 1918.

What was the result of all this noise? Surrealism on the one hand and on the other a few works of Hans Arp and above all of Picabia and Marcel Duchamp. If the works—painting, sculpture, graphic arts—executed by Hans Arp from 1916 to 1923 reveal more abstract art than the Dada spirit which appears, in certain other works, only in the taste which they show for the irrational and the fantastic, Picabia, on the contrary, has truly given to the uneasiness of Dada its pictorial expression. Sometimes using Cubist language and sometimes that of abstract art, and not despising academic formulas, it takes the greatest enjoyment in exciting the public by these banderillas which they call "works of art" combining painting and *collage*, introducing printed letters, showing proof of the most eccentric, the most unexpected imagination, with the minimum of illusions about themselves, they turn in mockery— without believing it too much—all the forms of art, traditional or avant-garde, and come up with a *Figure of a Woman* with a piece of string making up the contour and matches modeling the form. In such works, the Dada spirit accomplished itself plastically in Paris, as it did in the United States in the famous *Mariée mise à nu par ses célibataires mêmes* (1915-1923) a large work executed, on a floor af transparent glass, in tin, varnish and colors and making up, according to the artist's first admirer, the collector Henri-Pierre Roché, "*a mystico-mechanical epoch of the Desire of Love. The bride-fiancée hangs in the firmament by her antennae and communicates with the massive group of "her bachelors," red, standing... They receive the fluid of the bride and off in a distance spread out in a dramatico-mechanical and interstellar ballet on human love seen by a human being on another planet who understands nothing, as André Breton stated in the best terms.*"

Buried in 1922, Dada was going to come to life in another form, different however, systematic and totalitarian in the Surrealist movement.

It is to Apollinaire that it is indebted for its civilian status. As a matter of fact, the celebrated poet had dubbed his *Mamelles de Tirésias* as a "Surrealist drama"—a rather picturesque qualification which André Breton and Philippe Soupault took up again for this new school whose principal animators they became together with Pierre Naville, Benjamin Péret, Louis Aragon, Ribemont-Dessaignes and Crevel. Their first tribune was the revue *La Révolution Surréaliste;* André Breton lost no time in replacing Naville as head of it. Very much interested in the plastic arts, André Breton directed his thoughts to the problems of painting and published notably a series of studies that he took up again in his book, *Le Surréalisme et la Peinture* (1928). At the same time, several artistic manifestations affirmed the plastic pretentions of the movement. The first grouped in September 1925 at the Galerie Pierre the works sent by Hans Arp, Chirico, Ernst, Klee, Man Ray, Masson, Miro, Picasso and Pierre Roy. A new painting thus made itself felt with its center

at the Galerie Surréaliste from 1926 to 1929. But in December of the same year there appeared in the *Révolution Surréaliste* a second manifestation of Surrealism which stirred up Robert Desnos, Ribemont-Dessaignes, Vitrac, Limban and Jacques Baron against André Breton and Louis Aragon to whom their pamphlet *Un Cadre* was adressed. André Breton answered them with revengful notices which accompanied the publication of his *Second Manifeste* (1932) and allowing *La Révolution Surréaliste* to disappear, replaced it in July 1930 by *Le Surréalisme au service de la Révolution*, a revue whose title alone sanctified the unexpected shock between this movement and that of Communism. The passionate interest, which became more and more lively, that the Surrealists showed for politics did not prevent them, however, from being interested in the Fine Arts. Several exhibitions were organized, the one that caused

the most noise was that which was held in 1933 and another at the Galerie Beaux-Arts in 1937.

A movement—and here it differed greatly from Cubism—more philosophical than pictorial, Surrealism, according to the testimony of André Breton, is *"pure psychic automation by which one proposes to express the real function of thought either verbally or through writing or in any other way. A dictation of thought in the absence of all control exerted by reason, beyond all aesthetic or moral formation."* Anti-rational, with exasperation, resolute enemy of logic, rebellious against the positivist attitude, *"hostile,"* according to André Breton *"to all intellectual and moral play... made of meanness, hate";* according to its pontifical sovereign it is *"the dizzy descent in us, the systematic illumination of these hidden regions and the progressive obscurity of other regions, the perpetual promenade in open forbidden air"*, that it turns to in order to reach *"the source of all spiritual activity"* and of all true life *"there where our spirit dies, spying on its most secret and most spontaneous movements, those which have a character of revelation, an air of coming from somewhere else, fallen from the sky."*

Giving themselves freely to imagination, to dreams, to intuition, to all obscure forces which alone might bring us into contact with the fundamental and essential truths, the Surrealists thought of having access through this medium to this *"point of the mind where life and death, the real and the imaginary, the past and the future, the communicable and the incommunicable, would cease being seen in a contradictory way"*—to this absolute, in short, to which Rimbaud, Baudelaire, Lautréamont, Gérard de Nerval and the German Romanticists aspired without too much hope and which Saint John of the Cross himself knew well as: God.

What place does painting hold in this profane mysticism, cut off from its object? According to good logic, none; and André Breton was not wrong in professing scornfully that *"Surrealism is simply not interested in other contemporary artistic movements which masquerade under the name of art."* But as we very well know, reason does not always enlighten men's actions, especially when they are filled with scorn—the heart has always its reasons. André Breton's instincts inclined him towards the plastic arts which he preferred to music, and from this point of view he is in complete accordance with the Surrealist aesthetic who placed the emphasis on the visual rather than the auditory, and so began to paint.

And it is not only the example of their paragon, André Breton, which inspired the Surrealist not to banish the arts from their system. It is also the innate value of these arts, invaluable means of knowledge like poetry and by which it is possible to reach the absolute. Reduced in this way to play a minor role which is nevertheless quite important—namely, that of *"expressing even by unorthodox means the mysterious poetry induced by certain combinations of objects which are due either to chance or to the whims of a dominating intellect."* If André Breton and his comrades cannot look at a painting in any other way than *"considered as a window which naturally urges them to find out on what unknown sites it looks upon,"* at least they are well able to perceive or guess that beyond this window there lie strange realms which they thirst to explore. And they are not satisfied in practising the automatic writing discovered by Breton and Soupault, they insist upon the necessity of an automatic drawing, their spokesman being Robert Desnos. Max Ernst had shown the way to this new tendency in his *frottages* ([8]) and *collages*. And what better inspiration or guide could the Surrealists have found in their desire to explore those interior abysses where, they maintained, the absolute was to be found? This movement also engendered a school of painting which—to be quite frank—was rather incoherent and vague, and which found supporters—and here I only mention those painters referred to in the *Dictionnaire du Surréalisme*—in Dada members like Hans Arp and Marcel Duchamp as well as Salvador Dali, Max Ernst, Magritte ([9]), André Masson, Jean Miro and Tanguy to which we may add their precursor Pierre Roy, who also took part with Picasso in the Surrealist exhibition of September 1925.

But we must be careful of generalizations: if the accent is on painting it is not so much the plastic form which interests these artists, but rather the search for knowledge. Therefore their constant aesthetic preoccupation is to avoid confusing these two elements. And so they really intend, when they affirm that this art they believe in is a precious source of psychological and metaphysical truth, to subordinate form to content. What is important to these painters is what their painting *says* and not the *way* it says it. Form, therefore, is neglected. And they even insist on expressing their inner vision by means of the most unoriginal, conventional and anachronistic métier, which even the members of the Salon des Artistes Français would never dare to practise. What do we find? A conventional drawing devoid of all style as of all personal inspiration; arbitrary colors which touch on a chromatic quality and which are completely independent, only distinguished from each other by local colors, a scorn of light and effects of reflection and as empty of inventiveness as of subjective interpretation. A niggardly painted surface thinly applied by a miserly brush which in turn works regularly—one might almost say in the prosaic way of a good conscientious pupil; a mean technique like Meissonnier's; a provocative preoccupation with finish, a smooth appearance like that of waxed canvas, these are some of the characteristics of a good number of Surrealist painters and which spring mainly from their denial of the importance of fine technique and from their desire which was fulfilled to paint in an ironic way. *"The elimination from a painting of its essential pictorial elements seems to me exaggerated and can only result in chaos,"* said quite understandably Christian Zervos in his article *Du phénomène surréaliste* which appeared in *Les Cahiers d'Art* in 1928, in which he contrasted the example of Picasso with that of Dali, Tanguy, Max Ernst and Pierre Roy.

To belittle art so completely—and with what lack of spirit and force!—and to practise the most academic formulas in a much more practical way than Chirico and with considerably less taste, the Surrealists seemed to attain their principal objective which is nothing less than the creation of a magic universe whose significance is comparable to that of Hieronymus Bosch. The constructive critic finds many unsatisfactory elements in their work. What strikes us, for example, on seeing their paintings for the first time is the poverty of their imaginative powers. Refusing to experiment with line and color as did Odilon Redon, for example, or Paul Klee, they restricted their artistic exploration to the creation of fantastic forms and to the disquieting juxtaposition which in the ordinary course of things are diametrically opposed. But these highly unorthodox creations far from leading an organic existence as do Odilon Redon's monsters or even Granville's [10] fantasies are composed of badly unified elements such as the genital organs, surgical instruments or fiendish devices which we find in Tanguy's paintings; these borrowings from Hieronymus Bosch have no unity and make no definite, clear-cut impression on the spectator. The construction also is too obviously made up of these juxtapositions established by the Surrealists between various objects and whose aim can be summed up in Louis Aragon's words: *"The extraordinary is conveyed from the contemplation of the ordinary."* All this structure is too sought after, too cerebral, too lacking in that inspirational spark which we find in the Goya of the *Caprichos* or of the *Quinta del Sordo,* as well as in that strange, forceful undercurrent which we feel in the paintings of Odilon Redon. We cannot believe in Surrealist art because its inherent contradictions are too blatant. One of the most obvious of these is the disparity between its visionary or mystical tendencies and their pedantic realization based on formulas and facile technique.

But to trust in these appearances too much would be to disregard André Breton's warning: *"Personally, I consider a Surrealist image as strongest when it presents me with the highest degree of arbitrariness; this ideal image will take the longest time to translate into understandable language, either because one of its essential elements is missing, or because by making a forceful impact on my consciousness I believe in it implicitly, or again because of the fact that it justifies itself perfectly in an ironic way, or because it belongs to the realm of the fantastic, or again because it masks the abstract by its strong concrete element, or paradoxically because it implies the denial of even the*

65

elementary physical content, or finally because it urges me to laugh.'' With these words of André Breton as a warning, we can never forget that in the Surrealist world appearances are deceptive. And what of their famous academic use of perspective? Here again we must not be deceived—because far from being inspired by realist aims, the Surrealist use of perspective is dictated by a desire for poetic suggestion and for mystery, as in the work of Chirico, and doubtless also in that of his fourteenth century Italian models. At the same time we must recognize that this Surrealist preoccupation with an artistic form which suggests far more than it appears to mean is not used to create an illusionist impression or a realist *trompe-l'œil,* but is specifically intended to fascinate us by its bewitching presence. Its apparent objectivity is no more than the subtlest avatar of a subjectivity which demands a revivifying technique in order to combat the cliched modes of subjective expression. Far from being realist, academic, anti-modern, Surrealism radically changed pictorial standards and constituted the *nec plus ultra* of avant-gardism.

These clever Surrealist techniques could not exist in the void, but needed the support of the public. The principal fault of Surrealist art is its lack of conviction,

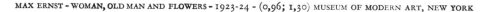

MAX ERNST - WOMAN, OLD MAN AND FLOWERS - 1923-24 - (0,96; 1,30) MUSEUM OF MODERN ART, NEW YORK

and the result is that we only half believe in its import. It is of little consequence, in fact, if the reason for this can be found in the lukewarm devotion of the Surrealists to their new artistic departure; or whether it is to be discovered in the chief contradiction of this system—namely, its materialist-mystic content, which is incapable of accepting these dark nights of the soul or any purifying catharsis as Michel Carrouges has shown in his remarkable study published in the revue *Rencontres* Number 5; or again whether we must seek the root cause of this weakness simply in the failure of an impotent technique to clothe the essential element of fantasy in satisfactory artistic form and so to elevate what is mainly literary to a visionary plane. We are only concerned with the tangible results of this aesthetic which, so far as painting is concerned, is the movement's failure to achieve fully its aims, although it has exercised a fruitful influence on many contemporary activities such as photography, cinema, posters, decoration, etc.

One would have to be a fanatical partisan of the Surrealist movement to deny the mediocrity of the plastic realizations of this school which, Picasso excepted, has produced only one great painter—namely, Miró. Max Ernst, of course, has succeeded in creating, before his departure for the United States, his own artistic universe consisting of a riot of luxurious and fantastic vegetation, petrified forms, various minerals crawling with strange insect life, a world which is unified and coherent and rich with disturbing echos.

Without doubt André Masson has also evoked a mysterious world with his fine sense of rhythm—a world which recalls the fluidity and preciseness of certain Chinese paintings whose influence he felt very deeply. However, the art of Pierre Roy and of Yves Tanguy, in spite of a certain poetic quality and finesse of execution, smells rather rankly of academism, a trap which finally ensnared Salvador Dali. There is nothing surprising, therefore, in the fact that from 1937 on, he whole heartedly embraced the most jaded formulas of Bolognese eclecticism and then, ten years later, those of Baroque art which nevertheless inspired his famous *Christ*. To be quite frank, his art has never stopped being both outrageously reactionary and conventional, since it is based on a meticulous realist search combined with the use of all those clichés so dear to the middle-class heart which he transforms with supreme mastery. Perfect drawing, smooth Vermeerlike surface, complete control of great detail—such were the rich resources which Dali brought to the service of an artistic cause more capable of giving weird titles to his paintings (for example, *Crâne atmosphérique sodomisant un piano à queue)* than of original creation. In fact, there is no need of any great imaginative power to change into ants the notes of a musical score, or to hang a spongy towel on someone's jacket, as we see in his composition at the Musée National d'Art Moderne. Nowhere else better than in this painting, whose only sincerity is a total insincerity (although there are certain valid elements, such as the obsession with certain Catalan landscapes and a certain eroticism inextricably mingled with a far too clever technique, and a marked penchant for exhibitionism) are we brought face to face with the insufficiency of Surrealist painting.

In radical opposition to this is Miró's work as simple and unsophisticated as Dali's is ingenious and tricky, as inventive and impulsive as his is conventional and methodic, as sensuous as his is cerebral, all instinct, all fantasy, all grace. A Catalan Klee greatly influenced by the Surrealists with whom he comes in contact in 1919, shortly after his arrival in Paris, and who were responsible for his renunciation of Cubism, so opposed to his nature, which he had tried for a while (1920-1921), is at the same time least influenced by Surrealism and its most powerful exponent. The least influenced, because his métier has nothing in common with that of his fellow artists. Already sure of his way in 1925 (the year of his first one-man show at the Galerie Pierre) and then maturing rather than evolving this style, enriching it with

68

JOAN MIRO – DUTCH INTERIOR – 1928 – (0,92; 0,73) MUSEUM OF MODERN ART, NEW YORK

the fruit of experiences taken from the other arts (theatre, ceramics, tapestries, wood engraving, graphic arts), Miró's career is from one end to the other homogenous and constant. His art has not the slightest touch of academism about it, because he finds inspiration from the prehistoric graphic art of the Spanish Levant, from popular Majorcan art, from Catalan folklore, and from child art. And this originality comes also from his conscientious craftsmanship particularly evident in the loving care with which he finishes his canvases and also in his search for the light quality of the thick paint surface, and finally in the precision of his free treatment. He achieves a perfect unity in his paintings by intimately harmonizing a lively or discreet background with light, firm, unexpected and nervous lines, which outline in sharp contour the spots of bright color, nearly always elementary and pure, which forcefully seize our imagination by their electriclike quality. And what of his subject matter? Here we find good sympathetic figures, there infinite infantile beasts; higher up bacterialike objects with long tendrils, further down crosses, moons concentric targets, small snakes, and so on. And his color—royal blues, vermilions, canary yellows, apple greens, blacks and whites, grouped in spotty arrangement with such freedom that they seem to dance like glistening fireflies behind our closed eyes. No modeling, no perspective, no light and shade, no composition—at least, not in the accepted sense. But on the other hand, there is always abundant evidence of the his fertile creation of new plastic symbols.

Extending in this way and doubtless without wishing it, the creative adventure of contemporary painting against which the Surrealists had so loudly reacted, Miró with complete self-assurance runs counter to these artistic tendencies of his fellow painters. This he does by the exuberance of his imaginative powers, and by his healthy ironic vein which is all the more convincing because of its completely spontaneous quality. We must not forget of course one of his richest gifts—his sense of humor—that is an integral part of his deepest artistic intuition and of his never failing inspiration. It is not so much the fantastic element of his work which makes it so inimitably his, but rather the sheer fantasy of his creative imagination. And what sincerity this fantasy breathes! It is enriched by his light lyrical approach never vitiated by malicious humor but always permeated by a laughing modesty and utter simplicity. It is above all its grace which attracts us, grace in the double sense of the world, which includes innate elegance as well as a miraculously preserved innocence. There is also an untainted quality about it which avoids tackling problems directly; a freedom, which enables it to solve these difficulties by preterition; spontaneously daring; unorthodox born of a sheer love of orthodoxy, Miró's painting brings us with it into an enchanted world where pure poetry mingles intimately with pure art—is this then the denial or the realization of Surrealism?

Had the Surrealist movement accomplished nothing more than inspire Miró to paint, it would have affirmed its right to be considered as artistically legitimate. But it has done more—it has exerted an incontestable and profound influence on the whole world of contemporary artistic endeavor. To point out merely some examples of this influence in the realm of painting itself, we would indicate the work of Lurçat and later that of the Transhilist painters of the Galerie Gravitations—namely Lafont, Marembert, Cattiaux, Ino, and of many artists such as Bertholle, Carzou, René-Jean Clot, Courmes, Coutaud and Labisse.

Their relationship with Surrealism is so obvious that it is hardly necessary to insist on the parallel, a better working method being to underline in what way they conflict with the Surrealist movement. First of all, they are not deeply interested in exploiting the *"themes provided by the subconscious, luck, madness, hallucinations or humor,"* which Maurice Raynal regards as the domain *par excellence* of Surrealism. Naturally these artists dream too, but as Lurçat has nicely put it *"they dream an exalted reality."* They use real objects then, as their staring point. (Coutaud uses an iron in this way.) If they re-create, transmute these objects by their vision, they refuse, on the other hand, to bring about a metamorphosis; in this way their world is not a fabricated one. Lurçat used to say: *"when I paint a tree, an egg, or a rock I embody these objects in their essential qualities of tree, egg and rock."* This statement is equally valid for all the other artists we have mentioned. According to the source of their inspiration, they vary their technique. These painters simply do not share the same revolt against reason, logic, and métier which the Surrealism loudly proclaimed: *"Even in the midst of his greatest lyric exaltation, the artist cannot allow himself to become a victim of utter chaos—the essential basis of all valid techniques and aesthetics is a strong dose of common sense and orderly imagination."* How little this statement of Lurçat's smacks of Surrealism, whose métier is diametrically opposed to that of Dali and Miró!

There is in Lurçat's art, as in that of Coutaud and Carzou, and even in that of Bertholle, a preoccupation with the decorative and monumental elements, his predilection for tapestry being responsible. Like Coutaud, he has devoted a great deal of attention to this artistic medium. Here as in the domains of photography, cinema, stage décor or posters, Surrealism has succeeded in penetrating into daily life. Surrealism, with Cubism, is the only modern pictorial movement to show such a rich variety of interest. But while this extension of Cubism was dictated by the need for clear logical expression, what a paradox we find in its results! To proclaim their scorn for an exclusively plastic art and to end up designing stage décor! To dream of metaphysical meaning and to find at the same time a source of fruitful inspiration in the walls of ultra modern interiors! But this apparent failure is nothing more, perhaps, than a proof of success—only those arts which dictate can create distinctive modes of expression. That Surrealism gave birth to one such original style is merely an indication of the great need artists felt, after the plastic experiments of Cubism, to escape into the rediscovered realm of the fantastic, where for almost the first time since the fifteenth century, painters had rediscovered the inexpressible delights of unfettered artistic expansion.

The Continuation
of
Pure Painting

BETWEEN the years 1914 and 1939 we find on all sides sharp reactions against the plastic experiments of Cubism and the spirit which conceived them. This revolt has many aspects: the deeply felt need for poetic expression in contrast to the exclusively plastic and intellectual preoccupations of Cubism; the urgency to exteriorise inner conflicts rather than to devote artistic endeavors to solving specifically stylistic problems; a revolt in the name of common sense, of conservatism, of the attachment to a traditional aesthetic as against unrealistic art; a desire to discover through a denuded art a dignity and at the same time to counterbalance the predominance of Cubism. This of course is not the whole truth—for as well as these four main expressions of a common revolt against the Cubist movement, the interest in, and the support of, pure painting continued to assert itself. Important works are born of this interest, which possess complete validity in their own right: for example, the Purism of Ozenfant and Jeanneret, the non-representationalism of Herbin, the work of Beaudin and finally that of Bissière.

During the First World War and above all in the years immediately following, Cubism turned its attention to stage décor (we should mention in regard to this its role with the Ballets Russes) and due to the influence of those great painters—Matisse, Dufy, Picasso, Braque and Juan Gris—who orientated it towards a more understandable mode of expression, Cubism had slipped into facility. A warning note was struck by two young painters, Ozenfant and Jeanneret, the latter to become, of course, one of the most distinguished and inventive architects the century has known under the pseudonym of Le Corbusier. In 1918 they edited a work called *Après le Cubisme* in which they proscribed the abandonment by the very champions of Cubism of those values they had formerly believed in. They recommended also a return to severity, the rejection of all superfluous elements and a new insistence on purity. Hence the name Purism with which they baptised their new movement. Seeking their models in the art of diverse civilizations—Ancient Egypt, Ancient Greece, the great Florentine painters of the fourteenth century, Giotto especially—they also find the art of Poussin, Ingres, Cézanne and Seurat pertinent to the aims of their new aesthetic. The two friends considered that the salvation of painting lay in the practice of a regenerating asceticism founded on logic, economy, construction and synthesis; the techniques of engineers and industrial designers offered them therefore a useful guide. A revue which they animated with a talent only equalled by their courage, served as a platform to expound their new ideas over a period of five years (1920-1925)—we mean, of course, *L'Esprit nouveau* ([11]) which considerably influenced not only painting but also the applied arts and even the cinema.

The best illustration of these theories is precisely the works they engendered: mainly still lifes constructed with great simplicity of line. These elemental forms flow into each other with an easy harmony—for example, the side of a bulging vase is juxtaposed against that of a slender violin, or the vertical line of a bottle is intim-

72

ately mingled with that of an upstanding book. In this way the composition achieves the unmistakable cohesion of distinct grandeur. All the more so because the two greatest exponents of Purism—Ozenfant and Le Corbusier—reduce contours and forms to their simplest. The contours become curved as the forms become level, very delicate modeling being the only element which prevents them from presenting a flat appearance. Outward form thus eliminated, and all detail abhorred, Ozenfant and Le Corbusier, faithful to the principle first formulated by Ozenfant himself: *"painting begins where reality ends,"* paint the entelechy of the object rather than the object itself.

This principle of Ozenfant's associated the two painters with the Cubist movement. On the other hand, these two men were already intimately involved with the same movement, at least during the years 1910 to 1912, by their use of color, by their paint surface and by their treatment. Painting in a monochromatic way, they use neutral and discreet tones exclusively: grays, olive greens, reddish browns which remind us of those of Greek ceramic art (and which Picasso at roughly the same time found so seductive), soft blue lavenders and ochres. We find also plaster white and blacks in the range of colors used by these two painters and whose function it is to fill in the ensemble so as to give form and suggest light. This use of economic light effects gives their paintings a spiritual quality reminiscent of that achieved by Louis le Nain. This predecessor of purist art succeeded in incorporating perfectly this particular effect of light and shade with his thin paint applied to his canvas with meticulous care. He succeeds in creating an impression of imperturbable serenity and anonymity.

Lacking variety though it may, this art nevertheless has real merits which are not sufficiently recognized today. The first of these is its genuine monumental quality which the two champions of this art refuse to banish from the design of their work. Their compositions are severely flat without contour or protuberance and have a fine architectural balance because of the arrangement of objects, the use of regular even lines and ideal proportions. This flat quality suits the wall perfectly —and we are not surprised to discover that Ozenfant devoted much time to the problems of mural decoration (*The Four Races*, 1928; *Life*, 1931). From the simple nobility which characterizes the work of these two painters, an impression of tender intimacy is evoked, like that revealed in the work of their contemporary Italian painters, Carrà and Morandi.

If the severity of its principles which are a little academic prevented Purism from recruiting supporters, at least it had the merit of defending severity and asceticism at a time when freedom in art was the cry, as well as that which is even greater of emphasizing the supremacy of pure painting at a time when less exacting voices commanded the greater audience.

The spiritual parallel between Purism and the current tendencies of abstract painting is obvious. During those intoxicating years before the First World War, this movement invaded the virgin lands of the abstract with an avid enthusiasm which took many forms—exultant in Delaunay's work, whimsical in Picabia's, and romantically lyric in Kandinsky's. But discipline was to follow this wild freedom; and Calvin-Mondrian follows upon the heels of Luther-Kandinsky.

A later recruit of the abstract movement with which he did not associate until the year 1915, Mondrian quickly gave evidence of the most fanatic devotion to the new cause. The puritan atmosphere of Holland (where he was forcibly confined for

CHARLES-EDOUARD JEANNERET
VERTICAL GUITAR — 1920
(1,60; 1,30) MUSÉE NATIONAL
D'ART MODERNE, PARIS

the duration of the First World War) greatly influenced him. In 1915 he lays the foundations of Neo-Plasticism with his associate van Doesburg. In 1916 and 1917 other Dutch painters support this new movement—Van der Leck, Huszan, and Vantongerloo—and all these painters spread the doctrines of their new movement through the medium of their revue *De Stijl (The Style)*. This movement belongs exclusively to Dutch art, but that did not prevent its having a marked influence on French painting, since Mondrian settled in Paris in 1919 and did not leave until 1938, and since Léonce Rosenberg organized in 1923 an exhibition devoted to the work of the *De Stijl* movement.

74

Mondrian's later evolution towards an increasingly austere conception of art is an excellent illustration of abstract art's deep-felt need for discipline after the first fine careless rapture of its early years.   In Russia where abstract art makes giant strides between the years 1912 and 1920 various movements such as the Suprematism of Malevitch whose manifesto dates from the year 1915, the Constructivism of Tatlin, the art of Babo and Pevsner, as expounded in their manifesto of 1920, are all symptoms of this new drive towards control, method, selection and at the extreme limit geometry.   And yet this abstract art which was triumphant in the Soviet Union in 1920, was the very next year put on the index, excommunicated and condemned; its champions had for the most part to become exiles—Pevsner settles in Paris, and so the capital is introduced to these contemporary Russian movements.

Central Europe was also gripped by the same obsession with discipline.   In Switzerland this abstract, almost geometrical art receives stimulation from the work of Sophie Täuber who, living in France with her husband Hans Arp in 1927, painted her masterpiece in Strasbourg during the following year: the decoration of the l'Aubette restaurant to which Hans Arp and van Doesburg collaborated.   These new abstract tendencies entered France by every frontier and finally reached Paris where several of their most ardent exponents, including the Belgian Vantongerloo, had settled. In Decembre 1925 an exhibition entitled "L'Art d'Aujourd'hui" took place in the hall at 18 Rue de la Ville-l'Evêque in which a considerable number of abstract paintings were hung among many other avant-garde paintings.   A good number of these abstract paintings were born of the austere spirit which we have just indicated: those in particular of the supporters of the *Stijl* movement.   Two years later Paul Dermée and Michel Seuphor organized in a gallery in the Rue du Cherche-Midi called "The Rite of Spring" *"exhibitions of abstract art and literary reunions,"* as Seuphor declared.   Still more significant was the Cercle et Carré Exhibition (in itself a characteristic name) which took place in April 1930 at 23 Rue La Boétie. With the exception of some figurative painters most of the participants in this exhibition were decidedly non-representative, and we can say perhaps that nearly all the most important European abstract painters, except for a half dozen or so, were well represented.   Two years later the "Abstraction-Création Movement" was born which published a revue during the years 1932 to 1936, and organized several exhibitions in the Avenue Wagram.

Essentially of an international character and mainly showing the work of foreigners, many of whom do not even belong to the School of Paris, these exhibitions, on the other hand, counted several French painters among their participants: some like Delaunay were the pioneers of abstract art; others like Gleizes, Jacques Villon, Fernand Léger were only influenced by this non-representational art for a short time.   But for certain artists who had just abandoned Cubism this conversion was permanent: we would point to the work of Reth, Charchoune, Closson, and above all to that of Herbin, the most representative perhaps of French abstract painters between the years 1920 to 1940, [12] and finally to Hélion's art who as a young recruit felt Mondrian's powerful influence in 1930.

Won over quite early in his career to the art of Braque and Picasso without, however, any striking results but with the most honorable intentions (from 1910 to about 1914), Herbin sacrificed everything for the first time, from 1917 to 1921, to a decorative and abstract geometry.   Coming back to figurative painting in 1922, in the landscapes painted at that time along with certain elements borrowed from

Cubism, others appeared which he deliberately took from abstract art. Thus we are not in the least astonished that from that time on he deliberately and definitely orientated himself towards this specific form of painting, from 1926 to be exact, and that it had since had an important place in the movement itself. Moreover, it was Herbin who contributed with Vantongerloo to the foundation of *Abstraction-Création* and it was he also who formulated a theory of abstract painted in his book *L'Art non figuratif non objectif* (1949). Cutting up the painting surface with squares or rectangles, he fills them in with solid colors and introduces other geometric figures: circles and triangles almost exclusively which also are filled in with solid colors. Often strident his color scheme combines the most vivid reds with strong blues and chrome yellows; black and white also appear on his palette which seems to include only primary and pure colors. The impassible, inexpressive, careful treatment brings out the striking effect of these pure color tones, the frankness of the contours heightening the contrast. Looking at these paintings which often remind us of roadway signs, we are tempted to ask ourselves if the artist, like his friends of the *Stijl*, has not mistaken abstraction and subtraction. ([13]) But the sincerity of the work on this point is quite evident, and the painter's persistence in this artistic path so obstinate that we cannot deny him a profound respect, nor the painting a marked attention which it deserves, if only for its historical significance in this phase of abstract painting. By its frankness it proves more than any other form of painting how necessary the most headstrong rigor, the most simplified geometry, the most scholarly discipline all were to abstract art. It was the means of finding again a definite intensity rather lost in the excess of Romanticism, and bringing to attention a form which has an exemplary virtue thanks to the desire for an avowed economy of means.

Repudiated by abstraction and Purism almost as much as by Surrealism, Expressionism and Neo-Realism, Cubism seemed destined not to have any future. We can believe this merely from the rare number of painters who about 1930 claimed any kinship to it. Among this small number mention must be made of Borès, Beaudin and especially of Bissière.

Faithful to those whom he first admired, Daniel-Henry Kahnweiler—the "discoverer" of Picasso, Juan Gris, Braque—gathered in his gallery, the Galerie Simon (which later became the Galerie Louise Leiris) the works of those painters who in certain respects continued the art of their famous precursors. The most interesting among them was André Beaudin who, in the words of Jacques Lassaigne *"considered that Cubism remained an excellent method of knowledge and of definition of forms, of organisation of colors and even of rhythmic expression."* Having come under the influence of Juan Gris during the last years of his life, he had benefited by his friendship with the painter by a taste and need of a more thought-out, methodic painting through economic, strained means. At first complex in its rhythms and forms, it became during the course of a slow evolution greatly and decidedly simplified—and, at the same time, filled with a profounder significance and with a more touching humanity. Reduced to a state of purity, the forms or rather the ideas of these forms are composed with a balance where a certain thinness does not, however, exclude a graceful quality, all the more so since the special color confirms this feeling of harmony and elegance. Softened to the paleness of pastel, it is made up of pink, mauve, straw yellow, viridian, gray and above all of many shades of blue : lavender

76

blue, sky blue, royal blue.   Delicate, exquisite, refined but of a sharpness of drawing and of a precision which does away with any danger of softness; a bit dry, but saved by its very flat quality which gives it a distinct flavor, this painting which leans to a certain mannerism and preciosity but avoids them by its sober quality, consistutes in a minor way the most expressive proof that far from being exhausted Cubism has more than enough to feed the other arts.   Without imitating it, nor even being attached to it by more confined and formal means, this painting developed one of the directions that Cubism had pointed out.   The same thing occurred with the painting of Bissière, but in an entirely different direction. ([14])

Ignored for a long time, it has only been during the last few years that this painter has drawn legitimate attention to himself and has acquired the place he deserved—namely, one of the most important among the painters of his generation.

Having approached Cubism about 1920 after playing with all the "-isms" during his youth, a Cubism whose decorative compromises he refused after the manner of the Purists (it was not for nothing that he wrote articles for *L'Esprit Nouveau*), Bissière from his early period showed decided qualities of seriousness, of force, of impressive depth which were the result no doubt of his keen admiration for

AUGUSTE HERBIN – VENUS – (0,72; 1,00) PRIVATE COLLECTION, PARIS

ANDRÉ BEAUDIN – THE BIRDS ARE CRYING – 1933 – (1,81; 2,30) MUSÉE NATIONAL D'ART MODERNE, PARIS

the great French painters of the seventeenth century and, especially, of the demands he made of himself. His *Still life with a Cello* (1921) at the Musée National d'Art Moderne is a characteristic painting of this manner of synthesis which he worked at between Cubism, Purism and classic tradition. Here we see him in love with pure simple forms with their sharp contours and peaceful surfaces which he excels in contrasting with discreet, almost scientific talent: the curves of the cello are brought out in all their compositional value by the straight lines of the frames hung on the background wall; and the roundness of the musical instrument, discreetly modeled, is exalted by the proximity of these rigorously flat objects. Made up of verticals and horizontals, the composition avoids any harshness as a result of the curved contours of the cello, and thus achieves a peaceful and majestic simplicity similar to the compositional purity of Louis le Nain. The color scheme derives its beauty from that of the Cubists as well as from his own; and all these severe gray paintings that Bissière does at that time have the nuance of a pale light subtly brought out by a few notes of color: olive green, tea rose, pale blue. Proud in its modesty of a popular and artisan aristocracy, this art is charged, more so than that of the Purists, with a fervent humanity. It constitutes, therefore, without pretending to and no doubt without realizing it, the French equivalent of the art of Carrà, Morandi and their associates, but with something severe and hidden which is rarely found in Italy and, on the contrary, is found so frequently in France: a heavy meditation, a proud refusal to reveal oneself, a completely Jansenistic aspiration of shedding all that is unnecessary give it a strangely spiritual quality.

From this time on, it is not astonishing that a man deeply involved in such a kind of painting would refuse immediate success in order to carry his searching elsewhere and further; he could have painted like Derain but in a much more authentic manner, capable at the same time of continuing the great tradition without repudiating any of its newness. A demanding person, he wanted more, with the desires at the age of forty that a young man has at twenty. Perhaps in this respect the contact he had with the young people he taught at the Académie Ranson did him a great deal of good: if they benefited a great deal from him, he benefited a great deal from them.

From that time on his art begins to change. A lonely, tormented soul, Bissière shows in his rare attempts at self-expression, by means of a fervent human quality which informs his art, an inexorable inner need for originality and intensity—two characteristic examples are *The Woman in Red and Green* at the Musée National d'Art Moderne (1937) and its pendant which we have reproduced on page 80. Cubism is always there, underlying and more prodigious in its spiritual message—a lesson of method, examples of construction—than in literary advice. And it is from Cubism that Bissière derives fruitful inspiration, if not for the very composition of his figures, at least for their rigorous design, composed of flat planes simply put together. It makes very little difference if this technique of his should give one the impression of subject deformation. The demands of a pure plastic art are greater than those dictated by anatomical interests, in the same way as those of precise color tones are more vital than those of an invented color scheme. The subject, formed of heavy planes each with its distinctive tone, is sharply and strongly defined against a discreet background, so completelely does it dominate the space it occupies. These figures of Bissière remind us of those of Romanesque art, that Romanesque art of his native district, the valley of the Garonne, where he had seen so many choice specimens. These figures evoke the Romanesque because of a certain impression of dynamic movement transmitted to us through a hieratic immobility, an *élan* bursting through the rigid form, making it tense by bestowing upon it a quality of flamelike elevation. His economy of means gives added strength to this intensity. This strength through discipline is one of the essential elements of his art—henceforth Bissière will only make use of simple, indispensable modes of expression, the very ones which characterize the art of this young and ambitious school. In fact, the period between the wars did not know many creations as important as those of Bissière's second manner where plastic purity, a complement to that of inner purity—is at the same time the source of that of human expression. During this time Bissière is essentially the same man who will declare years later (1953) in the revue *Premier bilan de l'art actuel:* "*When I put colors on a canvas I satisfy above all my need for self-expression... the validity of any work of art can be measured by the degree of humanity which it contains and which it succeeds in conveying.*"

Hardly noticed during this time, these paintings attracted no special interest and either because he was discouraged or because he felt a deep need for solitude and

ROGER BISSIÈRE – STANDING FIGURE – 1937
(1,62;0,44) GALERIE JEANNE BUCHER, PARIS

meditation, Bissière left Paris in 1938 and settled down in a farm in the department of Lot. Prevented from painting because of an eye disease, he proceeded to create highly original works of art, made from small, dissimilar pieces of fabric sewn together to create, surprisingly enough, a rather sumptuous and monumental decoration, like the famous Bayeux embroidery (the pseudo "Queen Mathilde Tapestry"). Well again and returning to his love for painting, and finally achieving sucess, he remembers these *"tentures"* and creates a compositional arrangement derived directly from them: planes of solid color, vertical or horizontal, rectangular or square, are juxtaposed in such a way as to leave a maximum of autonomy for each, and thus the signs take on their full significance, giving Bissière's compositions the effect of heraldic coat-of-arms filled with mystery and poetry. The color scheme also with its full, rich tones, has a quality of mystery and poetry; these deep, rigorous tones suggest a music that is both severe and limpid and forever pure despite the diversity, each composition supposing a predominating essence which often gives its name to it: this is the case with the painting *L'Harmonie verte* (Green Harmony) (1950) at the Musée National d'Art Moderne or the one a few years earlier which is entitled *Composition Blue and Yellow* (1950). The paint quality, transparent and deep, like stagnant water, increases the spreading effect of these tones, and gives the painting an aspect of crystal and velvet in perfect harmony with its musical quality. From now on it makes little or no difference whether there is still any reference to Nature or, at other times, whether Nature is completely abolished from his work. Semi-figurative or abstract, Bissière's paintings are, as an ensemble, the result of perfect plastic will and a need for restrained effusion. Manifestations of a pure, rigorous, inventive art seen as an ensemble; human and monumental, hieratic and tender, very different from the work of Paul Klee to which they have sometimes been wrongly compared, foreign to their fantasy, their impulsive verve, their elegance and grace but, on the contrary, wrapped up in themselves, secretive, meditative, almost religious, these paintings of Bissière, these objects of beauty and integrity, constitute one of the major expressions of contemporary painting. Far removed from Cubism, they are nevertheless the result of it, since they represent the accomplishment of a man who, during a period of thirty years, chose Cubism as a point of departure and dared, at a time of general reaction against Cubism, to claim it as part of his art.

THE AWAKENING
of
AVANT-GARDE PAINTING

IN spite of the upsurge, just before the outbreak of the First World War, of the Cubists and the first exponents of abstract art by a few artists who assured the continuation of the tradition of avant-garde but in the background and in a sort of pale darkness, the dominating character of the twenty years which separated the two World Wars had been, as we have seen, a sudden separation in regard to revolutionary searchings of pure painting which marked a period of stop. But suddenly it came to life again and moving forward brought into the pictorial career a whole new generation, audacious, innovating—and all this occurred in 1941. A paradoxical "moving forward" at least in appearance. Three-quarters of France, and Paris especially, strangely enough the setting of this awakening, were under the heel of the Nazi Occupation which professed a violent dislike of all "degenerate art" as they described it. But this "moving forward again" was in fact quite a normal thing and for which the exceptional circumstances of the artistic, intellectual and spiritual life of Paris during the Occupation were responsible.

First of all, there were no critics to speak of—at least, authoritative critics. Those who wrote for collaborationist newspapers were looked down upon for that very fact. They disapproved of the pictorial experiments of the younger painters, but the public chose to ignore them, inclined rather to take the opposite view of what they said. Thus for the new generation disappeared the wrangling of critical credit, more often than not hardly inclined to pay any serious attention to youthful experiments. And, at the same time, a whole group of new galleries was opened to this young new generation, the old ones for the most part having been closed down during the difficult years. The production of "their" artists had ended, and they were hardly interested in offering a chance to the newcomers. But suddenly, beginning in 1941, speculation along with an exceptional economic situation (currency which people hesitated in keeping before the fact that there was nothing to buy) provoked the opening of many new galleries. They found themselves in the position of a racing stable without horses, thus being obliged to appeal to the new generation of painters who, in view of the circumstances, were all, and could be nothing but, French. Those foreigners who were part of the School of Paris had returned, for the most part, to their countries, and the closing down of frontiers made it rather difficult to replace them.

81

CHARLES LAPICQUE — SAINT
CATHERINE OF FIERBOIS —
1940 — (1,15; 0,73) PRIVATE
COLLECTION, PARIS

And so for a while was separated from France this permanent Expressionism effusive and anti-plastic which so often brought new life to art abroad and which marked if not that of the School of Paris, at least of Montparnasse. Deprived of contribution from outside sources which is often an enrichment but which can also become unassimilable when there is too much of it and risk choking the national spirit, the French genius had every possibility to express itself anew: the field was open to the adventure of our young painters.

Now, the spirit of these painters tends to boldness because, on the one hand, they are living through a period of heroism and, on the other, the tempo, corollary with the war, had brutally given a historical place to those painters who were recently caught in actuality. What the conflict of 1914 had done for the Impressionists— disputed in 1913, classics in 1919—that of 1939 accomplished for Bonnard, Rouault, Matisse, Braque, Picasso, Léger, Dufy, Villon: disputed just before the outbreak of war in 1939, they suddenly were at such a distance that their true greatness came forth—a greatness so colossal, so majestic, so authentic, that there was no longer any question as to the value of what they had brought to painting. It made itself felt and imposed itself—and the young painters adhered to it because being cour- ageous, audacious and revolutionary it corresponded perfectly with their aspirations and the needs of the time. The very fact that the Nazis condemned it was sufficient proof of its truth. But it appeared at the same time to be the only French truth; and its defense and continuation became the only possible outlet for the young French painters. Knowing quite well that it was impossible *"to run away from the example of Matisse or Braque"* without *"following in the footsteps of Jean-Paul Laurens and Cormon,"* Bazaine was shortly before the war, like Buridan's donkey, before their example and that of their equals. He was wondering *"what to do in the face of this liberty of artistic inventions, this surplus of solutions which are both our great opportunity and our great danger,"* when the war and Occupation gave him the oppor- tunity, as well as his comrades, to solve this problem: *"On my return from the war,"* wrote one of his friends, Manessier, *"either by simple French politeness or by something deep in myself... feeling in such a moment of despair for the future of French painting that it was better to increase one's love for painting rather than to torture oneself, suddenly without my knowing it extremes met; what seemed to me impossibly opposed, Bonnard and Picasso, for example, I found complementary."* The answer to all this had come from the events themselves which forced avant-garde painting to go forward again. And so it was that on May 10, 1941 an exhibition was held at the Galerie Braun, Rue Louis-le-Grand, just behind what was the German Headquarters (what an irony!); this exhibition was entitled "Exposition des Jeunes Peintres de Tradition Française."

This exhibition grouped artists of various tendencies: those who belonged to Surrealism were found next to those of the Force Nouvelles movement; those who continued Cubism next to their friends who had touched slightly on Expressionism. But a new generation found a place in it, and for the first time, or almost, its best exponents were able to show their work: the leaders were Bazaine, Estève, Gischia, Lapicque and Pignon along with Le Moal, Manessier, Robin, Singier and others.

They all came from different places, but they all had already done considerable research in the field of avant-garde; and some of them by this time had accomplished work of importance: thus—if not Singier, Manessier and Le Moal, still too young to be on equal with the others but who had received the most useful advice from Bissière —Lapicque, Estève, Pignon, Bazaine and Gischia.

Six or seven years older than his comrades, Lapicque, who had studied at the Ecole Centrale, a self-taught painter, had during a period of fifteen years alternated rather conventional works and those, on the contrary, which were audaciously new. If he was reminded of Derain in certain landscapes painted at Paimpol in 1931 and 1932, he had, on the contrary, studied the work of the abstract painters when in 1927 he painted his *Homage to Palestrina* and that of the Cubists, even of the Futurists, in executing his *Portrait of Nelson* and his *Military Funeral of Marshal Foch*; and he finally let himself be drawn to the latter rather than to the former, and it was as much under the influence of certain artistic examples as those of his scientific and philosophical experiences and thoughts. Assistant at the Faculté des Sciences at the University of Paris, author of a thesis and of several contributions to optical science, a friend of Gabriel Marcel and Jean Wahl, he reached certain conclusions which none the less did not prevent him from breaking certain habits, like that—so often cited—"*the pictorial color, par excellence, for the sky is red, orange, or yellow*" and "*the pictorial color, par excellence, for the earth is blue.*" But this breaking away from pictorial tradition was helped by his admiration of Rouen pottery, of eighteenth century printed fabrics and above all by the tapestries, enamels and stained glass windows of the Middle Ages which taught him the lawfulness of measured plastic space different from that of perspective. We see him in this manner brought to his *Saint Catherine of Fierbois*, to his *Maritime Vocation* and to his *Joan of Arc Crossing the Loire* (1940) where he said of himself, "*A blue structure* ([15]) *sometimes figurative and sometimes abstract allows red and yellow to come through transparently. This space, however, is not univocal, but, like that of Cubism, it often has a certain ambiguity.*" He substitutes a moving space to static Florentine space, in which the forms are transparent and where a dynamic perspective reigns in harmony with the essential dynamism of the universe and of life.

About the same time Bazaine himself reached the same conclusions. He also had begun painting in a rather traditional manner, faithful to the examples of the Old Masters and to the picture of Nature. But having listened to Bonnard and Gromaire, he realized what had occurred during the past fifty years of pictorial activity and accepting this as a great lesson, evolved towards an art which, more than that of Bonnard and Gromaire, is indebted to the Cubists and Cézanne. Having learned from them the use of a new artistic vocabulary and of a new syntax, he applied all this to a more demanding interrogation of the exterior world which from now on he wished to understand in a more profound way. Mobilised in 1939 he comes directly into contact with Nature which he analyzes, pencil and pad in hand, during the war; he discovers that Nature is dynamism, and that it is the artist's duty to capture it and translate its secret and fundamental rhythms: he must learn "*the interior geometry of forms*" which attracts him, he admits, "*more than their appearances. A tree,*" he goes on to explain, "*a landscape, even a human face: I visualize them all by the complex network of lines going in all directions, by the lines of force*"—in short, by their intimate structure, which he excels in translating, beginning in 1940, but less by the contour which, he says, "*has never meant anything to me,*" than by the construction, the movement and the color, or, more exactly, by the "*colored values*" which are "*a value of space and of atmosphere,*" and thus set the object itself in the universe. In fact, between them there is no contradiction. *The more*

84

one penetrates into the interior of an object, far from closing in on itself, the more it opens out to an entire universe." And to support this affirmation, Bazaine can cite the example of Cézanne in his old age—the Cézanne of the *Bathers* and the *Bois de Bibemus*—who turned *"towards general forms bathed in an essential light... where the anatomy of the world is not that of a dead body on a dissecting table, but that of the great cosmic movements of living forms."*

It was less from the Cézanne of this tendency and more from that of the *Card Players* that Estève drew his inspiration. As a matter of fact, he had painted, in 1935, in his native village pictures already of majestic beauty: the *Card Game* and the *Blue Sofa*. In addition to the influence of Cézanne we must add that of Picasso *(Christine with Friends*, 1938*)* and that of Braque whose *Duo* painted in 1937 seems to have determined Estève's *Bach Cantata* painted the following year. In addition to the painters mentioned, Estève was influenced by Matisse and by his use of striped fabrics in the background in order to bring out the figures and the ensemble. Between Estève and these masters there existed elective affinities—an analogous sense of intimacy, of the secret life of things whose grandeur he felt so profoundly that he was able to create the equivalent in his paintings only by treating them majestically and animating them by an exacting geometry and by the transformation, due to the deformations, into objects of rigorous plastic forms.

The relationship is close between Estève's production just before the outbreak of war in 1939 and that, contemporary, of Pignon. These two young men had met not only at the Club des Indélicats, but also at the Belleville Drawing School. The subjects are often similar: still lifes filled with rather poor objects but touched by humanity—kitchen scenes or those of a meal; intimate scenes often inspired by family life. The style is analogous as a result of those of Picasso, Braque, Matisse, Cézanne. Similar reds, intense, choking the canvas in an almost burning sense, are associated with similar blues, also intense, with their muted glow. The coloring also is close to that of Estève's *Blue Fruit Dish* (Jacques Bazaine Collection) and Pignon's *Still Life with a Red Tablecloth* (Musée National d'Art Moderne) whose graphic quality also is very close with deliberately broken accents and systematic dissymmetry, this way of emphasizing the contours of the table through clearer or more somber color defining the separation of forms. Pignon's personality is no less different from Estève's—we see this, beginning at this time, in his painting. Aware of social problems, he turns quite often to popular scenes *(The Dead Worker)*, treating them in a less introspective style, more exterior perhaps, but also more ample and where an epic touch is felt. His color is less refined, but it has more force and violence. His form takes on mass: it is closer to that of a plastician combining powerful massive elements with those related to the Baroque than that of a musician skilful in heightening the melody of a subtle and definite arabesque.

But in all that they differed in artistic temperament and formation (and let us not forget Gischia, this lucid and determined creator of impeccable still lifes in which he combined the teachings of Matisse with those of Léger), all these artists, none the less, were brought to the same conclusions. They were quite evident in the paintings of the exhibition Jeunes Peintres de Tradition Française and in those they created or that were created by their comrades Manessier, Singier, Le Moal, Tal Coat, Fougeron, Robin, Burtin, Dayez and others during the four or five years that follow.

Could we define their works of that period as the heritage of Cubism? We are led to believe this from their choice of subject matter. Still life is popular, and its treatment is often similar to the manner in which the Cubists treated it. They like not only constructed forms which they compose through a rigorous scheme of diagrams, but also these forms are used and regarded as certain norms dear to the Cubists. Thus they all use a multiplication of view points—which permits Gischia, for example in his *Canvases*, to make us see what there is in a fruit dish whose upper part he sees from another angle than the bottom. The different planes of the table are also, in the same composition, examined and represented according to different angles in very much the same way, to cite another example, as in Estève's *Young*

Girl with a Pitcher or Pignon's *Woman with a Bowl* or Bazaine's *Still Life before the Window*, etc... Thus the composition takes on a mural aspect without, however, enclosing itself in a world of supported design, trying to respect and at the same time go beyond its demands: the presence of open windows in the background of the three paintings mentioned above is a revealing characteristic of this desire, which is not exactly a habit and yet frequently found in Lapicque and Bazaine, to give the forms a transparency which allows the spectator to see others behind it, without having to indicate them in this world of theirs where there is, so to speak, no perspective whatever. Nothing is more significant in this respect than the important pages of Lapicque entitled *The Factory on the Abdelle, The Big Talavera, The Battle Horse*.

87

Thus—as much as this transparency is inseparable, on the one hand, from a multiple, multivalent space, with no relationship whatever with tradition and Nature ([16]) and, on the other hand, from certain tributary deformations of those of Cézanne ([17])—they introduced in the painting a moving, living and fluid quality which, taken as a whole, gives the spectator the impression that the table moves, exists in time and makes up, as Lapique himself writes *"an almost irresistible invitation to dynamism."*

But here we are suddenly far from static Cubism and less disturbed by the problem of space than that of the object, of volume and of construction. If the young painters of the Tradition Française have utilised certain methods of this school, it is both because they fell into public domain and because it was necessary for them to make use of them, even if it was in order to try for different objects. Cubism was for them, to quote Bazaine, a*"point of departure"* which enabled them to seize the opportunity—but an opportunity which brought them where they had intended to go.

Was it towards the same horizon as the Futurists or the painters of the Section d'Or? Not at all. Their need of dynamism is something else entirely. Less descriptive, less turned inwardly, it is the very life of the world that they wish to understand and bring into their paintings which are not images of movement, but movement itself, time infused in space, becoming forceful in the very act of being. In regard to this shall we speak of Orphism? Not one of these painters had turned to Delaunay for inspiration and guidance, to a work which they had hardly paid attention to, and furthermore not one of them had thought of painting the cities, the machines, the modern life which were necessary themes to Delaunay's curiosity and to his personal experience of dynamism. On the contrary, when they get away from still lifes—and all of them, except Gischia, did not fail to do this especially beginning in 1942—it is often to paint landscapes: we see this in Lapicque's *Farm in Ile-de-France* (1942), Estève's *La Maison Perony* (1943), Pignon's *Orchard in Normandy* (1943), Bazaine's *Swimmer in the Reeds* (1943), Manessier's *Calvary in the Woods*. It confessed a leaning rather strange to Delaunay's art and a tendency to understand the dynamism of life less in human creation than in the things of Nature. As paradoxical as it may seem, it is not Orphism which is brought to mind in this respect, but rather the art of the Impressionists and still more that of Bonnard. In fact, it is not an accident that Bazaine, Estève and Gischia himself have always confessed a fervent admiration for Bonnard. The reason for this is that they discovered in his painting certain preoccupations with space and color analogous to their own and, as a result, found an answer to several of their pressing questions. Far from stopping at the appearance of this art, as did Brianchon, Legueult, Cavaillès, who saw in it merely the supreme flowering of the most Attic taste, they penetrated to one of its most fruitful secrets: this miraculous harmony that Bonnard achieved with the changing character of the world; this audacity with which, as though he had not touched it, he drained, so to speak, from each of his canvases, the very flux of life; this submergence that each of them makes up of the eternal moving essence of being and of existence. The universe for the Cubists was *immobility.* For Bonnard who, in this respect, had inherited the teachings of the Impressionists, it is *becoming.* And feeling it as such, Bazaine, Lapicque, Estève and their equals were led to turning towards the art of the patriarch of Cannet—and to borrow one of his fundamental resources—namely, color.

For more than anything else, it separates their painting from that of the Cubists: as much as the one confines itself to a neutral color scheme, both because it is voluntary and because it feels a need for nothing else, the other, by taste and necessity, calls for fresher and more intense tones, as powerfully effective in Matisse's work as in that of Bonnard.

Here, in fact, is the last spiritual father of their movement. Not that they found in him a fraternal soul sensitive, as they are, to the dynamism of life and to that of painting: on the contrary, no art is more static than his. But like Bonnard, not more so than Bonnard, but in a more evident way, because the Old Master of Vence, more agressive, prouder, more systematic, a majestic colorist, knew how to enlarge the domain of color and add new functions to it. Color is for him not only the means of translating objects and the light that strikes them, but it is a means of translating space as well because it is charged with proper spatial value. Rich in unique—and global—power of defining form and extension, it constitutes for the painter the totalitarian resource which enables him to evoke, synthetically, the ensemble of the exterior world. And there it becomes a resource all the more precious to him as it is in addition the place *par excellence* where the objective representation meets the subjective interpretation which the painter is able to give it. And through it the artist is able to express the totality of the universe with an ease, an economy and a freedom which makes possible all the daring liberties he takes, as well as all the accessible effects, even the strongest and the least known. We can understand that the young painters of the Tradition Française took care not to despise this color which was rather discredited, however, in the eyes of the avant-garde since the advent of Cubism and the rehabilitation by them of neutral tones. It makes no difference—or very little—that an Estève, painting in light touches à la Bonnard, likes to multiply the most varied nuances and provoke each tone by the contrast that he discreetly establishes with the one beside it, while a Gischia, using color in the manner of Matisse with large flat areas, establishes between them separate edges, and thus running against each other in a violent way, assures the painting of a supreme tension, and fills it veritably with an explosive electricity. If the means are different, the goal is the same. Similarly it is indifferent if someone like Lapicque takes a liking for colors more alive than striking, and fresh rather than intense; while a Pignon loves the most vermilion reds, the most saturated blues, golden yellow, emerald green, certain very special violets of a rare sumptuousness *(Maternity and the Coffee Pot)*. The color scheme can be different, but it allows the painter to achieve the same results: the creation of a canvas which, because it captures the dynamism of life, translates it and imposes its violence on us by works so denuded and so evident as his.

And it is in this respect that we can speak of the Fauvism of these artists. Not that they were ever led to pattern their works after a Derain, a Vlaminck : a trip to Germany that the painters made threw discredit on them precisely at this time. But it is because they shared one of the essential attitudes of the Fauves: their discovery of the fecundity of poverty and that, corollary, of intensity by means of economy. Like them they forced themselves, according to the words of Bazaine, *"to find again the essential through violence, the passion of expression based on a choice of colors and of elementary forms."* And rich, as they are also, *"in this nudity in the face of a chaste world, this purity and simplicity of intentions and means, this frankness and liberty which not one of them can call "clumsiness,"* they succeeded in being unburdened travelers and, from this very fact, ready to make all conquests. *"Neither Fauve nor Cubist, but inconceivable without them, young French contemporary painting seems to me to be situated in the evolution of French art and its effort to continue logically*

JEAN BAZAINE — LA MESSE
DE L'HOMME ARMÉ —
1944 (2,22; 1,40) WILLY
GRUBEN COLLECTION,
BRUSSELS

that of its elders." How could we not confirm, judging from this analysis, Jean Bazaine's conclusion which is an answer also to the questions he had asked himself shortly before seeing the contributions of Bonnard, Matisse, Léger, and the Cubists. *"Have we the right,"* he asked, *"to renounce the findings of such richness again and to close our eyes to it?"*—*"I have the presentiment that in this field one has gone as far as one can and that everything has been tried,"* Chapelain-Midi had written in 1935. To this the young painters of the Tradition Française answered in the words of Bazaine:*" the adventure of French painting during the past fifty years has been the only reasonable way."* Consequently, it was fitting to take up this way which had been forsaken since the First World War, and not only to take it up in 1941 in order to mark time, but to go ahead as well.

LÉON GISCHIA – THE CANVASES – 1944 – (1,00; 0,81) MUSÉE NATIONAL D'ART MODERNE, PARIS

Directly influenced by Picasso, Braque and Léger, but also by Matisse, Bonnard and Cézanne; finding again not so much by attraction as by necessity certain attitudes of the Cubists and the Fauves, and even the champions of Orphism; but gathering from these first fruits new conclusions and elaborating an art which, far from being an eclecticism, as we have sometimes seen, ([18]) is a continuation and, even more, a complement of these movements which it sometimes denies, sometimes achieves and which it always goes beyond; Lapicque, Bazaine, Estève, Gischia and Pignon, followed by Manessier, Singier and Le Moal, were not merely content to make a brilliant start at the Galerie Braun; during the following years they affirmed their viewpoint in a series of artistic manifestations which established the brief existence of their movement, at least as a coherent one. In 1942 an exhibition of their work was held at the Galerie Friedland; in 1943 exhibitions at the Galerie Berri-Raspail and at the Galerie de France; and at the Salon d'Automne of these two years and especially that of the Liberation where beside Picasso they triumphed in a room entirely devoted to their work. In the following year they drew the most attention at the Salon de Mai, which was the theatre of operation of their generation, created by Gaston Diehl (an art critic as courageous as he was active and perspicacious) with the help of Pignon, Gischia, Manessier and Singier. From then on they were on their way: Fougeron was awarded the Prix National in 1946. Recruits gave support to their movement: Burtin, Dayez, Fulcrand, Mouly, Tailleux, Moisset. Older painters leaned heavily in their direction, Chastel, for one, who following their example gave up the realism of his early period *(Les Enfants de l'Epicier)*, and followed a path which led to his meritorious award of the Grand Prix de Peinture of the first Sâo Paulo Biennale in 1951. Another example is André Marchand who in his *Hostages* and his *Fates* was won over to their intense and irrational color, to their violent drawing, to their deformations, and used everything for the sake of his early expressionism which as a result was reduced to more specifically plastic searchings *(The Bottle and Fruit)*. There is no doubt that this conversion was helpful, since the discreet amateur of cameos emerged as a powerful and rare colorist, and since it brought forth a precise and exacting draftsman as skilful in defining forms with the brush as he was in drawing from arabesques a subtle musical quality and a decided decorative power.

But already the group was breaking up: the Galerie Louis Carré had attracted Bazaine, Estève and Lapicque and had held a collective exhibition of their work in 1945, before giving Lapicque a one-man show in 1947 and one to Estève in 1948. Manessier, Singier and Le Moal were the "great hopes" of the Galerie Drouin in 1945 before joining Gischia, Robin and Fougeron in 1946 at the Galerie Billiet and, shortly afterwards at the Galerie de France, Pignon, who had not ceased exhibiting there since 1945. But this dividing was not only a result of the art dealers' choice, but also a result of the evolution of each of these painters. Their complex art had succeeded because of circumstances and because of this need so striking of French totality, felt from 1914 to 1945, to establish a balance between diverging tendencies. But this balance could be nothing else than precarious. As a result, it broke away, beginning in 1947, and each painter went his way.

For some it meant the complete giving up of painting, as was the case with Robin who since that date, almost ceased, unfortunately, to paint. For others, like Fougeron, it was the repudiation of political opinions; in 1948 he joined the camp of social-realism along with other painters inclined to Communist aesthetics: Amblard, Taslitsky, Vénitien.

Pignon, who also was a Marxist, did not believe, however, that he was obliged to join this group and remained instead faithful to himself, which nevertheless did not exclude a very marked evolution of his art. Social subjects become more abundant in his canvases, he likes to retrace the labor of Ostend sailors (1947), the sturdy frame of miners (1949), the sweat of a Provençal digging away in his field of olive trees (1950), the work of electricians among the wires (1955). Still life and even landscape give way to figures which are sometimes, as his *Nudes*, merely a pretext for a robust and healthy Rubenslike sensuality. Increasingly aware of Picasso's prestige, he allows drawing to take precedent over color. The sumptuous colorist of 1941 changes himself into a valuist but this rare valuist excels in giving to the grays a quality of light, and in bringing them out by pinks, blues, sometimes even by the red touch of a bloody sun. The expressionist wins out over the plastician, but does not destroy his profound and permanent originality. In fact, if an irresistible movement quivers through the order of the painting, based often on the diagonal or the vertical compositional pattern of Rubens or of Northern painters, it is because, as before, Pignon is in agreement with this dynamism of life of which henceforth he has perhaps even a vaster, profounder, more generous experience. In this respect we should look at his sails blown full by the wind, at his olive trees whose everlastingness is reconciled with the timeless setting of the sun, at his eternal nudes elevated, like those of Renoir, to the dignity of myths. And this feeling is always expressed only through spacial searchings: often making use of plunging perspective, raising the horizon line, superposing the distant objects on to the foreground designs, pushing the entire landscape before the canvas, Pignon reconciles his composition with his fundamental dynamism where everything moves and seems to breathe to great elementary pulsations.

The study of movement and its pictorial translation also drew more and more Lapicque's attention. It brought him round to painting racing scenes (1949) regattas (1951), marines, and even compositions like the *Liberation of Paris* (1945) and the *Battle of Waterloo* (1949). Anxious to express it through means other than traditional and more suited, by their very nuance, to render it more adequately, he turns to color which he increases to the point of making his marines a veritable puzzle of spots of pure color tones bordered by white. We can thus easily understand why he was so fascinated by Venice and the Venetian school of painting, especially Veronese and Tiepolo. Based exclusively on color, his art allows no place for volume any more than for composition, which he replaces by what one of his exegetes has called the "plastic discourse," suitable to expressing this dynamism of the world that Lapicque wants so much to translate that he refuses to resort to the abstract.

The art of Tal Coat is equally quite far removed from abstraction, and for the same reasons. Changing, less by versatility than by curiosity and uneasiness, coming from the Force Nouvelles movement to that of the Jeunes Peintres de Tradition Française where he brings a note all his own of Expressionism, if he leaves the latter it was, both properly speaking and figuratively, to make a pilgrimage to the Château Noir. ([19]) Having settled down near Aix in the vicinity, he drew from the sight of the old walls and the surrounding vegetation the same revelation as Cézanne in his old age: that of the essential life of the world. Helped by the influence of his neighbor and friend, André Masson, he discovered at that time in Oriental painting, in the landscape of the Sung dynasty in particular, the model or rather the suggestion of what he wanted to do; and he paints right off works which are without precedent in Western painting—landscapes where Nature is not viewed by a spectator from the outside but where it is seen and, still more, felt from the inside somewhat as if it could see itself by means of a spirit within, without, however, losing itself and take part in its inner growth.   As he finds the type of Oriental painting in plant sap as much as in the rustling of the wind and the light that cuts across space, he paints and signifies the blade of grass no less than immensity.   There is no scale: for it is the same life.   Nor is there any differentiation of material for the same reason.   Vegetable matter, minerals, water, air, all is identical, blown up by the activating presence.   And for the same reason, everything is movement, flux, manifestations of a force which he refuses to confine in a ridiculous contour or immobilize in a set form. His paintings are made of drippings whose colors flow towards a trembling background.   There is no affirmation either.   His paintings are merely propositions in which he achieves this prodigious quality of reconciling a great deal of passion with a great deal of silence for the greater good of an apparent ambiguity and of an indefinite movement which is life itself.

PIERRE TAL COAT — SOUVENIR OF DORDOGNE — 1955 — (1,00; 1,32) PRIVATE COLLECTION, PARIS

If Gischia also refuses abstract art it is for an entirely different reason. Remaining, like Tal Coat, Lapicque and Pignon, faithful to appearances—which he does not refrain from deforming and interpreting—he is as classic as they are baroque, as in much in love with rigor as they are with abundance, as exact in economy as they are carried away with themselves and brought to the heights of lyricism. There is little variety in his themes: still life always with some object, sometimes with figures shut in the interiors. Nothing moves in this world, and yet everything is extended, brought to a paroxysm of a crispation which fills the paintings with a strange energy. Removed of extraneous matter to a voluntary degree of dryness, the brushstroke embraces the forms with a cold demanding passion: a little more and it would strangle them. Blues, greens, lemon yellow are the painter's usual colors which tone the vermilion to the cold side. A certain metalic quality comes forth in his paintings, and their thin and very shiny surface, their execution belong even more to steel. An irresistible strength comes through in his work, especially since by his admirable décors and monumental costumes for the Théâtre National Populaire, he has developed a sense of architecture and of rhythm which the study of Romanesque painting had brought to a point of refinement. The Prosper Mérimée of painting, concealing under an exterior imperturbability a nervous sensitivity which he enjoys submitting to a keen intelligence and a lucid will, he knows, better than anyone else, how to be intense by being simple and how to enclose an inexhaustible potentiality of dynamism in the proud construction of his works and of his work in general.

But if these four artists remained attached to figurative art, it was not the same for most of their comrades of the exhibition of May 1941 who willingly, beginning in 1947, abandoned recognizable appearances in their works. If they did not consent to abstraction, they consented at least to the absence of all representation. In fact, they refused to paint in an abstract way similar to that of the members of the Salon des Réalités Nouvelles who, for their part, did not consider them as being part of their movement; and the heralds of abstraction—Léon Degand, for example—had nothing but sarcasm for these Bazaines, Manessiers, Singiers, Le Moals who, he thought, did not dare cross the Rubicon and deceived, as he says, their figurative wife with an abstract mistress. There is nothing more unjust than this tirade: for Bazaine, Manessier, Singier, Le Moal never for a moment thought of cutting themselves off from Mother Nature through whose contact they nourished their art as Antaeus from that of the Earth. The testimony of Bazaine, in his *Notes sur la peinture d'aujourd'hui*, is in this respect decisive and confirmed rather closely by Manessier, Singier, Le Moal. If abstract art is *"the absolute rejection of imitation, reproduction and even the deformation of forms derived from Nature"* [20] and if the proper attitude of these exponents consists in *"refusing to allow the outside world to enter into (their) art and forcing themselves despite all outside influence (?) to construct the drama of lines and colors,"* [20] Bazaine addresses a double criticism of prime importance: first of all, that all art is abstract and cannot but be this *"in the measure where it is not Nature, but a contraction of all reality,"* [21] and afterwards that *"the forms of a painting, as little figurative as they may be, must, even passing through us and coming out of us, come from somewhere."* [21] Thus Van Eyck's painting is abstract and as abstract—though in a completely different way—as that of Kandinsky; and what makes the beauty of the first one—which he does not deny—is also what makes the other one beautiful, as pure and as universal as the other: *"If there is not every-thing among the most figurative of our great painters, if there is not everything, and mathematics in a square centimeter of Vermeer, then burn down the Louvre and forget painting entirely."* ([22])   The fact that some of the painters thought it best to express themselves through recognizable objects—*"a horse of Uccello moves me more because I recognize not so much a horse but a Uccello horse"* ([23])—and that others preferred to dispense with these references does not imply on the part of the latter a progress but rather a poverty: to dispense with the world is to mutilate oneself, *"it is refusing to listen to oneself, it is a manner of suicide,"* ([24]) since after all this world is nothing but our own flesh; and it means also running the risk—which happened to Kandinsky—of seeking *"an incarnation which is refused,"* ([24]) and through this mistake painting does not achieve *"this mystery, this sympathetic magic of sensitive geometry, this going beyond geometry which we find in any one of the works of Klee."* ([24]) The sphere of an abstract is never anything but a sphere; Cézanne's apple is itself an apple and a sphere—an apple which is something else entirely than an apple, and more.   *"Art has never resembled anything in Nature; if it resembles anything it is Manand all that is least figurative in him: physical reflexes, impulses, sensations, conceptions of the world."* ([25])

Nothing is more different, therefore, in the attitudes of abstract painting than those of Bazaine and Manessier; nothing is more opposed to abstraction than their non-representation, all the more so since it seems to resemble the same thing to someone who has not been warned of the difference.   For the point of departure for these two painters is both Nature and life as opposed to that of other painters, and their paintings imply a long interrogation of the universe, pen, pencil, brush in hand. This fruitful study enriches the painter of the very life of the world.   In contrast to drawing in abstract painting which *"quickly becomes monotonous,"* the process of drawing from Nature allows for *"a deeper understanding of rhythms, forces and struc-tures than from the mere process of sight,"* according to the words of Bazaine, cited by Aimé Maeght.   And what Bazaine says of drawing "from a theme," Manessier will gladly say later on of watercolor and wash drawing.   If Bazaine's portfolios are full of studies made from plants, trees, rocks, stones, even of human beings, those of Manessier overflow with washed leaves at the country, at Crotoy in particular, where he seized upon a reflection of water, a play of light, a silhouette of a sail, a cloud, wind...   Taking as a point of departure these studies of the outside world, where they noted not so much its appearances as penetrated its structure, understood its living forces, they played a sort of winning game of retaining in their paintings this profound and moving life which they had felt at the beginning.   And if the finished work presents hardly any resemblance with the picture of the outside world, it is because it resembles it in profoundness as it does to all analogous sights.   They are the morning spaces Manessier painted, summed up, made significant, equalled, in his *Espace matinal* at the Musée National d'Art Moderne, and the essence of sea wind that Bazaine has expressed in his *Vent de mer* at the same museum.   Non-represen-tative art?   Rather an art in which the objects represented are not immediately identifiable because they are structures and essences; I would almost say the ideas of things (in the etymological sense of the word) and because by their generality they transcend the ever partial phenomena which strike or affect our senses.   Neither abstract nor figurative, this painting seems to deserve the title "super-representative," if this neologism by its very pedantry was not completely opposed to all that is authentic and true in Bazaine's painting.

Sharing this position of reserve in regard to abstraction and of distance in respect to an identifiable transcription of the universe, to which Pignon, Lapicque, Gischia and even Tal Coat remain faithful, in spite of their non-realism, Bazaine, Manessier, Singier and Le Moal still are very different from one another.

Organizer and star of the 1941 exhibition, Bazaine is the eldest of these painters. Evolving slowly far from the art he practised from 1941 to 1945, he arrived, from 1949, at a defined manner of painting which he seems just to have left. What characterizes his painting first of all is the need of going beyond the result which he achieves in his figurative canvases which, he says, "*enclosed... only a small portion of reality... Not because they were figurative, but because this figuration was, in a certain manner, short-termed.* Turning to reality more inwardly and at the same time intimately, he wants henceforth to translate the last stage of this act of possession—this act of possession of the world by himself and of himself of the world. "*Reality,*" he says, "*has reached its extreme tension point for me... it retains in itself the essential quality of its successive states, it exists through them, it thus remains open to the world, but if all that is essentially 'abstraction', it has nothing abstract in the ordinary sense of the word. I even think that this last term of these transpositions is simply reality.*" All the more so since there exists a harmony and a relationship between man and the world, between the universe and the artist—one of whose vocations is precisely to discover and to express this essential relationship through art: "*True feeling begins,*" Bazaine assures us, "*when the painter discovers that the bark of a tree and the swirl of water, are related, twins, the stones and his face, and when the world contracting thus little by little, he sees rise, under this rain of appearances, the great essential signs which are both his own truth and that of the universe.*" There is nothing astonishing, therefore, that from now on his paintings, in order to restore it better, will embrace the very structure and the very life of the sights of Nature which attract his attention so much, arouse his thought and, even more, draw him to meditation.

Feeling it more and more as an *élan*, and the world and existence and even God, as is the case in the majestic mosaic made in 1951 to decorate the façade of the Audincourt church, Bazaine constructs his works which he powerfully indicates with forceful lines, using diagonals or spirals which introduce always an ascending movement (*The Diver*, 1949; *Trees and Rocks*, 1951). He introduces a circular rhythm, not by closing in the lines but by tacking them on to the predominating obliques, which not only create a dynamism in the painting but also tend to enlarge this whirlpool to a cosmic dimension *(The Birth of a Day*, 1950*)*. Enclosed by directions often indicated by black, the color is carried away in this fundamental *élan* to which it adds a supplementary dimension: space, which it is part of his nature to create out of deep necessity. Between the grillwork of the parallel diagonals there thus opens a deep field of tones, all the more generators of the infinite as they are filled with light and, from this fact alone, they give not only an impression of atmosphere but also a suggestion of time. Often blues, mauves or violets, almost always cold, the colors which dominate the background are also brought to the surface of the composition by the warm tones—generally stronger and deeper—of reds, purples, yellows which Bazaine uses to fill up the foreground and with which he merges subtly the lighter harmonies of the background, thanks precisely to the blacks of his grillwork design. Thus the work possesses not only a monumental quality, but also an organic unity indispensable for it to be, if not the image, at least the equivalent of the sight at its far removed origin and of the closer experience of its creator. Powerful,

JEAN LE MOAL – THE WIND RISING – 1955-1956 – (1,30; 0,97) GALERIE DE FRANCE, PARIS

majestic, animated by a sort of vital pulsation, these compositions of Bazaine—generally of considerable dimension—saturated with colors, choked with forms, compact and yet full of air and light, have kept the promises made by the painter to those who would listen to him from the time long before the exhibition of the Jeunes Peintres de Tradition Française.

On the contrary Manessier, Singier, Le Moal, younger than he, hardly found themselves before this manifestation. It was shortly afterwards but to find themselves in more and more diverse paintings and where the personality of each of these painters was felt.

Despite the evolution of his art as revealed in his recent exhibition (1957), Le Moal is rather the man of still life—of the *Still-leben*, it would be more correct to say, of the silent life of objects which he feels so profoundly that the landscape itself—the tree, the water, the fields, the flowers—is felt in terms of silent beings. Everything in his art is peaceful and withdrawn. The composition is based on traced linear designs where the verticals are balanced with the horizontals and between which the color becomes more alive, richer, more discreet, more uniform, more melodious than before. From these architectural compositions with simple and numerous rhythms, vivified by a very exacting light, there emanates a feeling of amiable ease, of sober elegance, of purity especially which reminds one of Braque, Seurat, Corot, of all those who represent the "Racinian" tradition of France which Le Moal has inherited.

Serious, proudly modest, reserved, rather silent, his even tempered painting hardly resembles that of Singier, who refuses neither humor nor fantasy nor even an appearance of lightness and flirtation. Excelling in the most monumental decoration (his stained glass windows and tapestries prove this), but being also an incomparable water colorist who knows better than anyone else how to give a velvety quality to the sumptuous tones of little pieces of paper he likes to wet to the utmost, it is in his small or medium-sized canvases that Singier is most at ease and in which he gives the full measure of his abilities. Above all inspired by landscape, particularly attracted to water and light, he translates these sights which have moved him with a good humor and a good grace that save them from a preciousness to which he sometimes could easily fall. It merely proves that he has great taste, and a subtle and sure instinct of the exquisite. Light and indecisive, precise and airy, his brushstroke defines signs which the tone differentiates from a generally uniform background. Jade green, violet, lemon yellow, tea rose, they grind their sharp notes in the most stifled harmony of the background, as the grasshoppers their night songs in Provence. From these backgrounds of night-blue color but of ten different blues which Singier knows how to combine as though playing at some game, there results a transparency and a trembling quality of calm. Singier loves to animate this world of grace and fairylike beauty with a note of irony by making a pirouette, by amusing himself in painting it or having painted it: an excellent means of getting away from a decorative character. Warned against forcing his talent, treating everything thus with grace, relating his art to that of Klee and Dufy, his own has a rather special note—and quite a delightful one—in non-representative painting that results from the harmony—which apparently seems natural and yet is so difficult to achieve—of a vibrant sensibility, a naturally delicate taste and an intelligence which is rich in finesse and warmheartedness.

GUSTAVE SINGIER – CHRISTMAS NIGHT – 1950 – (0,38; 0,46) MUSÉE NATIONAL D'ART MODERNE, PARIS

Sensitive, like Singier, to water and light, but responding to their attraction with more depth, Manessier, who in this respect is closer to his friend Le Moal, allows himself not to define anything except in so far as it is related to himself. A pupil of Bissière, to whom he owes a great deal and in whose atelier he met Le Moal, taking part as he did and also Singier his neighbor and comrade, in the exhibition of the Jeunes Peintres de Tradition Française in 1941, he found himself, as they did, after this famous exhibition; and it was an elaboration of his first original style marked by his use of light and shade. As a result, his palette was not so bright as that of Pignon, Gischia and Bazaine of that period; the tones were velvety by their very depths and which the painter liked to bring close to one another and between which he enjoyed establishing some kind of a space. The paint placed on the canvas by a careful and slow hand, gives out a light which is both warm and glaucous, veritable and spiritual, which perfectly suits the religious themes Manessier treated dating from 1944 *(The Pilgrims of Emmaus)*.

Decidedly figurative at that period, at the same time that he veers away from representation of appearances, he evolves towards a new métier. His color scheme

100

ALFRED MANESSIER – THE CROWN OF THORNS – 1948 – (1,17; 0,90) COUVENT DE LA GLACIÈRE, PARIS

becomes fresher, more sensitive to half tones; the silky paint quality incorporates a mother-of-pearl light; the colored form becomes its own drawing, and an impression of ease and charm emanates from his works, less extended than his preceding ones but also less vigorous *(Waves in the Bay of the Somme,* 1949*)*.

The art of stained glass windows in which he excels (Bréseux church; Doubs church; All Saints' church, Basle; Trinquetaille church, Arles) brings Manessier to the heights of grandeur, and develops in him the need to make a painting something monumentally architectural. The composition becomes uniquely ascending, the contour makes itself felt, determinating a grillwork of circles, useful in reconciling the color which flees the surface, and the composition which organizes the design. The tones are more intense: golden yellows, deep reds, sumptuous violets, blues especially, midnight, deep blues, are harmonized between them by blacks of a rare intensity. The ensemble thus possesses an august majesty which harmonizes with the increasingly sacred character of Manessier's themes.

Wether the painting alludes to traditional Christian iconography *(the Crown of Thorns)* or whether it no longer does so, for example in the canvas (Eindhoven Museum) that Manessier painted after hearing, on Good Friday, the *"Tenebrae Service"*, and called by this name : in either case, all his work reveals a deep mystical fealing, which makes of the artist the greatest modern Christian painter, with Rouault. Finding the presence of God everywhere, each canvas is the result of his meditation on the sacred theme—and a means that his love has found of expressing it and of calling us also to that inner life. The getting rid of extraneous matter, the need confessed by his painting for simplicity, unity, fullness, to which it complies through discipline; the silence that it gives out; the peace that emanates from it, are all means by which Manessier communicates his religious experiences; but there is still another: non-figurative which seems, he has said *"to be the present chance by which the painter can better ascend towards his reality and become conscious again of what is essential in him. It is only from this recaptured point that he will be able to find his own weight and revitalize even the exterior reality of the world."*

Preferring to be alone, not frequenting the trio of friends whom we have just discussed, not even Bazaine, Estève came to analogous and different conclusions, original, through a path decidedly his own. Beginning in 1944 he also tends to give appearances a very distant representation. Often regarding the picture of the exterior world from unwonted angles and which do not prevent him from varying them in the same painting, he gives everything—plants in his *Aquarium* (1944), trees in his *Oak Grove* (1946), fields in his *Hill with Three Trees* (1948), the sea in his *Tree along the Bank* (1948)—an aspect all the more wanton because he enjoys in emphasizing this or that element at the cost of another and in granting to the things he paints proportions and an importance uniquely subjective. To this we must add the fact that the picture of Nature as he sees it, or rather as he feels it, is often represented by means of a foreground consisting of a grillwork of lines and colors, but a subtle, mobile grillwork whose movement he excels in suggesting: in the *Hill with Three Trees*, for example, the spectator truly participates thus in the swaying of the trees in the wind, and to an apparent movement that the landscape receives half seen through the branches. From the introduction of these references more and more allusive to the things in Nature, to their suppression pure and simple, there was but

102

one step to take, which Estève soon accomplishes. But it never was to make it abstract. A lived experience almost always nourishes his work and determines its name, usually immediately after he has finished it. Thus his *Padriac* (1956) is the expression of the anguish of the abyss and the translation of his character. But it also often happens that the work is a pure creation, an arrangement of forms necessitated neither by observation nor by the sight of Nature nor by the memory of an experience: thus this *Rose of Christmas* (1953) of which he writes, for example:"*"No allusion to December 25... I have... worked at this canvas till it became a sort of object, like something mechanical, like an organized corpse, ready to place itself in movement and already being an attentive eyewitness... A sort of bundle of plans and forms both drawn tightly together and overlapping... That could have been the rose of winds... Not having found a satisfactory title for this painting, I gave it this one the day I found again... the memory of the flower of the same name before which, as a child, I enjoyed a long and happy lesson in drawing.*"

But whatever the origin of the work, Estève's art nevertheless presents us with similar and perfectly defined characters. A color of a refinement and of a striking note unequalled since Bonnard is the most evident fact. Giving up the greens, the yellows and the blues of contemporary style of the Occupation, he turns, especially since 1946, to brilliant reds, chrome yellows, certain light and intense blues, proud like those of La Fresnaye. Warm and velvety blacks, which remind us that he is also a master of the pencil, a draftsman in the line of Seurat, above all white, blonde and luminous as snow, assure the harmony of these tones which he places here and there, willingly, in large flat areas, heightened, it is true, by a hundred touches which make them vibrate. The former grillwork has become an ensemble of arabesques made up of slow wavy movements, which give the composition a kind of ballet rhythm. Although the rhythm may not be the same in different canvases, it is that of a dancer we think of rather than that of these natural movements understood by Lapicque or Bazaine; it is so numerous and cadenced, submitted, spiritualized to the rightful measure. And so we get a more precise feeling of purified nobility, of sober elegance, of classic balance that this art gives, in which and by which a modality of non-representative painting is defined and achieved, very different from that shown by the works of Bazaine, Le Moal, Manessier and Singier, but rooted, like theirs, in its very newness, in ancient, permanent and sure values.

Pignon on the one side—on the side where we find also Lapicque, Tal Coat and Gischia; Estève, Bazaine, Le Moal and Singier on the other: the explosion was complete of the art which, favored by the Occupation, united the painters of the Tradition Française. From the moment when the atmosphere was no longer that of getting together and unity, each painter chose the elements which he felt drawn to develop in the balanced synthesis which had been their painting from 1941 to 1945. Thus for them partial arts succeeded to a total art that they had created themselves. We are not astonished that henceforth they accomplished what they themselves were not afraid to do and that some decided for figurative painting and others for abstract.

Two separate, aggressive positions faced each other: the successors of the Jeune Peintres de Tradition Française divided themselves sharply into two clans—two tendencies which will be the object of study in the following two chapters.

THE FIGURATIVE
REACTION

IT is from the year 1948 that we can date, if not the birth, at least the affirmation of a
movement which, rising up against the exclusively pictorial preoccupations of
the former painters of the Tradition Française and against their tendency to paint
less and less in a figurative style, returns to the imitation of appearances more or less
deformed by the expressionist concern for affirming their character, and claimed the
right of the painter to express openly in his paintings his personal conception of the
world, of life, of society, even of politics. The year 1948 marks, in fact, two revealing
events of this need—on the part of the artists and the public—for a painting both
realistic and expressionistic, fiercely hostile to the disinterested searchings of pure
art ("Art for Art's sake"), generators of non-representative non-realism: these two
importants events are, on the one hand, the exhibition entitled "L'Homme Témoin"
and, on the other, the sharing of the Prix de la Critique by Lorjou and Buffet.

In June 1948 there took place at the Galerie du Bac an artistic manifestation
grouping Michel de Gallard, Bernard Lorjou, Yvonne Mottet, Rebeyrolle and
Thompson. They proclaimed, through their spokesman, Jean Bouret, that man is
"someone who eats red meat, fried potatoes, fruit and cheese," solidly rooted in the
fundamental and daily reality of the world and of life and that therefore the painter
should give him true, direct, authentic paintings which he needs. Condemning the
"distillers of quintessence, abstractors, people who insist on splitting hairs," they call
for, as opposed to decadent bourgeois taste and that of byzantine intellectuals, the
right of common feeling, of solid popular good sense *"which insists on believing that
two and two makes four and that the earth revolves around the sun" ;* and reproaching those
painters who devote themselves entirely to the solution of pictorial problems for
not being *"engagés,"* even for being inhuman, they make known their convictions
that *"better days are coming"* for whose event they seriously intended to work.
The following year the group chose as its theatre of operations the Galerie Claude
where Bernard Buffet, Charazac, Simone Dat and André Minaux took part this time;
and the paintings inspired by familiar reality and treated moreover in the most
realistic way proved to the visitors that the painters' preoccupation was being the
witness of their time in portraying daily and popular reality—which is, in sum, a
rather slim conception, not to call it summary, of the testimony that a man
can bear of his time. Did Rubens, a painter of innumerable versions of Christ
and Venus, leave us with less an impression of Flanders in the seventeenth century
and of eternal Flanders than David Teniers in his smoking groups, his guards and
his village dances? And of France in the great age of Louis XIV, Cartesian, Jansenist
and Classical France, the testimony of a painter like Poussin is well worth that of the
brothers Le Nain equally witness to their time; but they expressed it less by the
scenes they painted inspired by peasants and the bourgeoisie than by the way in
which these paintings were made with a spirit of reserve, of rigor, of voluntary
system and of inner meditation. But finally each painter testified to his time accord-

104

ing to the idea that suited him or, better still, according to the idea of which he was capable. In any case, we shall not quibble over those of the champions of L'Homme-Témoin and of their two manifestations from 1948 to 1949.

Certain critics, however, meeting at the Galerie Saint-Placide—which was the first to defend these painters—had already during the summer of 1948 bestowed their prize on Lorjou and Buffet, champions of the movement, who not only shared the prize but by their work affirmed the tendency as well. Better off than Impressionism, Fauvism or Cubism, this movement saw itself supported from its very beginning by the important daily and weekly newspapers which used it as a weapon against the muddlings of abstract painting which the majority of these newspapers disapproved of.

In other words, the art of Lorjou and Buffet and their comrades knew how to get all the luck for itself. Assured of encouragement from the critics, it was covered from both sides. Brought so closely to socialist realism that Michel de Gallard, Rebeyrolle and Thompson also joined it (in respect to this we will note the exact harmony of their affirmations, since it was also in 1948 that Fougeron exhibited his *Parisians at the Market* at the Salon d'Automne and Amblard decorated the *Mairie* of Saint-Denis), it was keenly approved by those for whom abstract painting was the last mumblings of decaying capitalism and the expression *par excellence* of plutocratic and war mongering United States; but it attracted the approval of the French bourgeoisie who, conservative with tranquil obstinacy and always behind the times by at least fifty years but anxious also to be "up to date," was quite happy to find an alibi in this painting, as it had fifteen years before in that of Brianchon and Chapelain-Midy. The French bourgeois insensibility to specifically plastic qualities and its taste for the anecdote found exactly what it was looking for especially in view of its horror of novelty, its fear of effort, its taste for things already seen. Bankers, business men, fashionable women, politicians, antique dealers all vied for the paintings of Buffet and Lorjou, had them hung in galleries and reproduced in newspapers and magazines which they financed, created prizes for the sheer purpose of their "stars," [26] organized exhibitions of their work everywhere, from Japan to the United States. Not only was this a "rush" in the biggest way for these favored objects, it was "*la gloire*"—a glory such that in 1953 in *Le Premier Bilan de l'Art Actuel*, one can read—and it was nothing but the exact truth—that "*Bernard Buffet is without doubt the most famous young French painter.*" Never have artists benefited by such a dazzling success—since Fauconnet and Favory, ephemelar children cherished by the public and by success, about the year 1925.

From this sudden craze there resulted, naturally, a rallying of a host of young painters, attracted if not to this group, at least to this formula, all the more sincere in their belief that the expressionist pathos and violence of Buffet and Lorjou corresponded to the uneasiness and the anger of a youth which, alas, found in and around itself more subjects of anguish and indignation than reasons for hope and satisfaction. Innumerable young painters, often more authentic that those whose influence they felt—Aizpiri, Vinay, Verdier, Rosnay and, in a lesser measure, Clavé—turned to a realistic expressionism in their anxiety to represent contemporary life. Their meeting ground was the Salon des Moins de Trente Ans (Salon of Painters Less than Thirty Years of Age), a tribune strongly smelling of a certain political odor, and that of the Salon des Peintres Témoins de Leur Temps (Salon of Painters Witness to their Time), to which the attention was immediately drawn by magnificent catalogues sumptuously illustrated, by a frenzied propaganda of wise choices of summer places in the south of France, in Nice, Menton, Vichy and other tourist centers, as well as by the ingenious idea of giving the artists each year a different theme, such as Work (1951), Sunday (1953), Happiness (1955), the Portrait (1956), Sports (1957). And so the development of painting was deviated from its path of purity and non-realism, crushed, from 1941 to 1948, by Bazaine, Estève, Manessier, Pignon. Just as Cubism brought about the double reaction of a Neo-Realism and a new Expressionism (or Neo-Expressionism, as it is better known), so this art unloosened an analogous reaction, but whose originality is the contamination of a realism faithful to appearances and of an expressionism which interprets them in order to provoke the character and to translate the subjective emotion of the artist himself in the face of reality.

And thus it seems to appear in its work. For it has no doctrine and flatters itself at not having one: aside from the manifesto of the L'Homme-Témoin, it would be useless to look for definition of their searchings which were translated clearly only by those critics favorable to its ambitions, Bouret and Descargues in particular. Consisting also more of a tendency than of a group (aside from the initial group of the L'Homme-Témoin), it would have been equally impossible for the adherents of Neo-Realism to form one and to which in so many respects they bear such close resemblance. But this absence of an explicit program really makes very little difference—for there is no need of a key to open the way to their art. The works are themselves sufficient to tell us what they wish to say and without an equivocal meaning, for they are not only a direct access, but they cry and shout out their words and sources.

Among them the main ones are the art of Gruber and that of Courbet. Now despite the homage paid by the Salon de la Jeune Peinture to Desnoyer, who in fact was also the subject of another previously bestowed by the antagonist Salon de Mai, the influence of this giant of Sète on the art of these young adherents to an expressionist realism hardly seems to be evident. Constructor of forms willingly treated geometrically, a rigorous organizer of compositions submissive to mathematical schemes, a strong colorist, a descendant, in a word, of the Cubists and the Fauves, Desnoyer has always claimed a heritage which these painters, on the contrary, despised, and whose demand for pure plasticism they denounced as "formalism." Charged with great optimism, his production breathes a joy of life and a generosity which lie entirely outside their scope of feeling. For Gruber, on the other hand, we immediately see what they all owe to him; and it is not only this accent of anguish, this taste for ugliness and pain, but it is also an art that repudiates the discoveries of contemporary art since Gauguin, even since the Impressionists, in order to establish itself directly after that of Courbet— merely, of course, from the point of view of technique and plasticity. As for the painter of the *Stone Breaker*, if they possess neither his health nor his mastery, both full of the same assurance, they feel related to him, however, by their resolution to practise the traditional métier which, following him, Manet had brought to its perfection, and by their desire to paint their period and, like him, to draw from it a revolutionary beauty in the imitation of the reality of their time. We are astonished that they eventually were not drawn to Dunoyer de Segonzac and to Permeke with whom they seemed to share affinities, especially Minaux and Rebeyrolle.

106

BERNARD BUFFET – DESCENT FROM THE CROSS – 1948
(2,00; 0,97) MAURICE GARNIER COLLECTION, PARIS

The reason for this is that their painting is above all one of reaction. The traditional trinity—perspective, modeling, light and shade—is the object of their earnestness and if they lack it, it is not through a shifty desire to avoid it (and to every sinner mercy) but rather through a deficiency in their métier because they do not possess these trained resources—rather forgotten during the past fifty years—as well as Courbet, which goes without saying, or even as such painters as Carolus Duran, Edouard Detaille or Bonnat. Distrusting even Impressionism, they preferred the expression of local color to that of light and used, as though Manet had never existed, space and values in the most convenient way. Of all the taboos imposed by Renaissance aesthetics, there was only one which they deliberately dared to omit: the respect for anatomy—and that, corollary, of the true forms and proportions of animals and objects and whose expression made them exaggerate the character. But these deformations are hardly ever more daring than those of the caricaturists of the middle of the nineteenth century: they go less far in this direction than Rouault or Soutine whose succession they do not dream of claiming. On the whole, their instrument is that which has been proved by tradition.

And there is no reason why it should not be, since their object is also one of tradition: the imitation of Nature. Jean Bouret speaks the truth when, in the *Premier Bilan de l'Art Actuel*, he declares: *"The very fact that the year 1952 sees among the painters an obvious return to Nature, the fact proved by the substance of the Salon des Jeunes Peintres which is the best place to estimate the artistic production, proves to us that this very Nature is sufficient reason for the plastic expression."* What they want to imitate is reality and with the métier capable of allowing them to achieve this: but (and this is where they differ from the Neo-Realists of 1920 and their inheritors, the painters sometimes referred to as "Painters of Poetic Reality") the reality that they regard, feel, touch is an ugly, hostile, even cruel reality: Segonzac, Boussingault and, after them, more than they, Oudot and Brianchon observe reality and represent it as generous or noble, elegant or beautiful; whereas for them—and here is the real sign of our time—it is something else entirely that they like. Misery haunts them: the misery of poor people who are often the subject of their portraits; the misery of the faubourgs which often nourishes their landscape inspiration; the misery of country villages and the misery of animals, the unhappy and unfortunate companions of the peasants. Ugliness is the other object of their predilection: the ugliness of old age, the ugliness of death, the very ugliness of Nature which man earnestly tries to disfigure. It is through this aspect of life and Nature that these realists join the expressionists of the beginning or of the middle of this century, and from whom they take up again the art of explaining the character of things through systematic exaggeration. If the realism of the painters of the Poetic Reality group evokes the cackling of fashionable women having tea, their realism reminds one of the noisy clamorings of political meetings where grandiloquence flows in impetuous streams. How could they help but obtain the attention of a public which no longer knew how to listen to someone who spoke soberly and with meaning! Their success is often the result of an impudence which they knew how to drive to effect. The modern crowds, even the bourgeois, did not detest being forced. As for the stars of this movement, Lorjou and Buffet, the case appears to me not to have anything to do with art. As for the latter, a single merit does not suffer from discussion: that of having competed with the Renault Automobile Plant for the record of French production and having raised painting to the dignity of an industrial object fabricated *en masse.* As to the former, this Tartarin de Tarascon ([27]) of painting, for whom facility equals fecundity and *"tempérameng"* ([28]) talent, he has compromised another confusion and has identified Expressionism with exhibitionism. We are led to believe that "to have " (the expression is that of the person who wrote the preface to one of his catalogues) and "to show them" ([29]) is really all that his painting amounts to. All of which, in sum, is an insufficient idea of a kind of art practised by a great many ladies and which was that, among others, of Fra Angelico. It is better to shroud these cases in Noah's cloak and, like Dante and Virgil in Inferno, pass on...

Another reaction simultaneously developed, equally hostile to the exclusive searchings of pure painting, but whose sympathy with a Surrealism which it more or less openly tends to keeps to a path that leads to a return to a traditional métier and to an imitation of appearances. More interesting than the convulsions

JEAN DUBUFFET – LA RUE – (0,87; 1,14) JEAN PAULHAN COLLECTION, PARIS

of dying Surrealism—which was made quite evident at the exhibition in 1947 at the Galerie Maeght and as a survivor promised a doomed death and was kept going (without bringing it to life) by the painters of the Galerie de l'Etoile Scellée, under the aegis of André Breton—this tendency counts among its outstanding exponents Fautrier and Dubuffet.

Coming to Expressionism after a break of several years, Fautrier began a new style during the time of the exhibition of his *Hostages* (1945) in the short-lived and audacious Galerie Drouin, Place Vendôme, followed in 1955, 1956 and 1957 by those of his *Objects*, his *Nudes* and his *Partisans* at the Galerie Rive Droite. Greatly admired by writers and *littérateurs*, especially André Malraux, Jean Paulhan and Francis Ponge, he likes to accumulate on a prepared paper covered with a thick coating made of paste, a prodigiously thick *matière*, emphasized by a light graphic quality in ink which indicates, in a more or less allusive way, the contours of the pretext-forms of his work: heads of war victims, nudes, meager daily objects, fruit, etc. Of an incontestable originality, different from all that has gone before him, rich in paint quality, refined in color (Marcel Arland could speak of the "prettiness" of his *Hostages*) which remains figurative in spite of the spectator's difficulty sometimes in identifying the forms—he announces the *"informelle"* of certain abstracts by his taste for splash and spattering, his dragging of pigment, his happy accidents which he makes the most of; but he revives Expressionism by his pathos, his hostility to Cubism and to all those movements which place the plastic side of painting as a preoccupation of prime importance, his need to dissolve into his theme, to become with it an entirety, and the identification especially that he establishes between the painting and painter's anguished cry confronted as he is by the spectacle of the life around him, by the German occupation, the crushing of the Hungarian revolution or, more simply, domestic utensils. Effusive, he bases his art above all on the gesture, the spot of *matière* on the surface, as the Surrealists counted primarily on automatic writing.

The influence of Surrealism is equally felt in Dubuffet whose production was revealed to the public also in 1945 and by the same Galerie Drouin: an exhibition of a series of paintings entitled *"Hautes Pâtes"* aroused the enthusiasm of the same admirers. Other series followed: secret portraits, bodies of women, philosophical stones which, especially in the United States, drew attention to the painter. Alfred H. Barr Jr. wrote in 1945 in his *Masters of Modern Art*, p. 170: *"Possibly the most original painter to have emerged in Paris since the war is not abstract in his art. A man of exceptional intelligence and maturity, Jean Dubuffet combines a childlike style with bold innovations in surface handling and a grotesque sense of humor."* No better way can express this kind of painting which borrows its graphic quality from children's drawings, as well as from a graffito, already so dear to the Surrealists, giving the outstanding role to a bitumous *matière* triturated with a sort of scatalogical volup-tuousness and substituting the pathos of the Expressionists by a truculent *"Ubuesque"* [30] which conceals rather poorly an anguish similar to theirs. Voluntarily awkward, naïve, puerile even with science, this painting wants to be expressive as is the drawing of children, a direct expression, elementary, effusive to a state of purity; and it thus has the courage (or the irony) to perfect Expressionism, at least that of Germany before and after the First World War, as well as, even more, a certain Surrealism and Dada.

Thus, in the face of pure painting, effusion-painting becomes more arrogant than ever: Dada itself had not claimed so loudly such rights of anti-painting.

110

THE ABSTRACT
REACTION

SHORTLY after the affirmation of Fautrier and Dubuffet, heralds of *"a different art,"* [31] from 1945 on, shortly before that, in 1948, of Lorjou, his friends of the L'Homme-Témoin and co-laureate, Bernard Buffet, it was the year 1946 at the Salon des Réalités Nouvelles that affirmed the other form of the reaction directed against the art of the Bazaines, Estèves, Gischias, Manessiers, the reaction of abstract painters.

At that time abstract painting was almost forty years old, if it is true that its oldest manifestations first appeared in 1909 in the work of Picabia. But after a dazzling infancy, it spent a discreet youth during the two World Wars—at least in Paris, where, as we have seen, the activity of a man like Herbin was more or less shoved to one side. The arrival of Kandinsky fleeing Germany and Nazism did not bring forth any great glory (1933), but the departure of Mondrian, who left Paris in 1938 for England, then for the United States, did not sound its death note either. For a period of twenty years, abstract painting led a modest existence (which does not mean unfruitful) relegated to a secondary level by the more noisy movements around it. But suddenly it was going to have its revenge and pass immediately into the front ranks of actuality.

Premonitory signs had announced the explosion, but they were heeded only by those who were warned and already aware of what was happening. A modest gallery, L'Esquisse, had with rare courage exhibited on the Ile de la Cité abstract works before the Liberation and, in 1945, René Drouin had presented under the charming title of "Art concret" a manifestation grouping the first champions of this art, from Kandinsky to Mondrian, passing by Delaunay and his wife, Arp, Herbin, etc. At that time there were no young painters even though their number was legion—and here is the important fact—a year later at the Salon des Réalités Nouvelles.

Taking up a name which was due to Robert Delaunay who already in 1936 had spoken of *"nouvelles réalités,"* an antique dealer, Fredo Sidès who, in 1939 under this name had organized a manifestation at the Galerie Charpentier, founded in 1946 this new salon which, not content with paying homage to Delaunay, Kandinsky, Mondrian, van Doesburg, Kupka, Picabia, Gleizes and Villon, opened its doors to several hundred young painters of all countries. Immediately abstract painting appeared as the sure sign of a world fact and which, even more than in France, had already been developed in the United States where the Association of American Abstract Artists was created in 1936, and the inauguration of the Guggenheim Museum of Non-Objective Painting the following year. Abstract schools of very diverse inspiration flourished more or less everywhere, the most interesting being that in California known as the "Pacific School." The fear of being behind the Americans—who arrogantly noised their advancement—aroused the School of Paris, resulting in a rush of young painters towards abstract art and, soon afterwards, of a host of collectors towards their production. Galleries suddenly increased devoting themselves exclusively to their champions or making a fine place for them beside

111

their other painters. The Galerie Colette Allendy, ever courageous and in search of talent, offered a chance to many young painters of avant-garde art, the Galerie Denise René became the sanctuary of geometric abstract painters, the Galerie Lydia Conti revealed Hartung and Schneider to the public before they weretaken on by the Galerie Louis Carré, where they were joined by Lanskoy, Nicholas de Staël and Soulages. The Galerie Drouin revealed Wols. In 1947 the Galerie Maeght organized an exhibition of Atlan's work, followed in 1949 by two manifestations: *Les Premiers maîtres de l'art abstrait*, patronised rather paradoxically by the director of the Grenoble Museum, Andry-Farcy, who had not yet admitted them to his collection. In the same year the Salon de Mai opened its doors to the young painters recruited to abstract art, after having accepted Schneider as a member of its committee. Finally, an international exhibition of abstract art was held during the summer of the same year at Aix-les-Bains.

New names were revealed defended by new critics such as Charles Estienne, Léon Degrand, Michel Ragon, etc. A review, *Art d'Aujourd'hui*, was launched directed by an Algerian architect, André Bloc, who worked also in abstract sculpture without any happy results. He was not content merely to prone certain abstract painters of the School of Paris, but took pleasure in revealing to the French the abstract artists of abroad, and especially in those countries where his review would attract the greatest audience: Norway, Denmark, Sweden, Germany, North and South America. Finally several books reminded or taught the public the past of this art and of its principal masters. And so in 1948 the Association des Amis de l'Art, animated by Gaston Diehl, the founder of the Salon de Mai, published a small book *Pour ou contre l'abstrait* (For or Against Abstract), which greatly contributed to diffuse its ideas among the painters and the youth; and in 1950 Michel Seuphor, the hagiographer of the movement, gave Maeght his work *L'Art abstrait, ses origines et ses premiers maîtres*. In four short years abstract painting had achieved the right to establish itself in Parisian pictorial life.

Not much time was needed before abstract art affirmed its youthful imperialism: henceforth the principal galleries of Paris counted among "their" painters a more or less important contingent of abstract. Exhibitions of this tendency in art increased to such a point that it is hardly necessary to mention all of them. We would like to cite only the exhibition organized by Charles Estienne at the Théâtre de Babylone in 1952; the entry of diverse abstract artists—Atlan, Hartung, Poliakoff, Schneider, Soulages, etc.—in October, 1955 in the rather pompous Galerie Charpentier in favor of the exhibition of the School of Paris; the rather monotonous affirmation of international character of this painting in the exhibition organized in 1956 at the Musée National d'Art Moderne by James John Sweeney, the director of the Guggenheim Museum, etc. The succession to *Art d'Aujourd'hui* which ceased publication in 1954 was continued even before its disappearance by *Cimaise* published by the Galerie Arnaud beginning in November 1953. Critics favorable to abstract art grew in number and made themselves increasingly heard—among them were foreigners, like Roger van Gindertael and Mme Herta Wescher. One after another several books were published with this art as their object which they studied with an understanding often rather partial: *L'Aventure de l'Art abstrait* (1956) by Michel Ragon, *Art abstrait* by Marcel Brion (1956), the *Dictionnaire de l'Art abstrait* (1957) by Michel Seuphor, the extoller of Mondrian to whom during the same year he devoted a monument of fervent admiration.

Did abstract painting win a final victory? Far from it : a resistance grew up against it in proportion to its success and which, far from disarming, became greater each day. Despite a few exceptions, official milieux turned a wary face to it. For the most part, the critics of the big daily newspapers and those of the weekly remained irreducibly hostile: we can cite, among twenty others, Claude Roger-Marx in the *Figaro Littéraire*, Maximilien Gauthier in the *Nouvelles Littéraires*, Raymond Charmet in *Arts*, which was no doubt the most relentless publication to attack with perseverance avant-garde painting and to announce, periodically, its death. Those writers who obeyed Communist dictates cut it to pieces beginning in 1948 and saw in it the art *of "reaction"* which *"was not based on popular forces"* and *"serves nothing of value in social progress."* ([32])   They set up the art of L'Homme-Témoin against this abstract art and the Salon des Moins de Trente Ans against that of Réalités Nouvelles; while the advancement of Lorjou, as well as the creation of the Salon des Peintres Témoins de Leur Temps, is the ripost of those who, if they did not share the opinions of the Extreme Left, were not far from rallying to its aesthetic—and to an aesthetic which was esentially bourgeois. Books increased in which abstract art was attacked, more or less openly, more or less cleverly: *La Peinture Contemporaine* by Robert Genaille (1953), *La Peinture moderne en délire* by Watelin (1957) and especially the pamphlet, *Contre l'Art abstrait* by Robert Rey who, pursuing his hostility to avant-garde painting, which had already been felt during the Occupation in his opuscule *La Peinture Moderne ou l'Art sans métier* (1941), assures with *brio* the continuation of Camille Mauclair. A new avatar of the quarrel between the Ancients and the Moderns, between the classical powdered wigs and the long-haired Romantics, between Impressionism and Salon art, the battle of abstract art against its diverse enemies shows quite clearly that the war is far from won, despite such unexpected conversions as that of Jean Bouret in his book *L'Art abstrait, ses origines, ses luttes, sa présence,* published in 1957.

But affirming itself—and merely from continuing—abstract painting could not help breaking into different styles and, from this very fact, we can easily distinguish three tendencies: one geometrical and architectural, another "informal" and still another which is rather difficult to define because it is not distinguishable by such recognizable features and is not, fortunately, a "happy medium" between the two others, but one that seems to follow both the rigor of plastic form and the effusion of poetry.

Born out of the Neo-Plasticism of Mondrian, as well as the paintings of Herbin —the first who is equally indebted to Magnelli and Kandinsky in his last phase—the last tendency is the oldest of the three. Already in 1945 at the Galerie Denise René it made itself felt having found *Art d'Aujourd'hui* as its tribune. Its principal champions were Dewasne, Vasarely and the Dane Mortensen, ([33]) along with, though in a lesser degree, Deyrolle, the least orthodox of the group, the only one, moreover, who allowed himself certain escapades in the realm of fantasy and poetry. *"What I'm looking for,"* he wrote, *"is by the multiplicity and the combination of forms to achieve multiple significations... During the work reasoning constantly does not interfere, everything seems intuitive. There is no reason to get excited beyond a theory, almost all painters cheat more or less consciously at it... This cheating is a phenomenon of permanent invention and it nourishes the artist's evolution and prevents art from hardening."* All seem to claim for their drawing the impassible rigor of an architect's purity. Colored with a knowing equality the surfaces are heightened by these applied lines made pleasing to the eye by their strong tones, often quite frank and happy, which are disposed by flat areas made up of small parts without smudges or intrusions beyond the lines of the precise, dry edges. Deyrolle avoids bringing in the slightest intimate vitiation through the use of light and shade; there is no light, nor is there the slightest desire to suggest space of any kind. In fact, there is nothing but flat forms, perhaps through fear of falling into the proscribed allusions of reality. In these surface forms, where he is reminded of the most traditional designs of classical Euclidean geometry, he enjoys combing, without any charge of imagination, a series of forms closed in on themselves, which with a telling exactness fit marvelously into the restricted area. In sum, the painting is an ensemble, an entirety complete in two dimensions, made up of a flat architectural style. To this exclusively plastic ambition which, for want of complete novelty (it merely marks a continuation of Neo-Plasticism), lacks neither logic nor grandeur, the artist deliberately sacrifices sensuality, which goes without saying, but also sensibility, imagination, lyricism. It is in the light of cold reason, of an implacable method and of a puritan will that this painting is situated. The result is an unapproachable pride which is not without beauty, but its form borders on stiffness and its qualities recall that of the legendary sword of Charlemagne: Deyrolle's art, like the emperor's sword, is hard, flat and mortal. Going so far in his search for purity he ends up by no longer recognizing it, while at the same time he gives in to the temptation of disincarnation, of angelicism, forgetting—which is an astonishing omission in the land of Pascal—he who wants to be an angel... (³⁴).

Easy to explain, teach and learn, this art enjoyed a great success, principally about 1951, when Dewasne and Pillet inaugurated in 1950 the short-lived Atelier d'Art Abstrait, and Léon Degand, who for a short time was director of the Museum of Modern Art in São Paulo, assured the diffusion in South America: frightened at the idea of appearing avant-garde, it suddenly and without any transition—as though going from mule transportation to aviation, ignoring the railway stage—went from the most backward academism to this form of advanced art to which, in addition, it discovered the advantage of being its scholar and doctrinaire, and easily put it into practice. This success had to lead—and led—to a definite reaction, whose instigator was Charles Estienne, author of a pamphlet which appeared in 1950, *L'Art abstrait est-il un académisme*? Although André Bloc and the whole group of *Art d'Aujourd'hui* reacted vigorously and burned more incense before the idol of geometric abstraction of the Post-Neo-Plasticians, the return began. As prompt in getting out of it as they were in falling in love with it, avant-garde milieux saw in it nothing but mistakes where prior to this they saw definite qualities, novelty, audacity. The winds turned to the informal.

The origins of this tendency can be found in the works of Fautrier and Dubuffet and the poet-painter, Henri Michaux, whose influence, although thwarted by the success of the geometric abstract painters, was none the less felt on the young artists and critics beginning in 1946. Here is how Edouard Jaguer speaks of its intentions

114

JEAN DEYROLLE — BLAISE — (1,30; 0,96) GALERIE DENISE RENÉ, PARIS

in the October 1, 1946 issue of the newspaper *Juin*, "*a new phenomenon whose meteoric path illuminates writing as well*," where "*uneasiness, joy, hope, desire...*" are written "*in a form which is generally non-figurative*," and which is not "*a taking on of abstract painting by the Surrealist spirit*," but the expression "*of this same elementary force which blows through the countryside, changes the direction of cargo ships' smoke on the high seas and which, uniting flesh with flesh, unites man with his future.*"   In November 1946, the writer and painter, Camille Bryen, exhibited in a gallery in Basle, and presented by Audiberti, certain works whose proximity with those of Hans Arp, conferred upon it—in a way of speaking—the significant patronage of Dada.   He repeated (the offense) in November of the following year in Paris, this time at the

Galerie Luxembourg, where a month later a manifestation of Mathieu's works took place in a collective exhibition designated as "L'Imaginaire." Two other exhibitions H. W. P. S. M. T. B. and W. Black and White followed. In July 1948 it was the turn of the Galerie des Deux Iles to receive Bryen's works, presented by the person who was to become the Boileau of the movement, Michel Tapié. Finding the style of Dada again, consciously or not, he proclaimed it noisily in the catalogue after having thrashed to pieces mathematical painting founded on the Section d'Or: *"Hurrah for the teeming real numbers which reabsorb all these ideas of rhythm, style, plasticism, composition, dear to the hearts of impostor-professors: open the classes and the clinics, hurrah for the fair and microbes; the Incoherent and the Formless finally let loose to win over all painting, for they have the only magico-psychic force for it truly real: Inertia."*

Defended by another equally fervent champion, Michel Ragon, three Dutchmen, however, sensitive to the Germanic side of their nature and to the expressionist spirit of Fautrier and Dubuffet, Appel, Constant and Corneille, exhibited their work in 1949 at the Galerie Colette Allendy, before being taken on two years later by the Galerie Pierre. This time they were with three Scandinavians. Recognition in Paris was long in coming, and these artists did not achieve success till much later and in their own country: the Dutch devotees of Mondrian burned incense on the altar of their young compatriots, whose painting is the exact opposite of that preached by *de Stijl.* At least this tentative of Appel and his comrades confirmed the tendency of the young painters to insist on, even demand, the rights of thickly applied paint, of eloquent brush movement as opposed to the rigor of the Post-Neo-Plasticians. At the same time, there came forth a German painter living in France since 1932, Wols, who was soon to disappear. Two manifestations in 1945 and 1947 at the Galerie Drouin, the sanctuary of "L'Art brut" attracted the attention of a pleiad of fanatics who affirmed, through the pen of René Guilly, feeling before these works much more than a *"superficial pleasure which would appeal only to perception"* and finding in this art a sort of fusion of Surrealism and abstraction: *"Wols has achieved a polyvalent non-figurative painting, the painting of drama and of ambiguity, whose appearance has been necessitated by thirty years of speculative painting."* Aware of the pattern of moldiness, of splits, crevices and cracks, of rips in paper, of filth on walls, Wols uses these strange signs of Nature's capriciousness as a starting point in order to carry out sometimes large paintings, more often small water colors, joint products of spontaneous scribblings and a very elaborated métier. *"His painting,"* writes René Guilly, *"is 'that'* (the equivalent of these pictorial or graphic caprices of reality) *and other things even more irreplacable, a plastic structure and himself."* Nervous, paroxysmal, *"organized delirium,"* according to Michel Seuphor, his works combine small brushstrokes and strange colors, morbid and poisonous, without any concern for organization; and this painter knows how to make the most of the chance happenings of a feverish execution from which emanates, in the words again of Michel Seuphor, *"an extraordinary magnetism."* Wols died in 1951, but, before his disappearance and even more after it, he was regarded as a master by the young artists who followed in his path along the road of informal painting.

In 1951-1953 they were more or less everywhere. At the Galerie Nina Dausset in the Rue du Dragon, Michel Tapié brought together a little more than half a dozen young painters' works exhibited under the title *Véhémences confrontées* (March 1951). He repeated this shortly afterwards under the title *Peintures non-abstraites* and a

116

third time, at the Galerie Facchetti under the manifestation *Signifiants de l'Informel*. They were brought together again at the Salon d'Octobre founded by a young Turk, Nejad, unhappy about the way his paintings were hung at the Salon de Mai of 1952, and founded also under the impulsion of Charles Estienne. And so, four months later, in the Salle André Baugé, Avenue de Villiers, another Salon was opened. In April 1953 at the Galerie Craven in the Rue des Beaux-Arts, Degottex, Duvillier, Marcelle Loupchansky, Messagier, Arnal, the Princess Fahr el Nissa and Osorio organized an exposition contemporary with those that the Studio Facchetti and the Galerie Pierre devoted to the works of Riopelle and Mathieu. The movement was in full swing, proud of having received the benediction of André Breton who, in the Galerie de l'Étoile Scellée, though more strictly Surrealist, was decidedly sympathetic to it. It was encouraged by what was happening abroad, where analagous tendencies existed in Italy, Belgium, Holland, and especially in the United States. *"A certain number of individuals worthy of this name work in complete indifference,"* writes Charles Estienne, *"vis-à-vis classicism of which they have no nostalgia or refusal, in complete indifference, also, to all the new '-isms' which critics loaded with slogans are endlessly trying to give them... There are works... and there will shortly be a sufficient number of works, a posteriori, to elaborate the basis of an aesthetic according to its scale and to their power, an entirely different aesthetic which will be the best guarantee for a long and fruitful continuation, all apparent facilities reabsorbed once and for all."* These same individuals were finally to establish themselves at the Galerie Rive Droite which became the most brilliant center of their activity.

Attacks from all sides did not fail, however, to appear. The most important was that of a certain critic who, in Art d'Aujourd'hui, touched on the name *"Tachism"* [35] to designate the tendency which was made quite evident at the second Salon d'Octobre at the Galerie Craven in 1953. Protesting vehemently that *"if the Tachists resorted to spots it is exactly and in the same measure where the Fauves lived in a zoo and the Cubists resorted to cubes,"* Charles Estienne accepted the epithet for his *protégés* in an article which appeared in *Combat* March 1, 1954. Michel Seuphor had already used this terminology in his book on the American painter, Lee Heersch. Jean-José Marchand did all he could, in the April 5, 1954 issue of *Combat*, to protest against this name to which he preferred that of "Lyrical Abstractionists." Entirely conscious of recognizing the justice of his recriminatiom, Charles Estienne continued nevertheless to include this name in his vocabulary. Thus another school in "-ism" was born.

Where in this new school were the force-ideas expressed in black on white? In Michel Tapié's opuscule, *Un art autre* and that of Michel Ragon *Expressionisme et non-figuration*, but also in diverse texts of Michel Tapié, Charles Estienne, Camille Bryen, Georges Mathieu, etc., all included in issue 51 of the *Tour de Feu*. Let us question the writings before examining the paintings. What we notice, first of all, is an extremely violent stand against the geometric abstractionists, whom the advocates of informal art reproach both for not having brought anything new into the vision of art and for having created decorative and scholarly works. *"Beginning in 1944-1946,"* wrote Charles Estienne, for example, [36] *"until the present, a second generation of abstract painters began to develop a non-figurative style which was much more a decorative one than a protest against outward reality... Abstract art number 2 offered an art that was quite openly decorative and collective."* And Michel Tapié to go even further said [37] : *"The apparent facility of non-figurative art during the past years has*

117

*attracted so much mediocrity that everything worth while in this field... has become in-
creasily difficult to recognize in the midst of a production borrowed from such a nullity
and such an imbecility that—with all the good will in the world—we have had enough."*
Consequently, down with the Salon des Réalités Nouvelles, as academic as that of
the Artistes Français! Down with geometry: *"It is not a question of replacing nude
women with these purifed geometric forms more or less reduced to the same scholastic
ends (Michel Tapié)."* [38] Down with plastic searchings: it is necessary, following
the same augury, *"to throw oneself into a painting without any idea of composition,
without any idea at all, without seeking balance, nor a certain unbalance going on during
the execution, beyond preoccupations of beauty, intelligence, feeling, magical means, time,
'problem of color'..."* [39] Down with the desire for style and the concern for
former styles, the affiliation with yesterday: *"All style belongs to the past and has
been overtaken (Charles Estienne)."* [40] It is not a question of looking for this, nor
of regarding it as a point of departure: *"We are not departing from style, but from
ourselves. We are not looking for a natural painting"*, [40] affirmed the same critic in
Combat March 1, 1954. It was to find the principles of Dada and Surrealism again:
anarchic subjectivity, the taste of anti-art, the need of beginning again at zero, the
hunger for novelty and the unknown: *"Each one has taken on the indefinite domain of
the informal with his own temperament in a liberty vis-à-vis that which is called 'Art'
which allows him to let himself go in this vast field of the unknown which tempts him
with a total frankness vis-à-vis himself,"* [41] wrote Michel Tapié in 1951, echoing what
Camille Bryen had declared three years before: *"I would like it (the painting) to open
its work to itself."* [42]

Not only is it an expression of the painter himself, but the painting is also an
individual exploration of the Real (with a capital "R" as in Tapié's manifesto) and
the work a figure of the universe in whose nature it must participate by its very
creation. Some painters, Tapié affirmed, the informal painters ("informels") knew
how *"to force fulgurating points in this indefinite no man's land touched by the frontiers
of knowledge, but which interest only the true pioneers for whom a flock (a collective
artistic movement, for example) and knowledge (that others share and transmit) signify
a choking up."* [43] And these painters, if we are to believe him, *"in order to give a
chance to the total anarchy of the Real,"* [43] refuse composition, plastic research, thinking, as Camille Bryen had said, that *"the painting... is organized like a cosmic function"* [44]. Their productions therefore must possess these cosmic characteristics to
penetrate *"the real rhythms of Nature"* [45] to animate themselves by reconsidered
rhythms *"no longer to traverse the only possible calculation of entire numbers, but
through that of real and hypercomplex numbers"* to be structures related to the *"more
general and richer notions of continuity and proximity of the actual topology whose
classic geometry is nothing more than a small and extremely particularized chapter"* [46]
and to make a place in space for a space linked *"with the theories of the Groups of
Gauls and the ensembles of Cantor, with the actual metalogics explaining the beyonds,
and with the dynamic logic of the contradictory of Lupasco."* [46] Let it be observed
that we are here quoting Michel Tapié.

Out of all these ambitions, in which we have no difficulty in finding again the
last avatar of the spirit which was already expressed in Surrealism and Dada, in
Expressionism—especially German Expressionism—and in German Romanticism,

what were the plastic results? Canvases generally immense in size—those of Mathieu especially—where the signs are brought to life by violent brushwork, happy in triturating a thick paint quality, I will say almost a gluey surface, taking advantage of all the happy accidents of its downward flow. More than spots (Tachism), they are quite often spaces of abbreviated signatures, of immense vibrations, which act upon the backgrounds sometimes bare (Mathieu), sometimes filled with compact forms (Riopelle), or with kinds of multicolored and fluent foggy forms. Although very different according to the individual painters, the color scheme seems, in a general way, rather in love with neutral and muted tones: to the re-establishment of black to a place of honor, so characteristic of contemporary abstract painting, the works of the Tachists have not been foreign. There is absolutely no composition. The forms do not converge towards the center, nor do they obey the injunctions of lines of forces or of rhythms; but running across the canvas in all directions, they evoke the disorderly flight of ants when a catastrophe has destroyed their hill. The limit of the canvas does not stop them: fusing confusingly, they aspire to go beyond the limits imposed by the rectangular space, to lose themselves in space. The result appears to be a rapid creation, independent of all directional thought, obeying only itself and the drunkenness of its own gestures (the painter's brush).

It is of course too early to estimate these results without the weight of time which judges everything. But perhaps we show an excessive severity when we think that they are neither at the height of the movement's aspirations nor so new, so "other" as these theoricians put forward. The same adventure had already happened to Dada and to Surrealism. Interesting in its testimony to certain needs of today, this art of the informal has doubtless not given birth to any decisive works, or even equal to those of Wols (who were themselves far from having the value of Klee's, their source). No doubt they have the merit of being more alive and, in a certain measure, more original than those of the Post-Neo-Plasticians, but, in spite of these qualities, neither Riopelle nor Bryen nor Mathieu—the Dali of the informal group—appears to have succeeded in giving to his searchings the translation which was necessary to it. Their poetry itself seems subject to caution, more verbal than truly lyrical. Who knows if the result of their aesthetic is not precisely here, and if the informal can find its chances in the universe of forms which is painting? Unless the absence of forms is not itself form... But if it is only a question of a new form (and not exactly new, since there have already been Turner and Monet, who at once returned to a paradoxical actuality), if it is a question of nothing but an additional form, why did they denounce the geometric abstractionists as followers (which they are, in fact) when nothing more was done than to replace the imitation of Mondrian by that of another? There is possibly less novelty than they pretend in the realizations of the Tachists as in their aesthetic-ethics, and more conformity than is thought among their recruits: at least it is Michel Ragon who leads us to ask this question when, in the September-October issue of *Cimaise*, he denounces the rottenness of this tendency: "*abstract art, yes, of course, I still like it, but I preferred it when it was young. It is beginning to smell bad.*" And to denounce the Tachist followers, as well as those of Atlan, Chapoval, Hartung, Kolos-Vary, Lacasse, Lanskoy, Palazuelo, Piaubert, Poliakoff, Marie Raymond, Schneider, Soulages, de Staël, Szenes, Ubac, Vuilamy, Zack, representatives of a third tendency of abstract painting which is neither the formalism of the geometric abstractionists nor the Tachism of the informals.

The fact that this tendency—unnamed till now—is not easy to define results, it seems, from several factors of very different order. First of all, nothing exists in common among the painters that we have mentioned (and we could easily have doubled or tripled the list); there is no common denominator of age, nationality, evolution or experience. Some, like Schneider, are approaching sixty while others are thirty years younger than he; Chapoval, who died too soon in 1951, was born in 1919, and with his disappearance abstract painting suffered one of its cruelest losses. Some of them are French and others are not; and among this last group some have been living in Paris for a long time (Ubac, Poliakoff, Zack, etc.) and others for only a short time. For some of them abstract painting is not at all new—Hartung had been experimenting with it since 1922—while for others it is a recent adventure. Some came to it through Cubism and through movements derived from it, others through Expressionism or through other fields of art. Mondrian and Kandinsky were the idols for some while others preferred different gods. Thus nothing seems to unite these painters, not even friendship nor a common destiny. They hardly mingle with one another; some do not even know each other, and if some prefer to exhibit at the Salon des Réalités Nouvelles others prefer the Salon de Mai. It is not astonishing, therefore, that their painting is so different in spirit: classic in Palazuelo, in love with rigor and reserve, romantic in Schneider, Lanskoy, who also like dynamism, abundance, effusion. Constructors are opposed to colorists, exploiters of abundant paint quality and expressive treatment to those who refuse the one and the other. What similarities therefore exist among them?

First of all they refuse the mathematical abstraction preached by *Art d'Aujour-d'hui*, as the Tachism so dear to Michel Tapié. Though Ubac, Hartung, hung their painting next to those of the informal painters at the Galerie des Deux-Iles or the Galerie du Luxembourg, their art is no less impossible to confuse with that of a Mathieu or a Riopelle. There is neither geometric formalism nor informal Tachism: this double characteristic first of all defines their production. But it is not sufficiently satisfying to characterize their work negatively; it posesses a defined allure and points to precise ambitions. To be plastic and lyrical all in one, and to express itself in finished pictorial forms filled at the same time with a subjective poetry: here seems to be the aspiration of these artists and the fact that sums up their achievements: perfectly incarnated forms, brought to life by a paint quality which is neither the magma o fthe Tachists nor the anonymous pellicule of the geometric abstractionists, by an expressive, free brushstroke but placed at the service of a thought which directs it—these forms live their own life and transmit their message to us, that of a whole man whom no mutilation has reduced to the happy chance of things nor to the slave brain of a method. On the contrary, he allows his entire being to speak for itself: sensuality, sensitivity, intelligence, will, without excluding either his body or his soul. Less partial than the other abstract tendencies this one is richer and its realizations, from this very fact, acquire more complexity and more diversity—a diversity which they owe to the affirmation of the personalities of their authors.

Among those, that we regret not being able to study one by one, the most characteristic and the most exemplary—by that I mean those which seem better to define a certain tendency in a spiritual and plastic way—seem to me to be those of Atlan, Hartung, Poliakoff, Schneider, Soulages, de Staël and Ubac, the best known, as well, of these artists.

JEAN-MICHEL ATLAN
REDOUTABLE – 1956
(1,46; 0,89) DENISE
ATLAN COLLECTION, PARIS

Among them, Atlan, in a certain respect, is the one who comes closest to the Tachists, if not plastically, at least spiritually. Marked, as they are, by Surrealism, he is the most visionary of all the abstract artists (it is not astonishing that he likes Redon), the most sensitive to mystery, to the fantastic, to the primary things of life, and the one who forces himself most to give of his painting something of this cosmic or the visceral which breathes across the infinite life of universal existences: "*It* (my vision) *does not break with the telluric forces of the world, nor detach from them, but attempts to join further with its forces,*" he declared one day to André Verdet: which permits him to protest against the name "abstract" that is given to his work: "*How could it be abstract when, on a canvas, a form that has just been put down, even something entirely strange, wanton, begins to palpitate? When it breathes and the air circulates about it, how could it be qualified as abstract?*" A being almost alive because it is animated by the same forces that animate the world, a being magical also and given strange powers, his painting is still related to those of the informals by the important role that is played by the paint quality. Whether he uses pastel or oil, Atlan demands a great deal of the paint. In his own words "*all is there.*" But it was to add—and this is where he turns his back to the Tachists: "*it should not be seen* (in other words, it should not be obvious), *it should submit to the general laws which govern the composition of a painting.*" For, far from repudiating order, grouping, rhythm, plasticity, color, drawing, he makes them his principal preoccupations. Enclosing his powerful contours with deep colors, he lightens his ochre-reds, blue-greens, sulphur-yellows, his blacks, warm and dense, with a chiaroscuro which creates a suggestion of light and of space, while at the same time he infuses an element of mystery. Reminded, no doubt, of African and Oceanic arts, perhaps also those of pre-Columbian America and pre-Roman Europe, he submits each painting to a powerful rhythm: organic pulsation, sacred dance which brings it to life, emphasizing each of these forms and making them as definite as those of the Tachists are indefinite, as incontestable as the others are vague and, from this very fact, as fruitful in poetic emanation as in plastic robustness.

Atlan by his magical sense is related to Ubac, who, like him, possesses a powerful feeling for paint qualities and the incarnation of form in constructive materials: the most remarkable of his productions are perhaps his engraved slates with a rigor and an intensity worthy of Romanesque sculpture. But his drawings and paintings with their overwhelming blacks equally possess a grandeur to which it is difficult not to be sensitive, all the more so since this tragic intensity, both majestic and pathetic, is obtained by voluntarily meager and marvelously certain means, by a forceful soberness and a reserve which is the best sign of a rich and proud soul.

Soberness, intensity, majesty: it is even more by these three words that Soulages' art is defined; for his also is "Romanesque" and its nervous solemnity evokes that of the Conques church (the painter's spiritual homeland) where balance is born of the neutralization one by the other of opposed forces. There is little color in his work, but it has depth and is dense enough to conciliate transparency and saturation. On a uniform background, bluish, greenish or brown, but one that is varied by the half-light, the form-signs detach themselves in bottle green, Prussian blue, in

SERGE POLIAKOFF – COMPOSITION – 1955 – (0,90; 1,31) PRIVATE COLLECTION, PARIS

ochres, and especially in sumptuous blacks, velvety and hard, strong and profound, amply colored in a single tone, diversified and enriched by a thousand precious nuances: we immediately think of a ball of porphyry or onyx. This painting possesses also the tight grain quality of porphyry and onyx. The largeness of the treatment, the decision of each brushstroke take nothing away from it; on the contrary, they add to the richness of the paint quality, full, compact, without ever achieving a quality of heaviness. The brush draws at the same time that it gives play to the heavy paint. Long bands—we are tempted to say long boards—rise, meet, cross each other, like branches of a tree or the arms of a cross. From their different directions, whose evidence heightens the effect of dynamism, a movement would issue forth if their opposite direction did not bring about a definite serenity—but a serenity that creates an irresistible ascending verticality, recalling that of medieval edifices or even menhirs, both objects of Soulages' admiration: in this respect we note the artist's predilection for upright rectangulars as opposed to horizontal. But if he is seeking height, he has no fear of the opposite direction. Like Atlan and Ubac,

123

he makes use of a half-light to create an opening among this network of forms for the infinity of space, in the same way as the infinity of the sky comes through the openings of a Venetian blind. The studied element is not missing which gives to the painting its monumental quality as incontestable as that in medieval stained glass windows. An impression of power imposes itself, an instinctive and studied power, frustrated and refined, which is born of the direct and reflected art of a man both talented and determined. Essentially and exclusively plastic, this art nevertheless has a profound musical element, like that of a plain song, with its gravity, its tension and its fullness.

This same vigor and soberness characterize the art of Serge Poliakoff, a white Russian who after living in France for quite some time came to abstract art rather late. (47) Rich and vibrating in its paint quality, richer in color than most of these abstract paintings, and despising neither azure blues nor golden yellows nor reds nor

124

whites, without, however, resorting to pure color fresh from the tube, his paintings remain powerfully sober by the simplicity of the forms which he combines to achieve a peaceful immobility—I would almost say, a heavy sleep. Nothing whatever troubles their serenity: they are different from those of Atlan because they are not situated in any kind of space, nor are they touched by any sort of chiaroscuro—in short, they are undeniably flat. Poliakoff himself speaking of his art to Michel Ragon stated that for him the outstanding difference between abstract and figurative art lies in the fact that *"with abstract the shadow values no longer count. One no longer knows where the background is. All parts of the composition can act as form."* And in his art (Poliakoff's) this play is serene, submitted to *"certain rules that help me to find,"* he

PIERRE SOULAGES – COMPOSITION – 1957
(0,80; 0,60) COLLECTION OF THE ARTIST

HANS HARTUNG – T. 56-19 – 1956 – (1,80; 1,36) GALERIE DE FRANCE, PARIS

says, *"the balance of my compositions."* This essentially static balance of a rather rough fullness, harmonizes perfectly with a certain rustic quality which heightens the impression of well-being and authenticity which the painting creates.

Brought, like Soulages, in his search for a mute and full color scheme, to oppose form-sign to a flat background, to achieve power through economy of means, Hartung differs from him no less profoundly as Romanticism differs from Romanesque art. His art is more nervous, more refined, more lyrical. Turning to abstract very early in his career, going ahead and through his paintings of 1922 announcing Tachism (which never boasted of this origin for fear, perhaps, of the comparison), he soon elaborated a graphic element which even now characterizes his painting. Light and definite, thought-out and spontaneous, like Japanese calligraphy (which Hartung seems not to have been acquainted with), the brushstrokes cross the canvas, here, there and everywhere, meet and unite, like sprays and splashes, making up a kind of hieroglyphic, whose vigorous capacity is none the less full of novelty as a result of this special treatment which creates it. Sometimes it is only the aspect of a trembling line on the background, like a blade of grass agitated by the wind. Sometimes dark, these lines contrast with the lighter background tonality where waves of vibrant and limpid light pass. Carried out with the care of an Oriental lacquer artist, by several coats of scumbling and glazing, the background achieves as much finesse as solidity—qualities the artist arrives at as the result of long hours of work, of great care and exactness, but with the desire, also, of giving the impression of spontaneous freshness. The signs tremble against a trembling background—and the ensemble acquires an allure of movement, very different from the dynamic calm of Soulages. Everything, in this art, vibrates and creates a natural and scientific lieder poetry, as simple as it is precious, diaphonous, airy, enveloping, bewitching: we think of Heine and Schumann and, like them perhaps here is the best of German genius expressed in the art of this German wounded in 1944 while serving in the French army and now a naturalized French citizen, one of the most exquisite abstract painters of today and one of the strongest of our art.

Still more romantic is the work of Schneider, a Swiss from Jura—like Le Corbusier—which differed from Hartung's in that it came to abstraction very slowly, but suddenly found in it its spiritual climate and the means of its realization. A great admirer of Cézanne and Poussin, it is mostly the major musicians of the middle of the nineteenth century whom he evokes: Berlioz, Liszt, Wagner, Brahms. In his painting, the color, which has evolved more and more towards a wild violence, is used in waves that follow one another, cover themselves and separate in order to unfurl, break up at the side, covering in flowing areas the large surface of the painting— generally oblong, while in the case of Hartung, Soulages, Ubac and Atlan it was rather vertical. From this unfurling element where violet waves mingle with those of blue or gray and give out isolated areas of red, yellow or white, there emanates a powerful impression of dynamism, confirmed by the disposition of the forms in whirling spirals and the largeness in which they are treated. Schneider prefers force to refinement and even a certain paroxystic lyricism. If Hartung's painting is chamber music, his is an orchestra—while that of Lanskoy is a dance.

127

What trepidation in his art which reminds us of Moussorgsky, Borodin and Stravinsky *(Petrushka)* all in one; it is the wild and reckless rhythm of a popular Russian holiday that has made its way into the painting of this noble man living in exile in France since the fall of the Tsarist régime. First of all figurative, coming to abstract art after the Occupation, he seems, like Schneider, to have found the medium best suited to the realization of his artistic talent. Enamoured of strong colors, which he enjoys bringing out strikingly among beautiful blacks, heavy browns and grays, he confers on these jumbled up accents of vermilion, purple, green, blue, violet, yellow, stridence and verve by the decision of his brushstroke. Although his paint quality is thick, sometimes even compact, a nervous animation is assured: like the colors, the paint quality also dances a ballet. Crossed by evident lines of force and all the more dynamic, the composition receives from these obliques, these spirals and these ellipses, an agitated, vibrating allure. It is the drunkenness of a carnival where poignant melancholy, anguish, fever seek to allay their griefs and which adds a profoundly human extension to this art both refined and barbarous, common and aristocratic, and always plastic: the art of a born painter whose science merely confirms his instinct.

Born in Russia, like Lanskoy, of an aristocratic family which preferred exile to the new régime but with this difference that he left Russia at an early age and so retained very little memory of it and, therefore, is less Russian, Nicholas de Staël also is a man of tumultuous instinct to which are added a warm sensuality, an extended will, a necessary anguish to question everything and a métier of incredible *brio*. Converted to abstract painting in 1942—at that time he was only twenty-eight years of age—he did not wait long, after a few promising experiments (1942-1944), to impose an absolute originality. Small—or more often—large, his canvases are covered with a thick coat of paint, which however is neither heavy nor choking nor muddy. Soft (in the melted sense of the word), or built up, according to the paintings, or, in the same painting, according to the places, it is the product of a work that is both wild and slow, artisanal and inspired, often executed with a palette knife, which enjoys accumulating colors and uniting them in one lump. The tones, generally mute, rarely high in value, always possess the brilliancy of a gem. Night blue and sometimes blood-red, the predominating harmonies are more often discreet: grays, ochres, greens toned down, yellows whose brilliance has been softened are brought together in large and long flowing areas, and all from the same source organized with a very subtle sense of relationship between warm and cold tones. An indestructible unity is born, reinforced by the fact that, different from Soulages, Schneider, Hartung, de Staël, like Poliakoff, places all his forms on the same plane: which does not prevent him (and here he is obviously more subtle than his compatriot) from giving them a needed nuance, to nurture them, to make them live and by discreet shadows accord them a poetical quality. The presence of these works affirms them as organic, autonomous, palpitant beings, and a powerful lyricism manifests itself, a lyricism controlled but warm, emanating from the evidence of flesh and blood as from the disquietude of the soul.

We feel in each of his strained works, under their appearance of unanswerable affirmations, a perpetual interrogation and a requestioning, before each, of all painting, and we are not astonished in the evolution of de Staël's work. Witnessing a soccer match at night at the Parc des Princes in April 1952, along with the discovery of the countryside, forbidden until then because of poverty, brought him slowly, almost invisibly, towards a painting attentive to Nature: he had always denied he painted in an abstract manner, he who confessed to me his antipathy for what he jokingly called "the gang of avant abstraction" and had requested me in 1950 not to hang his *Composition in Gray and Green*, which the Musée National d'Art Moderne had recently acquired, in the same room as the abstract paintings. Beginning therefore in 1952 he has no fear—and will no longer fear—of portraying the exterior world: landscapes *(The Roofs, 1952)*, animated scenes *(Football Players, 1952; The Musicians, 1952)*, objects *(The Bottles in the Atelier, 1953)*, Figures *(Standing Nude, 1953; Large Orange Nude, 1953)*. His technique is modified. He prefers the trowel to the palette knife. If he is still painting in a thick manner in 1952-1953, he becomes later on more economical in his use of pigment in his landscapes of southern France and of Sicily. Rather sober at first, he leaves the domain of grays for a warmer scheme of reds and blacks, his palette becomes increasingly intense. With an audacity unprecedented since van Gogh he throws oranges against violets, vermilions

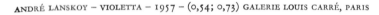

ANDRÉ LANSKOY – VIOLETTA – 1957 – (0,54; 0,73) GALERIE LOUIS CARRÉ, PARIS

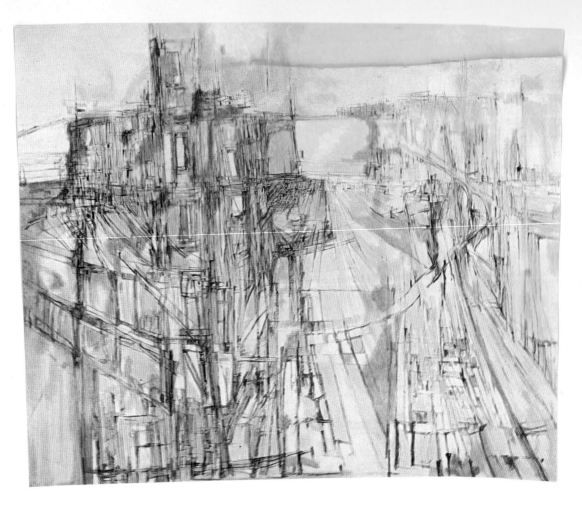

HELENA VIEIRA DA SILVA – LES HAUTS CHANTIERS – 1957 – (1,15; 1,37) COLLECTION OF THE ARTIST

against Prussian blues, and all the more violent in that he disposes them in large uniform areas. The painting reaches an almost unbearable tension—and which de Staël did not bear.

In fact, beginning in 1954, on his return from Sicily, the color scheme is less intense and becomes almost tender: pale blues, creamy whites, grays make up the background *(The Seagulls, 1953; Sleeping Nude, 1955)*. The paint quality becomes thin, the treatment rapid. The form is less powerful—except in the drawings which force us to ask if certain characteristics that we notice in his painting, cannot be explained by its unfinished quality—an unfinished quality due to a tragic event: de Staël's suicide at Antibes on the morning of March 16, 1955.

Unafraid of probing into a mystery which should be regarded simply with respect, certain people have insinuated that this death was inextricably bound up with de Staël's anguish, torn as he was between abstract and figurative painting.

130

NICHOLAS DE STAËL — LE PARC DES PRINCES —
1952 — (1,95; 0,97) PRIVATE COLLECTION, PARIS

A silly calumny which neglects the fact that, for him, there was no opposition, no frontier between these two domains of painting. In fact, most of the works inspired by reality profess such a re-creation of this reality, a rethinking in function of pure plasticism, that they are as abstract as the non-figurative pages whose pictorial essence, on the contrary, is such that they end up by evoking real objects and by being even living and concrete things. Synthetic to the extreme, retaining from the picture of Nature—landscapes, animated scenes—only the most general traits, the drawing harmonizes with the execution by large "moons" of colored paint so as to suggest as the more allusive forms, made of large empty designs and which, more than the images of women, beaches or bottles, are pictorial compositions. Transposed, even invented, the color makes no pretense of recreating that of things and objects: in a certain Mediterranean landscape, "the large blue" is black! It becomes in turn red in a Sicilian landscape. Orange beaches, violet skies reveal the painter more anxious to harmonize complementaries than to represent the exterior world. All the more so since from one end to the other of his production, it is the same Nicholas de Staël who creates the same confidence and gives up to us the same ardent man, volcanic and tenacious, generous, excessive, and more anxious to consume himself in a dazzling flame than to abandon himself; only little by little and with economic prudence. Lyrical and plastic, abstract and figurative, his painting reveals the arbitrary of these oppositions that any great work transcend.

It was equally the case of the painting, less powerful, less ample, but more exquisite, of two artists, Maria-Helena Vieira da Silva and Zao WouKi, whom it is difficult to place either among the abstract or the figurative.

Influenced by Surrealism, but more spiritually than when the plastic element is concerned, Mme da Silva has since 1947 created a universe belonging only to herself and whose bewitching sortileges are difficult to avoid. It is sharp and airy drawing, thought-out and full of the unexpected; a limpid color like light itself. In contrast to the tones of 1947-1951—striking red, electric blues, sulphur yellow—she prefers pinks, linen blues, water greens, straw yellows, especially white, multiple whites spread across the canvas without its becoming empty, monotonous or dull; a water-color quality, a thin surface but as firm as that of a fresco; and a treatment which is the author's own, with its touches of rectangles and squares recalling a mosaic whose transparency the painting possesses. But more than anything else Mme da Silva brings us to a new conception of space, a fantastic and floating space, which has depth and design, both determined and uncertain, constructed and yet phantasmagoric, a world of light and a world of dreams. What are these impalpable forms that people this unprecedented space: real? invented? figurative? abstract? Each of us according to his own ideas, can see an open street veering towards the infinite with its façades flickering with a thousand lights, the shelves of a library, blades of grass trembling on the immensity of a plain or of a water design, or nothing concrete, nothing known to experience, visions of beautiful dreams that have never been made. But out of this magical world flows a strange, ambiguous poetry, very soft, very pure and almost morbid, pleasing and full of fever and whose light leaves us uncertain as to whether it is that of shadows or hallucinations. What difference does it make, since the artist's song resembles no other and, good or bad, it is pleasant to abandon ourselves to its charms.

132

Less ambiguous than this feminine universe, that of Zao Wou Ki possesses nevertheless the troubling mystery of distant China from which the painter seems to have come merely to unite the tradition of the Far East with that of modern Western painting under the sign of Paul Klee. Of an abstract aspect when they were figurative and seeming to represent both familiar and unknown objects, now that they give themselves up to the abstract, his paintings have never failed to achieve the rarest technical perfection and the most discreet lyricism, and also the most refined. The paint quality is as precious as that of lacquer. Rather thin, its richness is not the result of an accumulation of coats of paint, as in de Staël's work, but the fruit of a slow work on a carefully prepared surface and the consummate usage of scumbling and glazing. In its subtle finesse it unites forms and backgrounds which make up only the foreground. Opposition does not exist in his work—the very opposition of foreground and background as in the work of Soulages and Hartung—as if this crafty Chinaman knew how to volatilize it by a compromise inexplicable to our Western sense of logic. The tonal unity reinforces this unity, taking in everything in the same predominating harmony—a generally minor harmony, based on grays for a long time (his views of Venice, 1951) and now of deep browns and reds like those of exotic wood. Though they are of the same tonality and of the same substance as the background, the forms are quite distinguishable. In a brushstroke whose dexterity goes back centuries, these were figures yesterday—women, dogs, monuments or boats—and today are pure and simple forms. But they always reveal the same agility and intelligence and the same mobility also in their daring calligraphy. The precise brushstroke do not imprison them. Overflowing their contour, going beyond the spot, they seem to come to life but in obedience to precise cadences whose exactness takes nothing away from their lightness. Products of an art as perfect as it is nurtured by a sure and aristocratic taste, these paintings nevertheless are filled with the most seductive poetry. Often strong, sometimes even tragic, their proper domain is grace, a "courteous" elegance, and also a reserve which makes their discreet incantations all the more irresistible.

Thus not halfway between but outside and beyond the abstract and the figurative, painters reveal the vanity of these classifications, as the best of the abstracts, beyond and outside Tachism and the geometry of the Post-Neo-Plasticians, bring out the poor basis of partisan attitudes. Today more than ever, the works count more than the doctrines and the individual painters more than the movements: here is the truth of which the young painters seem to be convinced, to study even rapidly, as it remains for us to do, their nascent production.

THE YOUNGEST
FRENCH PAINTING

IN the face of these diverse movements and of the work of all these artists whose powerful personality often lies outside (and quite happily) the scope of schools, what is the attitude of today's youth—by that I mean the painters who, born between 1920 and 1930, begin to possess their personalities and impose their names? The answer to this question is not an easy one. In fact, these young artists are less known than their elders, and any one of them could be left out of this examination, and yet in two or three years—even less—on the contrary attract more attention than all the others. Then too, it is more difficult in this domain than in any other to speak objectively: one wants so much to have youth on one's side that one is sometimes tempted to appropriate it unduly for oneself. On reading the articles of Maximilien Gauthier, of Claude Roger-Marx, of the collaborators of *Arts*, one would believe that the young painters were deserting abstract art *en masse*, which would already have been dead for several years. To which its defenders have fair play to answer them in the words of the personage of Corneille's *Le Menteur: "The people you kill are looking quite well..."* free after that to solicit the facts and to proclaim that all youth paints only in the abstract. And if Léon Degand sees in it nothing but budding little Mondrians, Michel Tapié thinks that informal painting is the only object worthy of its aspirations. And each to repeat with satisfaction, "Youth is on our side."

The truth appears more complex. The young painters are, in fact, everywhere. There is nothing more natural than their turning in diverse directions; for their age is one both of interrogation and of availability. And it would be rather silly for them not to profit by the multiple tendencies of contemporary painting and in particular that offered by the co-existence of two languages: the figurative and the abstract. And it is a question for each person to judge for himself and to know which of these two languages will enable him to express himself, to be sincere with himself and with others; and it is a question, also, for each person to make the choice, a free choice, which his inner necessity imposes upon him—free to turn back on it during the course of his evolution if other needs dictate other tendencies: the important thing is to be sincere. It is not astonishing therefore that of all the tendencies or almost all that we have analyzed in this work, the continuation seemed assured by this or that section of youth.

Inheritors of Besnards, Cottets, Lucien Simons, of all those who, since a Delaroche and a Horace Vernet, have attempted to find a third way between avant-garde and academism, the Brianchons, the Cavaillès, the Chapelain-Midys, the Oudots have—and it was impossible that they should not have—successors, often rather different from them, less concerned with good taste, less anxious to please and rooted better than they and more intimately in things. Less exact in repeating the letter of their art than in extending its spirit, the young painters are the champions of this happy medium which solicits prudence at each period or answers the needs of sensibility and temperament accorded by Nature. One has merely to visit the Salon des Tuileries or the Salon d'Automne to notice ten painters there and a hundred here all anxious to conciliate the audacious novelties of yesterday with tradition and all masters of an excellent technique to achieve this with brio. Some of them have even struck a note of sincerity, a loyalty, a correctness which can only draw respect and sympathy: I am thinking in particular of Montane, of Jean-Pierre Capron whose pale and nude landscapes, constructed with exactness and bathed in a sensitive light, have a decided authenticity and show a rich reserve of delicate tenderness which, beyond Oudot, permits an evocation of the Chirico of 1912 and his poetical quality of the beyond. Entirely different, with temperament rather than sensibility

JACQUES BUSSE – VERRERIES – 1955 – (0,55 ; 0,46) COLLECTION OF THE ARTIST

PIERRE DMITRIENKO – THE QUARRY – (1,15 ; 0,88) PRIVATE COLLECTION, PARIS

Calmettes carries away his still lifes, painted with great virtuosity and whose fiery passion does not prevent them from remaining sober in color and vigorous in construction revealing the artist as the painter's painter of the generation. He reminds us not so much of his teacher, Friesz, as of Courbet.

The grand favorite of the bourgeois public since 1950, the last version of Expressionism—exemplified by a Lorjou, a Buffet—rapidly became the one before the last, as it soon shot out in a new branch. Buffet's "miserabilism" resulted especially in a school of imitators, and one no longer counts the young painters who, in a drab range of colors, created, in delineated forms, anaemic figures or mournful landscapes, still lifes consisting of pathetic meats or popular and dismal *genre* scenes. Dauchot, Lersy, Commère, Verdier, Guerrier stand out among the most remarkable champions of this Expressionism. The version portrayed by Maurice Rocher, who is principally a religious painter, seems to me more interesting; the influence of Permeke—as well as his sacred subjects—took him away from the morose delectation of Buffet and oriented him towards at ense and inward art. If Lorjou has created less of a following than Buffet, his colorful and blustering expressionism has nevertheless exercised a certain influence on contemporary painting. We find traces in the art of a Cottavoz, a Fusaro—but less superficial, less disconnected, decidedly prouder—who seem also indebted to James Ensor: his biting poetic element prevents their art from being vulgar and from his teaching their palette has acquired a finesse and a luminosity foreign to their other model. Moreover, a desire for construction saves Patrix from the redundancy of this Expressionism to which, however, he may be associated. With all these artists—in addition to whom we can name Dany and Belias—figurative painting is not deserted, and it would be rather excessive to proclaim, as some people have, that it is breaking up.

But it would be equally false to announce the defeat of non-representative and abstract painting practised by at least as many young artists. Among those who, turning away from the picture of Nature or the experience of Nature, interpret the fundamental ideas to the point sometimes of making it difficult to identify them—we have called them the "non-representatives" — the most interesting seem to me to be the former adepts of the Group de L'Echelle, Busse, Cortot, Dmitrienko, not forgetting their comrade Ravel, nor three of their elders, Marzelle, Lagrange and Prassinos. Strongly influenced by Cubism and still more by Cézanne, they all turn to the exterior world as the source of their constructions, their rhythms, their elements of re-creation. Less instinctive than the Expressionists, proceeding more by reflection and method, conscious of their goals and their means, wilful, it is a question for them at the same time to interpret the springboard spectacle in its sense, the sense of profound Nature, of its essential truth, and in the sense of the work at hand, including also in this translation that of their own personality. From this fact, among all of them, whatever the—considerable—differences in their paintings, the same necessity to remake the real—making it almost unrecognizable in the finished work—for having been rethought-out, it becomes both the more truthful vision of the painter himself, a plastic thing and the expression of him who rethinks it. From now on three elements make up their works: a fundamental element, an interpretation of this element, and a plastic searching based principally on form, space, rhythm, order. More architects than draftsmen, colorists or culinary artists of savory paint qualities, they reconstruct their forms in a space itself reconstructed as the purpose of the painting and its demands and, conceiving the ensemble as a sort of complete monument, they give it a supplement both of unity and of life through the rhythms to which it is submitted. Here is their unity, by which the landscapes of Arcueil inspired to Lagrange by the sight of the aquaduct resemble those that the Alpilles suggested to Prassinos, the Mount Sainte-Victoire to Marzelle, the forest of Carnelle to Dmitrienko, the port of Dives to Ravel, a glass service to Busse and some human face to Cortot. As for the other characteristics, what diversity! Lagrange is reserved and humorous, Marzelle reserved and serious, Prassinos tense and lyrical; influenced by Jacques Villon, Ravel poeticises his luminous constructions by a kind of chaste tenderness; more uneasy and ambitious, Cortot, more of a colorist, is not afraid of a certain preciosity nor of an almost abstract decorative hermetism. Voluntarily dry and apparently cold, seeming to identify drawing with diagrams, elaborating, in virtue of his intelligence, impeccable constructions, rid of extraneous details and scientifically spread out, Busse is thus the opposite of Dmitrienko. Enamoured, he also, with reddish brown and deep tones—blacks, grays, ochres, purples, whites—and also with a thick and velvety paint quality, placed on the canvas in large strokes and with a great deal of sensuality (in this respect he is closely related to Nicholas de Staël), this Russian born in Paris excels in painting portraits of landscapes where the exterior world, spiritualized completely, resembles itself in an inner resemblance. There is nothing less abstract than these works; but nothing less figurative either—the more so as the rock, the quarry, the forest, the water, the wind, the light are perceptible there, felt rather than identified. Essentially a painter to the point sometimes of abandoning himself to the temptation of *brio*, Dmitrienko is voluptuous in his painting. But he is also a musician, talented in happy dissonances, in rhythmic syncopes, in large movements of grand dances; and it is above all an instinct of Nature that he sees at its center and whose grand hidden and omnipotent life of the world he makes visible to us as well. And finally he is the proof—as Vieira da Silva, Hartung, Soulages, Bazaine, Manessier—of the insufficiency of our distinction: abstract-figurative. The abstract works have existence and plastic worth only if they possess an organic existence which confers upon them an allure of reality. But reality is clothed in abstract appearance, when one sees it from the inside. What do I say? when one sees it: when one photographs its intimacy. I have before my eyes a microphotograph of eighteen by twenty-four centimeters, taken at the Saclay laboratory, which represents two microns on three of an alloyage of silver and cadmium crystal. It is like an abstract painting or, more abstract still, a landscape made by Dmitrienko from the bauxite mines of the Var or the rocks from the forest of l'Isle-Adam.

Going from this non-representative to abstract painting is easy and indeed certain expressions are closely related, notably those, of Lapoujade (b. 1921) and Bernard Dufour (b. 1922.) Whether he starts from reality or not, whether he proposes to give an illusion of it in his work, Lapoujade knows—like Dufour whose paintings have no source in reality, nor do they tend to evoke it—how to manifest in his work a personal life, an organic reality which are the best proof of plastic authenticity and of human resonance. Both artists paint in large transparent spots of light and bright rather than intense colors; but it is without being Tachists (even

138

ROBERT LAPOUJADE — NUDE WOMAN IN
AN INTERIOR — 1957 — (1,90; 0,75) GALERIE
PIERRE, PARIS

though certain canvases of Lapoujade in 1950 are the precursors of and announce Tachism). They are so far removed from informal painting that their spots are forms which, within an indistinct but present contour, quiver against the light backgrounds. The vibration of this universe is the fruit also of the execution: hardly prodigal in paint quality, they nevertheless achieve an expressive treatment and their paintings are clothed in an expressively living allure. For this reason Lapoujade and Dufour are the most typical champions of their generation of this form of abstract art which is called "abstract lyricism."

This abstract lyricism becomes more concerned with formal problems in the works of the young artists among whom we can name Huguette Bertrand (b. 1923), Martin Barré (b. 1924), Kallos (b. 1928), Germain (b. 1915), René Legrand (b. 1923), Rezvani (b. 1928), Pichette (b. 1920), Lesieur. Doubtless they are different from one another, some, like Huguette Bertrand, more interested in graphism, others, like Germain, in color; Martin Barré turns towards Neo-Plasticism, Kallos towards a less formal abstractionism. But the taste for a clear rather than a raw palette, a fine and pearly light, a careful execution, although light and decided, seems to me their common character, along with a very strong interest in form. For example, if we look at the thought-out and scrupulously organized compositions of Pichette: the form is immobilised, contained in an insistent contour and imbedded in a thick paint quality—here are the signs of interest in pure plasticism. Not that he had sacrificed on the altars of Vasarély or Mondrian any more than the other artists I have named, with the sole exception of Barré. It is rather to Cubism that he is indebted—or still more to the painters belonging to its movement. From a La Fresnaye, from Jacques Villon, he appears in fact to like elegant soberness, purity without stiffness, refined naturalness: all characteristics that he desires to achieve and that, it seems to me, are also achieved in different ways and in various degrees by Huguette Bertrand, Lesieur, René Legrand, Germain, Rezvani, Kallos. If the lyrical tendency of Lapoujade and Dufour is close to that of Impressionism, theirs is rather that of the Section d'Or movement.

A third orientation of lyrical abstraction is that of Gillet (b. 1924), Doucet (b. 1924), Debré (b. 1920), Nallard (b. 1918), of all those who cherish a mute and heavy color scheme with dominant earth colors, ochres, grays, blacks and where there is an obvious search for a truculence of treatment and for a paint quality which, thick and crusty, has nothing in common with the lava that jets from the informal volcano, nor even with that sputtered by the Cobra abstract movement. It is voluntary, fabricated, in no way effusive but plastic and an element of plasticity itself. And finally, through it a sort of melancholy lyricism pervades the whole of the work and places this form of lyrical abstraction in the regions of Expressionism.

From this Expressionism we so decidedly cross the border that we pass also that of Surrealism with the last variety of abstract painting practised by the young artists of today: that which is defended by Arnal (b. 1924), Serpan (b. 1922), Maryan, etc. Passion for paint which they fanatically pile up on the canvas; a taste for violent color (whether it is high or mute); a desire to make something of any happy fallings out of the brush: all these are placed at the disposition of a delirious imagination, which can be taxed of morbidity and who knows—better than that of the Surrealists, with the exception perhaps of Max Ernst—gives a pictorial existence to these terrifying worlds. But here, the worlds are abstract—different on this point from those of Picasso to whom, all the same, they owe something. A musty smell of blood, sexuality and death emanate from these works whose atmosphere is also heavy, as filled with miasma as that of a tropical forest. The drama loiters... we are far removed from the worlds of Pichette and Dufour, still more from that of Vasarély. In fact, the distance that separates the abstraction of the latter from Neo-Plasticism is almost as great as that which separates Max Ernst from Purism, Picasso from Seurat, Delacroix from David. And thus the truth comes forth in full evidence: that the domain of abstract art, far from being reduced to a pure formalism, is quite as vast as that of figurative art to which it is parallel.

They are, in fact, two languages and two languages which have their proper genius. But however different French is from German, for example, the reasons are not different which make the verse good (or bad) in one or the other. The sonority of words, their resonance, their rhythm, the rhythm of verse, the very law of verse are no doubt not the same in this case, but a beautiful verse is here and there a verse where the musical quality of the word harmonizes with its resonance, where the

JAMES PICHETTE – MEDITERRANEAN JOY – 1956 – (0,325; 0,50) COLLECTION OF THE ARTIST

rhythm of thought and that of the verse harmonize, where the image becomes music and the music image, where... But this is not the place to develop certain aspects that we have wished to introduce or rather indicate only as subjects of comparison. As a matter of fact, if abstract and figurative art are also two distinct languages, within these languages, and taking into account their specific demands, the quality of a work arises and ripens from the same characteristics or, more exactly, from analagous characteristics. The authority of brushstroke, the harmony of color, the force of form, the unity of composition, the musical quality of rhythms, the pungency of paint surface, the living quality of execution: these are for an abstract work,

R.-E. GILLET – COMPOSITION – 1957
(1,30; 0,89) GALERIE DE FRANCE, PARIS

FRANÇOIS ARNAL – THE DARK HOLIDAYS OF FLESH – 1957 – (1,40; 2,00) COLLECTION OF THE ARTIST

entirely as for a figurative work, some of the proper elements on which its beauty is based. The reasons are the same, *mutatis mutandis*, for the value of *Udnie* and that of the *Fin d'arabesque* where Degas and Picabia described movement and expressed dance by similar means (belonging each time to the special genius of the two painters between whom, naturally, we are not thinking of establishing a parallel).

But the profound unity of the reasons for which, beyond all the languages, the beauty of poetry is due to the same reasons is in no way incompatible with a diversity which results in the fact that within the same language, two prosodies, even opposed, can and should give birth to beautiful poetry for different motifs. From this the same demands of tone, rhythm, image, a line of Jean Racine and a line of Blaise Cendrars impart their quality from distinct sources. Likewise, a painting by Léger and a painting by Poussin have distinct sources, even though the two of them paint in a figurative manner. The language is the same, the prosody is no longer—neither the syntax nor the grammar. Except for certain fundamental and ineluctable laws, the precepts are no longer the same for the means of expression of both painters. Perspective, modeling, light and shade, unity of point of view, respect for anatomy, use of values, etc., made themselves felt in the painting of the seventeenth-century master, while the master of this century seeks a two-dimensional painting where modeling is expressed by quite other means than by values or light and shade, where the multi-

143

plicity of the points of view and the deformation of human anatomy are made into principles, where the syncopated and the discontinuous replace transitions. From Cézanne (and perhaps even from Manet) to Léger, passing by Gauguin, Rouault, Matisse, Braque and Picasso, figurative painting constituted a new grammar which permitted therefore a new use of the old vocabulary—the things of Nature. It speaks a language received from new laws. The abstract painters speak another language.

But they have not taken the trouble to give it its grammar. In fact, they borrowed different grammars from the figurative language: some Cubist grammar, others that of Expressionism, some even that of tradition. There are some abstract painters who do not despise perspective, modeling, light and shade, as there are those who practise the respect for design in the painting, the cult of flat form, incompatible with the light and shade, etc. All the tendencies, from figurative painting to traditional academism and from Impressionism to Cubism and to Orphism, find themselves again in abstract art.

And so, we sometimes come to the point of asking ourselves if the quarrel between the figurative and the abstract is merely a quarrel over subject matter, analogous to that which in 1830 opposed the "Medievalists" and the "antiquomanes," and, twenty years later, painters of contemporary life with those of the ideal existence of former times. On the one hand, the paintings in which one finds again, though it be by illusion, the things of Nature, and on the other, those where one does not find them again: *"A painting should be called 'abstract' when we can recognize nothing in it of objective reality which constitutes the normal milieu of our life,"* professed Michel Seuphor in this respect, the legislator of his Parnassus, on pages 2 and 3 of his *Dictionary of Abstract Painting.* One is therefore tempted to think that the artistic war of today is much too eager for such stakes.

It is not that it is vain. The choice of a subject always implies more than the subject itself, and when Delacroix preferred the Middle Ages to the Greece of David, or Courbet the picture of the life of his time to the mythological conventions of Cabanel, the choice of these themes implied that of a certain style in which to treat them. But, finally are not these stakes less important than those of the Cubist mêlée and the Impressionist battle? A new syntax is a more important creation than new subjects.

But no: there is more in abstract art than new subjects. In fact, it offers the possibility of a different expression of other messages, to whose translation it is perhaps better suited. Previously I compared it to a different language. Would it not be more exact to compare it to music and to establish between it and figurative art the relationship that we can draw up between it and literature, even poetry? Now they are not the same geniuses which express themselves by means of the written word and that of a musical note, nor the same object which is proposed by these two distinct resources. Likewise, painters abstract and figurative are and should be—if they are sincere—of different temperaments and have other things to say, whose translation dictates the choice of the adequate art—figurative or abstract.

Annexing the domain of the abstract, painting has doubled its empire and offers multiple chances to those who practise it. It is up to them not to be mistaken in the choice they make of the one or the other of these paintings. If they have more chances than their elders, they also run more risks. It is up to the painters, then, and to them alone, to stake their claim and to make good use of this new liberty, for the future of their art depends upon it.

144

1 – One sees, for example, two : one at the parochial church of Saint Nicholas of Véroce and the other in the Chapel of the Chatrix, near the same village, purchased in Vienna by some of these Savoyard merchants who, after having made their fortune there, returned to their native village.

2 – To point this out I should like to relate this rather significant anecdote. Seeing a child one day drawing a pot which he had before him, and in the drawing indicating the handle which, from where he was, he was unable to see, I amused myself in asking him why he represented this invisible handle. " Because all pots have handles," he answered. Just as Mr. Jourdain (in Molière's *Le Bourgeois Gentilhomme*) spoke prose without knowing it, this child made Cubism without his realizing it, if Cubism consists in preferring the realism of knowledge to that of the senses.

3 – In regard to this let us remember the words of Segonzac : " *The spirit of the true tradition is to be to contemporary life what the ancients were to their own, without any imitation or pastiche of the past.* " Cited in Gaston Poulain, Dunoyer de Segonzac, *L'Art vivant*, 1934, p. 18.

4 – An outdoor exhibition of paintings and drawings held near the Sacré-Cœur. - *Tr.*

5 – Allusion to the title of the book *Le Cafard après la fête*, published by the critic Adolphe Basler.

6 – Villon and Duchamp. - *Tr.*

8 – From the French meaning "to rub." - *Tr.*

9 – Whom Belgian painting claims and whom we gladly give to it.

10 - A famous nineteenth century illustrator - engraver. - *Tr.*

11 – To which *L'Elan*, published by Ozenfant from 1915 to 1917, had given the preliminaries.

12 – Let us equally mention Félix del Marle (1889-1952) who went from Futurism to the Neo-Plasticism of Mondrian, to veer as a result towards Surrealism and to return to abstraction just before the Liberation. Animator of the revue *Vouloir* in the North, he tried to diffuse abstract art in this region and in Belgium.

13 – Let us note, however, his effort to attach significance to this décor and to make a language out of it. In fact, he establishes an entire system of relationships between the lines, the colors and the forms, on the one hand, and the letters on the other ; and he wants, in this way, to give pictorial translations to the words.

14 – And also, in a certain measure, that of Borès, who offers certain analogies with the art of Beaudin.

15 – In relation to a scientific experience that he has formulated in this terms : " *The human eye... is tainted by a fault that is called ' chromatism ' and which causes a slight disassociation of colored elements making up the incidental light... The part of the spectrum formed of lights of short wave length, in other words blue, is decidedly deviated in its course: it takes on the contours of the image, forming around it an edge, a halo, of—naturally—blue color.* "

16 – Cf., in regard to this, his words : " *The twelfth-century Limoges porcelain makers reserve their golden brass indifferently for the objects or for the background ; but also their space has hardly any relationship with classical space: it is discreet, interior, abstract, incommensurable with that of Nature... We search in vain in this Nature for a picture taking on the objective justification, incontestable, of the space or the colors, in a Champlevé enamel of Limoges, in a fourteenth-century tapestry, in a Chinese décor of Rouen or in an abstract painting of the modern school.* "

17 – In regard to this let us recall the words of Lapicque : " *Immobility* (during the Renaissance) *settles down at ease and reigns during three centuries. Then along comes this crazy fool Cézanne with the idea of deforming objects. In the light of what precedes, we can more justly qualify these so-called deformations: they are deformations for those who move, they are movement for those who consent.* "

18 – Robert Genaille in *La Peinture Contemporaine*, p. 284, writes : " *These painters are eclectics exactly as Brianchon, Legueult, Planson, Limouse and Cavaillès were in 1930.* "

19 – The place where Cézanne had lived at one time. - *Tr.*

20 – *Notes sur la peinture d'Aujourd'hui*, p. 47. We are citing the second edition of 1953.

21 – *Ibid.*, p. 47.

22 – *Ibid.*, p. 63.

23 – *Ibid.*, p. 58-59.

24 – *Ibid.*, p. 62.

25 – *Ibid.*, p. 60.

26 – It was thus that malevolent minds insinuated that the prize founded in 1949 by the newspaper *Opéra* was instituted in order to be awarded to Lorjou, to whom a jury, no doubt poorly selected, preferred Desnoyer : a gesture that brought about the suppression of the prize the following year. We are bringing to mind this opinion without, however, its being our own.

27 - The principal figure of three novels by Alphonse Daudet which are satires on the Meridional character of southeastern France. - *Tr.*

28 - The word *"tempérament"* in the heavy accent of southern France. - *Tr.*

29 – *"...Seul le bouc en a"*. Preface by Maurice Lacour. Exhibition of drawings *(Le Bouc et l'Arlequin)* at the Galerie d'Art du Faubourg, July 6-August 5, 1956.

30 - Referring to the works of Alfred **Jarry**, especially his *Ubu Roi*. - *Tr.*

31 – The expression is that of Michel Tapié, panegyrist of the movement, who gave this title to a book which appeared in 1952.

32 – Jean Marcenac, cited by Michel Ragon, *L'Aventure de l'Art abstrait*, p. 45.

33 – One will note, in this respect, the craze for the art of this tendency in the Scandinavian countries, where its champions went to exhibit, paint decorations, etc.

34 - He is referring to the famous phrase in Pascal : "L'homme n'est ni ange ni bête, et le malheur veut que qui veut faire l'ange fait la bête." - *Tr.*

35 - From the French meaning "a stain, a spot, a blob." - *Tr.*

36 – In *Combat*, March 1, 1954, cited by the *Tour de Feu*, No 51, p. 84.

37 – *Ibid.*, p. 79.

38, 39, 41, 43 – *Ibid.*, pp. 80-81.

40 – *Ibid.*, p. 86.

42, 44 – *Ibid.*, p. 78.

45 – *Ibid.*, p. 79.

46 – *Ibid.*, p. 93.

47 – One will note, in regard to this, the number and the importance of Russians in the genesis of abstract art (Kandinsky, Baranoff-Rosiné, Sonia Terk-Delaunay, Gontcharova, Tatlin, Malevitch, Pevsner, Gabo (etc.), as in its blossoming (Chapoval, Lanskoy, Poliakoff, de Staël, Zack and many others). It was as though pictorial Slav genius, annihilated by the examples of Western realism of which it achieved in assimilating only the most mediocre appearances, came forth suddenly in all its glory and finding again its ancient atmosphere of Byzantine non-realism, was capable of giving it its fullest measure.

BIOGRAPHICAL NOTICES

ALIX, Yves

Born at Fontainebleau August 19, 1890. In 1908 at the Ecole des Beaux-Arts, where he studied in the ateliers of Baschet and Royer. Left the Ecole des Beaux-Arts for the Académie Ranson where Bonnard, Vuillard and Roussel were teaching along with Maurice Denis and Sérusier. Exhibited for the first time at the Salon des Indépendants of 1912; worked with Denis on the decoration of the Champs-Elysées Theatre. Like every artist his age, he was attracted by the Cubist movement, but he soon revealed an independent personality related to that of the Expressionists, Gromaire particularly. "He proceeds," wrote Roger Allard, "by dark and luminous masses, and it is at the edge of each mass that the outlines are revealed. His suggestion of spatial relations which is particularly strong does not need the artificial means of a jewel setting which gives the illusion of definite firmness." He has evolved towards a more colorful art and one that is more submissive to the appearances of the outside world which he interprets less.

ARNAL, François

Born at La Valette (Var) October 2, 1924. His mother was Spanish. After studying at the lycée in Toulon, he enrolls at the Faculty of Law and Letters at Aix-en-Provence. For a time he is an instructor in judo. In 1940 he begins to paint instinctively with the spontaneity of a child *(Fort Apache, The Grape Gatherers)*. Already one finds in his first paintings the hieroglyphic signs which appear in his later work. Drawn to Paris, Arnal arrived one day in 1948 with four canvases under his arm and full of hope. He soon discovered the jungle of painting and the controversy over abstract art. After a troublesome and discouraging period, he turned his back completely to all the established rules and paints with a passionate freedom. Forms in intense, rich and vibrating colors (the red often predominates) burst forth from his canvas without any concern at all for "prettiness." Everything is sacrificed to the expression; the object and its "sign" are juxtaposed, creating a feeling of mystery and magic. A thick coat of paint worked over with a palette knife takes on life and becomes land, sea or a melting metal. Prix de la Jeune Peinture in 1949. Arnal exhibited first at the Galerie Drouant-David (1950), and then at the Galerie "Rive Droite."

ATLAN, Jean-Michel

Born in Constantinople January 23, 1913. His parents, who had a small business, sent him to Paris where he received his degree in philosophy. During the war he had to feign madness to escape deportation and was interned at the Sainte-Anne Hospital. Tempted by painting in 1941, it was not till the Liberation, in 1944, that he could devote himself to it entirely. Already in the Expressionist paintings of his beginnings one can recognize Atlan's African ancestry. Towards 1947 he turns to abstraction but soon finds his actual form of expression in the different sorts of fantastic animals which leave a choice of interpretation in the spectator's imagination. Of a very rich surface, these forms are made from a mixture of oil, pastel and chalk, and they are often encircled by a strong black outline which divides the canvas into a suggestive rhythm. Atlan's harsh style asserted itself rather slowly. His first exhibition took place at the Galerie Maeght in 1947, and afterwards at the Galerie Bing in 1956. In 1957 the Palais des Beaux-Arts of Brussels and the Museum of Antibes devoted their rooms to him. Atlan sends work regularly to the Salon de Mai, and also takes part in international exhibitions (Liège, Tokio). He has published a collection of poems, *Le Sang Profond* (1944) and has illustrated the *Description of a Fight* by Kafka (1947).

AUJAME, Jean

Born at Aubusson May 12, 1905 of a bourgeois Auvergnat family. Admitted at the age of seventeen to the École des Beaux-Arts of Rouen, he then entered upon his law studies. He established himself in Paris in 1930 and began by doing strong Fauve painting. His art improved during the course of the following years: trips in the Creuse (1931 and 1932), Holland (1932), Spain (1933), and during these trips he painted many landscapes. In 1935 he received the Prix Paul Guillaume. Important decoration for the Palais de la Découverte in 1937 *(Découverte des eaux souterraines)*. During a captivity of two and a half years (1940-1942) he concerned himself entirely with the theatre. Returned to work, he sent paintings to an exhibition in Copenhagen (Galerie Corner) (1945) and had an exhibition at the Galerie de Berri (1946). He was awarded the Hallmark Prize in 1949.

147

BALTHUS

The artist who had adopted this pseudonym was born February 29, 1908 of a family of artists of Polish origin. He has always painted, and since the age of sixteen has devoted himself exclusively to painting. Part of his childhood was spent in Switzerland. Rainer-Maria Rilke becomes interested in his childish paintings where already his special world appears. He has no teachers but soon knows Bonnard and Derain who often visit his parents. One of his fundamental themes which is strikingly evident in his early canvases is "the obsession with attitudes, with secret relationships and conducts which mark the change over from childhood to adolescence" (Georges Bernier, *L'Œil*, March 1956). Always living a life apart and hostile to publicity, he has retired to the country after having worked for a long time in Paris. Each year sees a deeper regard to his work to which he devotes himself with restless energy. In addition to painting he has designed theatre décors, notably *La Peste* and *L'Etat de Siège* of Albert Camus. In the field of book illustration he has made drawings, which remain unpublished for *Wuthering Heights*. He exhibited in 1946 at the Galerie des Beaux-Arts, in 1948 at Renou and Colle's, and in 1956 at the Galerie des Beaux-Arts.

BAUCHANT, André

Born at Châteaurenault (Indre-et-Loire) in 1873. At the same time that he was going to public school he was helping his father, a gardener. In 1900 he married and came to Paris on his honeymoon to see the Universal Exposition. In 1908 he gave up his nursery in order to devote himself to art. In 1921 he exhibited nine paintings at the Salon d'Automne among which were sketches for a panorama of the Battle of the Marne. Le Corbusier and Ozenfant bought his paintings. He did the décor of *Apollon Muzagete* for Diaghilev. He sent his paintings to different salons, but beginning in 1929 he limited himself to the Salon d'Automne and to the Salon des Surindépendants. From 1927 to 1941 Jeanne Bucher showed his paintings. In 1948 there was a large retrospective exhibition of his work at the Galerie Charpentier. After having painted primarily historical pictures *(Pericles Rendering an Account of Public Funds, The Battle of Thermopylae, The American Declaration of Independence)*, Bauchant paints, after 1929, landscapes, flowers, birds and also Biblical scenes among which was *The Creation of the World*.

BAZAINE, Jean

Born in Paris December 21, 1904. His family, originally from Lorraine, made him go on with his secondary studies, but after receiving a degree in letters, Bazaine, who since childhood had worked in sculpture, enrolled at the Ecole des Beaux-Arts, then later at the Atelier Landowski. It was at that time he turned towards painting which he never gave up. At his first exhibition at the Galerie van Leer in 1932, he met Bonnard, who encouraged him and gave him advice, and also Gromaire —the beginning of a lasting friendship. Bazaine has exhibited at the Salon des Tuileries since 1930, and at the Salon d'Automne since 1931. In 1938 he was awarded the Blumenthal Prize in painting. Mobilized in 1939, he drew from Nature "barks of trees, stones, whirlpools, bodies of men taking a bath, etc." It was there he discovered his true expression, this search for the profound reality of beings and things which he does not cease going after by a slow and continuous evolution. A figurative painter at the beginning and now less concerned with appearances, Bazaine always leans towards the living forms which are around him. In 1941, he was one of the organizers of the exhibition called "Jeunes Peintres de Tradition Française." He exhibited at the Galerie Jeanne Bucher, then at the Galerie Louis Carré, and since 1949 he has been showing his work at the Galerie Maeght. In 1952 he was selected jury member of the Pittsburg International Exhibition. Bazaine executed three stained glass windows for the church of Assy and a mosaic for the church of Audincourt. He is also an art critic and has published many articles and an essay entitled *Notes sur la peinture d'aujourd'hui*.

BEAUDIN, André

Born at Mennecy (Seine-et-Oise) February 3, 1895 of peasant origin. His formation is elementary, and he takes a school certificate successfully. He came to painting through drawing, "in little steps," as he says. From 1911 to 1913 he studied at the Ecole des Arts Décoratifs. In 1921 he took a trip to Italy. His admiration has remained faithful to Matisse, Juan Gris, Picasso. The subject for Beaudin tends to become a theme. He studies it and is penetrated by it, afterwards he interprets it by removing all that is extraneous. For instance, we notice thus a series of *Horses*, a theme to which he often returns; the *Villas* and the *Pavillons*, the *Flowers*, without forgetting the very modern theme of *The Bicycle*. He follows his proceedings with an untiring will, transforming everything by light. There are

148

no spots, few arabesques and modulations but a light scumble where sometimes the colors are smeared on in large flat areas but without insistence: each of his works is a rustle, like that of leaves. His first exhibition was held at the Galerie Percier in 1923, with a preface by Max Jacob; a recent exhibition was held at the Galerie Louise Leiris, with a preface by André Frénaud.

BERTHOLLE, *Jean*

Born at Dijon June 26, 1909. His father was chief inspector of the railroad. He took courses at the Ecole des Beaux-Arts of Lyon, but after his arrival in Paris he spent only a short time at the Beaux-Arts. He was influenced at that time by the Surrealist milieu; the mystery of man in the world haunted him. As a result of his Surrealist and Cubist experiences, his art retained the simplicity of lines and volumes, the will of construction which for him are a means of expressing allusions to a secret world and of bringing forth the hidden connection of things.

BISSIÈRE, *Roger*

Born at Villeréal (Lot-et-Garonne) September 22, 1888. Having finished his secondary studies, Bissière enrolled at the Ecole des Beaux-Arts of Bordeaux. At the age of seventeen he had painted his first picture, "without having seen anything." He comes to Paris in 1910, and in order to earn a living he becomes a journalist. He meets Lhote in 1919, Braque in 1921. He exhibits for the first time at the Salon d'Automne of 1919. From 1924 on, he teaches at the Académie Ranson. He continues to work very much alone; reality ceases to satisfy him and his work evolves towards a new art (1936). In 1939 he had been living for a short time in the family house of Boissierette, in the Causses; he remained there during the five years of war. For him the agony of Occupation aggravates the fear that he may lose his sight, having had his first attack of glaucoma in 1939. Just as he loves his country life, he loves the popular song: "*Je me sens... à l'aise à l'ombre d'Edith Piaf*" (quoted by Max-Pol Fouchet), he writes in the preface of his catalogue, when he exhibits in 1947, at the Galerie Drouin, paintings as well as tapestry hangings made from pieces of dissimilar material, sewn together. His operation, in 1948, for glaucoma was successful, and his work becomes more optimistic. He exhibits in 1951 *Images sans Titre* at the Galerie Jeanne Bucher; second exhibition in 1952; he is awarded the Grand Prix National des Arts. In 1942 he publishes with wood engravings the *Hymn to the Sun* of St. Francis of Assisi (Edition Jeanne Bucher). In his paintings of the last twenty years one frequently finds a style of composition which recalls that of his tapestry hangings parallel bands themselves formed very often of superposed rectangles.

BOMBOIS, *Camille*

Born at Vénarey-les-Laumes February 3, 1883. His father was a boatsman. In several paintings one finds again the influence of his life on the water. At twelve years of age Camille Bombois becomes a farm hand at Migennes. He begins to draw at sixteen. Of athletic force he becomes regional wrestling champion, and afterwards joins a traveling circus as boxer. Wishing to know Paris he comes there on foot. He becomes a roadman, then a laborer on the subway construction. But finding that he does not have sufficient time to paint, he prefers to work at night in a printing house. As a result of his conduct during war of 1914-1918 he is awarded the Military Medal. About 1922 he begins exhibiting his canvases in the street. They are noticed by Noël Bureau, who writes an article about him in *Rythme et Synthèse*; Mathot and Uhde buy all his paintings. He is thus allowed to leave his work and devote himself to painting.

BORES, *Francisco.*

Born in Madrid in 1898; a few months previously he would have been born at Manilla, since his father was the last Spanish governor of the Philippines. He begins painting at the age of seventeen in a private academy and copies Velazquez for a long time at the Prado.

In 1925 he exhibits for the first time at the Salon des Artistes Ibériques. It was then that he came to Paris and settled down. This young Spaniard could not help being influenced by Picasso and Juan Gris, but he really felt that his elders had said everything in the road that they had opened before them. He did not even bother to go from figurative painting to abstract, but he wished to discover a personal expression, going back to the findings of Cubism. He was tempted for a time by Surrealism. He reckons with the geometric spirit, renounces the object in itself; he sought at that time to suggest the dynamism of the objects, and had his first exhibition at the Galerie Percier in 1927. The more he advances, the richer his themes become. He is brought by life to multiply the figures and all things in movement, like a ball of strings, as well as garlands of beads; he even introduces a baroque point of view, submitted to a movement not of flight but of expansion. In 1929 he undergoes another stage of evolution. "It was from his stay at Grasse, a period from which one can date," said Jean Grenier in the September 1956 issue of *L'Œil*, "his full originality derived from a new poetic interpretation of geometry." Exhibition at the Galerie Louis Carré in July of 1956.

BOUSSINGAULT, *Jean-Louis* (1883-1943)

Born in Paris March 8, 1883 in a milieu of scientists; his grandfather was a chemist and a teacher at the Collège de France; he died in Paris May 17, 1943. He enrolled at the Ecole des Arts Décoratifs and at the same time took an evening course in an academy of drawing on the Ile Saint-Louis. In 1901 he took part in a contest for art workers as a lithographer and poster designer, and from this period he considers his métier with great esteem. In 1902 he did his military service at La Flèche and there he meets Dunoyer de Segonzac. On his return he works at the Académie Julian, then at the Académie de la Palette, where his work is noticed by Desvallières and Laprade. His comrades in the atelier are La Fresnaye, Jean Marchand, Segonzac, L.-A. Moreau, and in 1908 he spends a brief time with them at Saint-Tropez. He leads a rather elegant existence, earning a living drawing for magazines which were then in fashion. In 1911 he executed for the couturier Paul Poiret his first large composition, *Promenade* (19′69″ × 8′20″), exhibited at the Salon d'Automne of 1913, a painting in which traces of Cubist stylization are quite evident. Just after the war, in 1914, he takes a trip to Egypt. For Boussingault the period after the war is one of uneasiness and searching. He runs away from all influences and seeks to express himself in compositions, figures, and still lifes which he exhibits from 1923 to 1927. But he never paints landscapes. He emerges enriched by this period of solitude, and his work attains its fullness between 1930 and 1940, fruitful years during which he paints nudes, flowers, portraits and above all still lifes. His treatment becomes more and more heavy but without pigment thickness or violent colors which betray his virtuosity. His art sometimes achieves gracefulness from the strength of his drawing and from a full and serious style which is almost austere. He has also left some vast and powerful mural compositions.

BRAYER, *Yves*

Born at Versailles November 18, 1907. Pupil of Lucien Simon at the Ecole des Beaux-Arts. In 1927 he received a government grant which enables him to visit Spain. Grand Prix de Rome in 1930. Travels in Italy, in Morocco. From 1944 on he spends several summers in Provence and Camargue. He is a painter of landscapes as well as compositions and figures, and if he respects the great traditions he is none the less interested in new searchings in art.

BRIANCHON, *Maurice*

Born at Fresnay-sur-Sarthe January 3, 1899. His parents owned a cider distillery. His vocation was precocious. After he had finished his studies at the Collège of Le Mans, he spent some time at the Ecole des Beaux-Arts of Bordeaux, but he soon returns to Paris. He spends eight days at the Ecole des Beaux-Arts, then enrolls at the Ecole des Arts Décoratifs, where he stays six years and where he meets Oudot and Legueult. In Montparnasse he shares an atelier with Legueult. During his early period he is influenced by Bonnard and Manet. He paints interiors, nudes, seascapes (Brittany and the Basque country). In 1920 he exhibits for the first time at the Salon d'Automne. In 1924 he receives the Blumenthal Prize. In 1931 he makes a trip to Spain. In 1928-1932 he frequents the circus, the music hall, the artists backstage. Together with Legueult he designs décor models. He marries Marguerite Louppe, but collaborates with her only on the three decorative panels at the Conservatory (1942). In 1947 he becomes a teacher at the Ecole des Arts Décoratifs. In 1939 he is awarded the Carnegie Prize. Brianchon's taste has made him a painter of femininities which he translates into refined colors. He is also a landscape painter, but especially of an urban nature. In 1956 he takes part in the exhibition called "Peintres de la Réalité Poétique" held at the Galerie Romanet. He is teaching at the Ecole des Beaux-Arts.

BUFFET, *Bernard*

Born in Paris July 10, 1928. He was a bad student and was expelled from the Lycée Carnot. In 1943 he took an evening course in drawing. The following year he enrolled at the Ecole des Beaux-Arts; then worked alone in his room, Boulevard des Batignolles. He forms a friendship with Aujame who makes him known. The Galerie des Impressions d'Art devoted a small exhibition to him which had no success whatever (1947). After sending work several times to the Salons, it is towards 1948 that he develops a personal style; he is awarded along with Lorjou the Prix de la Critique (Galerie Saint-Placide). From that moment on Bernard Buffet's paintings take a predominating place in the art market. The Galerie Drouant-David organizes several exhibitions (1952, *La Passion;* 1953, *Landscapes;* 1954, *Nudes;* 1955, *The War*, three large canvases; 1956, *The Circus;*) in 1957 the Galerie David et Garnier presents a series of canvases having as subject matter the monuments of Paris. In his still lifes or in his landscapes, as well as in his thin, drawn out nudes, Bernard Buffet, following the tradition of Gruber has always portrayed a tragic and hopeless world. Buffet had done many illustrations, especially in etching, *Les Chants de Maladoror* of Lautréamont (1952), *La Recherche de la Pureté* of Jean Giono and *La Passion.*

BUSSE, *Jacques*

Born in Paris December 22, 1922. After secondary studies which he would have liked to continue right up to a degree in philosophy, he enrolled at the Académie de la Grande Chaumière and devotes himself to painting (1942). He took part with Calmettes, Cortot, Patrix in the formation of the group called "L'Echelle." A forced worker for two years, he exhibits on his return (1945) at the first Salon de Mai, to which he remains faithfully attached and is named a member of the committee in 1956. After a so-called "rhythmic" period (dunes, waves), then Neo-Cubist (still lifes), Busse gets away from representation with its rather vivid colors reminding one of "glass making." Impressed by a brief stay at Les Baux, he now paints his "stone quarries" in more austere grays, dividing his canvas according to strict straight lines. Like his companions of the "Echelle" group, Busse has been influenced by Cubism and has tried to adapt his lessons to create his actual form of expression. Since 1957 he has been exhibiting at the Galerie Jacques Massol.

CAILLARD, *Christian*

Born at Clichy (Seine) July 26, 1899. Secondary studies at the Collège Rollin. Prepares for the Ecole Centrale. In 1921 he gives up science and enrolls at the Académie Billoul, where he meets Eugène Dabit. From 1929 to 1932 he travels around the world, stopping in Indo-China, Bali, Bora-Bora, Martinique. In 1923 he meets Loutreuil with whom he works for several years. From 1926 to 1928 he is in charge of an art gallery and spends the winters in Morocco. On his return he exhibits at the Galerie du Portique, and since 1933 at the Galerie Bernier. In 1934 he is awarded the Blumenthal Prize and later discovers Spain. In 1936 he is awarded the Prix de l'Afrique du Nord. Spends the winters once again in Morocco from 1936 to 1939. He is taken prisoner in June 1940, and is liberated after a year of captivity. Caillard has decorated notably the Palais de la Découverte (1937) and the lecture rooms of the Musée Guimet (five large frescoes on the life of Buddha). Exhibits with the Groupe de la Réalité Poétique at the Galerie Romanet in 1956.

CAILLAUD, *Aristide*

Born in Moulens (Deux-Sèvres) January 28, 1902. When only a child he looked at the sky and saw things there. At the age of five he liked to draw. That Caillaud was a butcher at Asnières is certainly picturesque, but it is of little importance. What is important, however, is that he is a born painter. At the age of twenty he paints for his own pleasure; he becomes interested in the work of Picasso. But his revelation takes place when he is forty years old. Prisoner of war in 1943 at the Oflag IV D, he undergoes an inner moral crisis. With great luck he is able to procure paints and brushes. And, in a profoundly religious sense, Caillard covers the walls of his barrack with large compositions. On his return, after the war, his vocation has definitely decided his objective in life. Louis Chéronnet gives him advice. Caillaud translates into painted forms the things that his childish eyes have seen and his mind has dreamed: the farm, the chicken coop, the brook, the village circus. But after a trip to Venice he translated his impressions of the unique city into a large canvas which was bought by the Musée National d'Art Moderne in 1957. A religious painter, each of his works: *Christ Child in the Manger, The Baptism of Christ, St. Francis of Assisi,* is a spontaneous emotion which classes him among the most valuable painters in the renewal of *art sacré.* Caillaud has not only the genius of invention but a sense of color and construction as well. His way of transgressing the laws of perspective in such paintings as *Panorama of Paris* and others, the astonishment that is created by such an unexpected aspect of bulk and mass, of colors or of light, bring about a feeling of something almost fairylike. And one should not find fault with his painting *The Helicopter* which he paints in full flight! He exhibits at the Salon de Mai and at the Galerie Bénézit (1957).

CALMETTES, *Jean-Marie*

Born at Wissous (Seine-et-Oise) April 15, 1918. After secondary studies, he enrolls at the Ecole des Arts Appliqués, then at the Ecole des Arts Décoratifs. At that time he was doing sculpture under the direction of Wlerick (1935-1937). Calmettes shortly afterwards turns towards painting and enrolls at the Ecole des Beaux-Arts (1938-1939). Mobilised, he returns to Paris in 1941 and took part in the formation of the "Echelle" group, which has its first exhibition in 1943. In 1947 he is awarded the Prix Carrefour de la Jeune Peinture, the Prix Othon Friesz in 1954, and the Prix du Dôme in 1955.

151

CAVAILLÈS, Jules

Born at Carmaux June 20, 1901 of Languedoc ancestry. In 1922 he enrolls at the Académie Julian, where he is the pupil of the brothers Pierre and Jean-Paul Laurens. He exhibits at the Salon des Indépendants, at the Salon d'Automne, at the Salon des Tuileries. In 1936 he receives the first Blumenthal Grant for French thought and art. If the Fauves had at first taught him intensity, he dared to return to nuance. Cavaillès is a painter of atmosphere. His poetic liberty, his taste for pure sensation which he translates into clear and vivid tones, the pleasing quality of his composition—all go to make his paintings mirrors, reflecting the joy of life, as it were. In 1949 he is awarded one of the Hallmark prizes. In 1956 he exhibits at the Galerie Romanet with other painters of the Réalité Poétique group.

CHAGALL, Marc

Born at Vitebstk (Russia) July 7, 1887. His father was a Jew employed in a herring warehouse and who had ten children. Chagall studied first in the atelier of the portrait painter Pen, and soon afterwards left for St. Petersburg. Thanks to a pension he is able to come to Paris in 1911. He settles down at La Ruche, discovers Fauvism, then Cubism, and becomes friendly with Blaise Cendars, Apollinaire, Max Jacob, André Lhote, Delaunay, Gleizes, La Fresnaye, Modigliani. In 1914 Chagall has a large exhibition of his work at Berlin; the canvases that were shown to the public were chosen by Apollinaire as among the most expressionistic. In 1914 Chagall turns to Russia and in 1915 marries a young girl who had greatly aided and influenced him before he had gone away. During the revolution of 1917, he is named superintendent of the Fine Arts and is founder of a State academy at Vitebstk. But after a disagreement with Malevitch he resigns and goes to Paris in 1922, stopping at Berlin. In 1931 he was invited to attend the inauguration of the Tel Aviv Museum, and he takes advantage of the invitation to visit Palestine and Syria. During the war he went to the United States. His first wife dies in 1944. In 1945, he designs the décor and costumes for Stravinsky's *Firebird*. In 1947 he returns to France. An exhibition devoted to his works is held at the Musée National d'Art Moderne. He has illustrated numerous books: *Dead Souls* of Gogol, *The Fables of La Fontaine*, *The Bible*, etc. He has also worked in ceramic (decoration of the baptistery of the church of Plateau d'Assy).

CHAPELAIN-MIDI, Roger

Born in Paris August 24, 1904 of Beauceron ancestry. Finished his secondary studies at the Lycée Louis-le-Grand. Encouraged by his parents in his taste for painting, he enrolled at the Ecole des Beaux-Arts in the atelier of Cormon. He remains there only four months, and after his military service works in the free academies of Montparnasse. In order to live he is obliged to do publicity, decorative and journalistic work. In 1930 he is commissioned to do the decorative panels of the *"Mairie"* of the IVe arrondissement. From this date he takes part in numerous exhibitions in other countries. In 1949 he is awarded the Hallmark Prize.

CHASTEL, Roger

Born at Paris March 25, 1897. Studies with Jean-Paul Laurens at the Académie Julian. On leaving the atelier he does political and literary caricatures. Awake to the atmosphere of the time, if he admires Braque and uses him as an example, as does Modigliani at a time, he knows also what he owes to Matisse or Picasso (especially baroque, it seems to him). He begins by doing Cubism and makes his start in 1926 with Max Berger (Galerie Vavin-Raspail). About 1929-1930, progressively returned to a more objective art, he undergoes a neo-realist period of very sensitive inspiration *(Les Enfants du Boulanger*, 1932-1934, Musée National d'Art Moderne). Beginning in 1939 he goes through a baroque phase, where the excess of forms is united with the exaltation of color. *The Piano Lesson*, 1946, achieves a sort of expressionism, but leans less to the excess of the character of the individual than to the exaltation of the intellectual and poetical theme. *La Coiffure*, 1945, in light flat grays, blues, mauves, greens and light yellows, marks a rigorousness of construction which responds in Chastel to the other side of his nature, and which shows him well on his way to his present period. His nature would be of an almost austere reserve in the color if, in the predominating deep tones, a strong spot did not always brighten the picture *(Herring and Pitcher*, series 1949-1954). This hieratism which Chastel has today achieved—"because it is lasting"—remains close to the figurative.

His searchings, sincere and complex, are those of a romanticist who dreams of classicism. Is it for this reason that, for nearly thirty years, Chastel works every day, near the noble windows of Louis XIV, in the place that he has chosen for himself at Saint-Germain-en-Laye? Supported in his beginning by Paul Guillaume, he exhibits at the Galerie Jeanne Castel, and afterwards at the Galerie Maeght, for whom he illustrates the *Bestiaire* of Paul Eluard in colored etching. He exhibits now at the Galerie Galanis. He was awarded the Grand Prix de la Peinture at the first Sâo Paulo Biennale in 1951. In the field of tapestry, Chastel gave the Gobelins in 1952 a large design *The Fourteenth of July at Toulon.*

CHIRICO, *Giorgio di*

Born at Volo (Greece) July 10, 1888 of an Italian family; his father was originally from Palermo and his mother from Genoa. For two years he attends the School of Drawing in Athens, then works a year and a half at the Munich Academy. In Italy he follows no school of art but copies the Old Masters in the museums. From 1911 to 1915 Giorgio di Chirico lives in Paris where he makes the acquaintance of Raynal, Apollinaire, Picasso, Paul Guillaume. In 1915 he returns to Italy where he is forced to remain till 1924, living in Rome and Florence, but without abandoning his travels. At the end of 1924 he goes to Paris with the intention to settle down permanently, but he leaves the city for Rome, where he becomes the semi-official painter of Fascism *(Portrait of Edda Ciano).* The work of Chirico is divided into four periods. The first is that of large urban landscapes inspired by the paintings of Paolo Uccello and Piero della Francesca. These paintings of Chirico show large deserted places with accented perspective and under a strong light which throws fantastic shadows. The second period, known as the Germano-Italian, shows the influence of Munich Symbolism. On his return to Paris in 1924 he took an active part in the Surrealist movement. His Surrealist period extends from 1924 to 1929. During this period he painted series of gladiators, horses, interiors in the open air, figures composed like mounted pieces having the appearance of ghosts. Then he adopts an art submissive to appearances (still lifes, nudes), influenced by academism, in very soft tones and with the forms much less precise. In 1946 he exhibited a significant ensemble of his work at the Galerie Maeght. He designed décor-models for the theatre. Aside from his work as a painter, he occupies an important place in the modern art movement with his literary work *(Hebdomeros)* and his writings as art critic.

CORTOT, *Jean*

Born at Alexandria, Egypt February 14, 1925. Studied in Paris. Tired of trying for an unobtainable *baccalauréat*, he entered the atelier of Othon Friesz in 1942 at the age of seventeen, and exhibited the same year at the Salon restricted to painters less than thirty years of age (Salon de Moins de Trente Ans). He took part in the formation of the group called "L'Echelle" (Calmettes, Busse, Patrix, Dalmbert, Laran) and exhibited with the group at the Galerie Jacques Blot in 1943. His first exhibition was held at the Galerie Visconti in 1944. Then till October of 1945 he was a soldier. Since 1947 he has been exhibiting regularly at the Salon de Mai. In 1948 he was awarded the Prix de la Jeune Peinture. A exhibition of his work was held at the Galerie Vallotton in Lausanne; in 1954 he exhibited with Calmettes, Busse and Dmitrienko at the Galerie Apollo in Brussels; the very same year he exhibited with Davy (tapestries) and Cesar (sculpture) at the Galerie Lucien Durand in Paris. Since 1957 he has been exhibiting at the Galerie Jacques Massol. Cortot remembers the Cubists' example but seeks incessantly a new form of expression. He devotes a period of time to themes that he develops: ship construction at La Ciotat (1947-1950), austere landscapes of the Ardèche (1951), the human face itself: all of these are an opportunity for personal expression. He always starts from reality. Still life painting is his unchanging artistic form of expression. He is passionately fond of excavations—chipped flint implements as well as fossil molusc, whose characteristic groove is found in the graphic quality of his recent canvases.

COUTAUD, *Lucien*

Born at Meynes (Gard) December 13, 1904. He has been painting since the age of sixteen. Spends two years at the Ecole des Beaux-Arts of Nimes, then at the free academies in Paris. Spends his military service in the Rhineland. During a long stay in Italy, he discovers Piero della Francesca. Alone, he works on the same lines as the Surrealist movement: he reads Rimbaud, Lautréamont, Raymond Roussel. In 1928 Dullin asks him to design décor and costumes for the *Birds* of Aristophanes. He does a great deal more work for the theatre among which are *As You Like It* by Shakespeare, at Florence, for Jacques Copeau (1939); *Le Soulier de Satin* of Claudel at the Comédie Française (1943). He is also a decorator *(Palais de la Découverte*, 1937), etc. As a tapestry maker he has made several sketches *(La Harpe des Eaux*, etc.). From 1942 on he has been exhibiting at the Salon d'Automne, at the Salon des Tuileries, and in 1945 at the Salon de Mai.

DALI, *Salvador*

Born at Figueras (Catalonia) March 11, 1904. From his early childhood he felt an intense need for making himself noticed, going so far as to throw himself down a flight of stairs in order to be admired by his comrades. At the age of ten he had already made two paintings: *Joseph Greeting his Brothers* and *Portrait of Helen of Troy*. Dali was drawn during his early period to the nineteenth-century Spanish painters of war scenes and also to the French Impressionists, but after spending time at the Escuela Especial de Pintura in Madrid in 1921, he is visibly influenced by the Italian Futurists. In 1924 he is expelled for insubordination and shortly afterwards sent to prison for his anti-governmental political activity. Hesitating on different styles, between 1925 and 1927, he is inspired by the Dutch painters of the seventeenth century, by Cubism, by abstract art as well as Neo-Classicism. From 1927 onwards dates Dali's obsession with the subconscious. In 1928 he leaves for Paris (in a taxi) with the purpose of meeting Picasso, and during a second trip he signs a contract with the Galerie Goemans where in 1929 he exhibits for the first time. He is then influenced by Chirico, Max Ernst, Tanguy. He collaborates on the film *Le Chien Andalou* and begins to paint double images. In 1931 he collaborates on the film *L'Âge d'Or*. In 1932 he paints pictures from the Freudian conception and from the legend of William Tell. In 1933 he has his first New York exhibition at the Julian Levy Gallery, followed in 1934 by his first visit to the United States. Towards 1937 he returns to his early admiration of Vermeer, and during a trip to Italy he becomes enthusiastic over the Renaissance and Baroque painters. In 1940 he settles in the United States and designs costumes and décors for several ballets for which he has also written the book *(Bacchanal, Labyrinth)*. But his triumph is in posters, and Walt Disney asks him to collaborate on his cartoons. In 1941 he has two important exhibitions, one at the Museum of Modern Art in New York and the other in Hollywood. He returns to Spain where he is well received in Falangist milieux, and paints religious pictures in the most academic style—pictures which, it seems, the Pope would have appreciated, but whose sincerity leaves one with a rather sceptical feeling. Gifted with the genius of publicity, he has published, among other books, a biography of more than 300 pages entitled *The Secret Life of Salvador Dali* (1942). A museum for his works is in preparation in Cleveland under the direction of Mr. A. Reynolds Morse, a passionate collector of Dali's work and who has brought together a considerable number of his paintings. A recent Dali exhibition was organized by Felix Labisse in the summer of 1956 at the casino of Zoute, near Ostend.

DAUCHOT, *Gabriel*

Born at Gargan-Livry near Paris May 10, 1926. His father is an architect. He paints already when he is fourteen years of age, encouraged by his parents. After the inevitable time spent at the Ecole des Beaux-Arts, he follows the advice of Yves Brayer and Othon Friesz. He admires Utrillo and Soutine. His efforts and aims are for unity and moderation, and after varying his techniques he tends to attach himself to the pictorial *"matière"* which best translates his subject. Above all, he wants to remain human: he has been defined as a painter of tragic reality. In Paris he has exhibited at Cardo's and at the Galerie Durand-Ruel; special exhibitions of his work have been held in Los Angeles, New York, Geneva, Zurich, Basle.

DAYEZ, *Georges*

Born in Paris July 29, 1907. He began painting very young, frequented the Ecole des Beaux-Arts, and worked notably in evening courses under the direction of the sculptors Arnold and Wlerick, a very lively atelier where he met Edouard Pignon. Afterwards followed a period of years of independent research, a part of the time devoted to manual labor, as an ordinary worker, then as technician in a printing establishment. He meets André Lhote, to whom he owes a great deal, and is influenced by Braque, Picasso, Matisse and others. He joins a movement which results in the formation of the Salon de Mai in 1945. Since 1948 he has been exhibiting regularly at the Salon d'Automne, at the Salon de Mai, where he is a member of the committee, at the Salon des Tuileries, as well as in numerous galleries in France and in other countries. Georges Dayez has also worked in engravings and in tapestry; he has executed a stained glass window and a monumental mosaic.

DESNOYER, *François*

Born at Montauban September 30, 1894. In 1912-1913 he is a student at the Ecole des Arts Décoratifs where years later he will teach. He is friendly with Marquet, Gromaire, Villon, Goerg, Walch, Lotiron, and he exhibits with them. He travels, visits the musuems of Europe and copies the Old Masters: El Greco, Titian, Veronese, Delacroix, Bruegel, Cranach, Grunewald, Fouquet, the colorists especially. From 1922 onwards he exhibits at the Salon des Indépendants and at the Salon d'Automne. In 1924 he is awarded the Blumenthal Prize; in 1937 the Gold Medal of the Exposition. Invited to exhibit at the Salon de Mai of 1946. Desnoyer has painted landscapes: Languedoc, the Riviera, the Sarthe, Epte, North Africa,

Italy, Holland, but he is interested above all in people and still more in living groups, itinerant fairs, markets, ports: "Everything that moves, cries out, is pushed about, is shoved" (G. Besson). He wanted to reconcile Fauvism with Cubism. He paints with passion. "Don't let him have your house while you're away on a long trip," writes Georges Besson. "For when you return you'll find the interior walls covered with compositions, the ceiling plinths, the windows decorated, the façade painted in a fresco manner, with the help of a neighboring mason. And on the mantlepieces you'll find ceramics, and in your sideboard a polycromatic set of dishes which you had not left there at all." Desnoyer is also a sculptor. He has illustrated the *Dies Irae* of La Fontaine and has made several tapestry drawings.

DESPIERRE, *Jacques*

The son of Céria, Despierre was born at Saint-Etienne March 7, 1912. After secondary studies he enrolled at the Académie Colarossi, then at the Académie Scandinave where he studied under Dufresne and Friesz. He exhibited at the Salon de l'Œuvre Unique in 1935 and at the Salon des Tuileries in 1938. He was awarded the Prix Paul Guillaume. Teacher at the Ecole des Arts Décoratifs. Following the example of Dufresne and the great Italian decorators, Tiepolo in particular, Despierre likes compositions that are both large and well ordered, grouping a certain number of figures held together by a common action. It is a "famous subject" scorned by many, and in surface richness whose lively tones of blue, vermillion, Veronese green, are like precious stones against areas of white and gray.

DEWASNE, *Jean*

Born at Hellemmes-Lille (Nord) May 21, 1921. He began to paint when he was only twelve years of age when his studies at the lycée and those of music left him free time. There are pointillist paintings of his made at the age of eighteen. After the *baccalauréat* he devotes two years to architecture, but he does this solely in order to be better prepared for painting. For five years, every morning, he draws from plaster casts and from the nude. He becomes passionately interested in the behavior of insects. Either by curiosity or by necessity he has been engaged in manual work of different kinds. Then, one by one, he became a perspective teacher, cinema assistant, journalist. Member of the group of the Galerie Denise René from its formation, he has been exhibiting there regularly (1945-1956). Together with Pillet he directs the Académie d'Art Abstrait (1950-1952). Dewasne excels in large mural composi-

tions. In his easel-picture paintings the very lively colors, in striking opposition, sometimes split the frame, in spite of the solid architecture of the composition. He wants his painting to bring forth the joy of life.

DEYROLLE, *Jean-Jacques*.

Born at Nogent-sur-Marne August 20, 1911. His family was originally from Brittany where he spent his childhood. Studied publicity in Paris, where he began to paint without a teacher to guide him. He took a trip to Morocco and one to Spain 1932 to 1937, then returned to Brittany in 1938. At that time he came under the influence of Sérusier and is afterwards fascinated by Braque. From his experience with these two masters he catches a glimpse of the possibilities of abstraction, a tendency which strengthens his meeting with Domela. Jeanne Bucher buys his first non-figurative paintings. In 1946 he receives the encouragement of Wilhelm Uhde. Several brief stays in Denmark, in Germany. After the Liberation he exhibited at the Salon d'Automne of 1944, classified as an abstract painter. In 1945 and 1946 he exhibited at the Salon des Surindépendants, and since 1945 he has been exhibiting at the Salon de Mai. Since 1947 he has been exhibiting regularly at the Galerie Denise René. Deyrolle composes free architectual paintings in tones of shaded tints; his work is dominated by a scientific and patient analysis of values.

DMITRIENKO, *Pierre*

Born in Paris April 20, 1925, of Russian origin on his father's side. He studied architecture and painting in Paris. In 1944 he works with Arnal and Rezvani: this is his so-called "Romantic" period (portraits, landscapes, seascapes). The following year, having been influenced by Gleizes, he turns towards Cubism, then is enchanted by Klee. Afterwards he returns, until 1950, to formal austerity. In 1951-1952 Dmitrienko paints principally factories, rhythmic constructions in a range of blacks, grays and whites which will soon break out in vivid reds *(Gennevilliers, Crucifixion, 1953)*. *Les Inondations* (1954) is of graphic research strongly related to the Japanese. After a return to black and gray *(The Petrified Forest, The Big Port)*, his palette now is richer in color and his large canvases in strong and precise forms are of an exceptional luminosity. Dmitrienko is essentially a painter of exteriors: ports, rivers, stones quarries, forests, factories, farm courtyards—all of these are subject matter. He has recently settled down in a small country village of Dieudonne, in the Oise. His first exhibition took place at the Galerie Maeght with the group called "Les Mains Eblouies" (1948). He exhibits there again in 1949 and 1950. Together with Arnal, Dufour, Gillet, Lapoujade, Quentin, Rezvani, he participates in several art exhibitions in France and in other countries (Galerie Blanche in Stockholm, Hugo Gallery in New York, the Gallery "Palette" in Zurich). Since 1950 he has been exhibiting at the Salon de Mai.

DOUCET, Jacques

Born at Boulogne-sur-Seine in 1924 in a bourgeois milieu. Finishing his secondary studies he develops an interest in the poets and novelists of his time. He becomes friendly with Max Jacob and often stays with him for short periods of time at Saint-Benoît-sur-Loire. Encouraged by Max Jacob, he begins to draw and paint. He is imprisoned by the Vichy government and is freed at the Liberation. He travels in central Europe, in Italy, in Switzerland. His artistic evolution is indebted to Matisse, who taught him color and schematisation, then to Klee and Miro. He has found his true language in non-figurative art. He exhibited for the first time in 1948 and regularly since at the Galerie Colette Allendy. In 1954 he exhibited at the Galerie Ariel. He has exhibited also at the Salon de Mai. In 1950 he took part in the exhibition called "Les Mains Eblouies" which was held at the Galerie Maeght. Special exhibitions of his work were held at Basle, Zurich, Genoa, Brussels.

DUBUFFET, Jean

Born in Le Havre in 1901; his father was a wealthy wine merchant. He was a brilliant student at the lycée and a spoiled child at home. At an early age he shows a taste for drawing and a gift for caricature. He paints when he is still a child. In 1918 he comes to Paris, enrolls at the Académie Julian, but hardly remains there. He does not scorn a certain snobbery, even to dressing in a rather picturesque manner. In 1922 he is a soldier and a meteorologist at the Eiffel Tower. But above all he is a dilettante, he spends his time only with his chosen friends, travels for his own pleasure in Switzerland, and shortly afterwards in South America. His perfect liberty of artistic searchings—this invention of surface material and forms—resulted in his first exhibition at the Galerie René Drouin, in 1945, when he was already forty-five years of age. He has given up the paint brush for the trowel: he uses tar, stones, coal, broken bottle ends—creating a heavy surface "matière." New exhibition at René Drouin's in 1946: Hautes Pâtes (Mirobolus, Macadam et Cie). Brief stays at El Goléa in 1947, 1948, 1949. He organizes an exhibition called "Art Brut" in 1948 at the Galerie Drouin, and then a few years later he organizes an exhibition of wild, wretched painters, most of whom came from psychiatric wards. This exhibition was held in the publishing house of Gallimard, N.R.F. Finding a large following in the United States, he resides for a while in New York in 1949. In 1954 at the Galerie Rive Gauche he exhibits small statues made from newspaper, then his so-called "assemblages" in 1956. Looked upon by some people with disgrace, this despiser of all the established rules found fervent admirers in literary milieux: Jean Paulhan first of all, then Paul Eluard, Antonin Artaud, André Fraigneau, Francis Ponge, etc. Dubuffet has published several stories: Ler dla Campane, Anvouaiage, Plus Kifeklermoinkon nivoua, Labonefam Abeber.

DUFOUR, Bernard

Born in Paris November 21, 1922. After his secondary studies he was sent to Germany by the S.T.O. (Forced Labor Orgazination), a period which lasted from 1943 to 1945. On his return he finished his engineering-agriculture studies; while, at the same time, he frequented the academies of Montparnasse and the Ecole des Beaux-Arts. Since 1949 he has been exhibiting at the Salon de Mai; in 1949-1950 he took part in the exhibition called "Les Mains Eblouies" which was held at the Galerie Maeght, and he took part also in the Salon d'Octobre organized by Charles Estienne (1952-1953). An important exhibition of his work was held at the Galerie Jeanne Bucher in 1951, 1952, 1953; and since 1954 an important exhibition of his work has been held at the Galerie Pierre. If the work of Bernard Dufour is outwardly marked by a need for mobility and sensual dynamism, it is marked inwardly by a very strong sense of analogy, by the complexity of the sway of reigning influences, by the ambivalence of the elements. "I notice in my contacts with Nature that often landscapes of quite different appearances arouse in me feelings that are almost identical, and I ask myself then what is the unique and secret language by which I thus perceive, accidently, the various fragments." As means: "graphic-drawing and the color that is outside Nature, which the creators of imaginary and visionary worlds as the Irish monks created in their illuminated manuscripts, the sculptor-painters of New Guinea, the Romanesque, joined by Gauguin, Cézanne in his old age, Kandinsky."

DUFRESNE, Charles (1876-1938)

Born at Millemont (Seine-et-Oise) November 23, 1876, died at La Seyne (Var) in August 1938. At an early age he took courses at the Ecole des Beaux-Arts and worked at the same time as an agent at Alexandre Charpentier's. He began painting about 1905 and from that year on exhibited at the Salon de la Nationale and at the Salon des Indépendants. From 1906 to 1910 he frequents the music halls, the cafés-concerts, the circuses, and executed several paintings from sketches he had made at these places. In 1910 he is awarded the Prix de l'Afrique du Nord which offers him a chance to spend two years in Algiers. And it was there he became fully aware of his painter's personality. During the war he serves in the camouflage service where he meets Dunoyer de Segonzac whom he knew in 1912 during the same time when he knew Luc-Albert Moreau and Boussingault. After the war he spends a few years teaching at the Académie Scandinave. He goes through a dark period during which he paints massive compositions whose forms retain a certain Cubist aspect. Then his painting becomes more and more light in color, and his search is directed towards the opulence of tones. In 1924 he supplied the tapestries for a furniture ensemble by Sue and Marc which had a great success at the Exposition des Arts Décoratifs of 1925. He designed décors for the Opera and tapestry compositions for interriors owned by the State. In 1937 he painted two panels for the Palais de Chaillot (Le théâtre de Molière) and also mural compositions for the School of Pharmacy.

DUNOYER DE SEGONZAC, André

Born at Boussy-Saint-Antoine (Seine-et-Oise) July 16, 1884. From his father's side he belongs to an old Quercy family and from his mother's to the Franche-Comté. He spent the major part of this childhood at Boussy-Saint-Antoine and was a rather mediocre student at the Lycée Henri IV. His parents greatly desired that he enter Saint-Cyr, but he rather preferred to study painting. He worked with Luc-Olivier Merson, but leaves him after his military service and though he studies at the atelier of Jean-Paul Laurens and at the Académie de La Palette, he remains in both places only a short time. Finally his mind is made up and he decides to work alone, sharing a studio with Boussingault at 37, Rue Saint-André-des-Arts. In 1910 he exhibited a painting called *Les Buveurs* at the Salon d'Automne and another, entitled *Village Scene* at the Salon des Indépendants of 1911. He works chiefly in watercolor, which is perhaps the most interesting medium in which he seeks to express himself. During the war he serves in the infantry, then in the camouflage section of the Third Army where he has under his command Dufresnes, Camoin, Puy as well as his other comrades Boussingault and André Marc who along with Jean Marchand, Luc-Albert Moreau and himself

form the "Black Band." After the war he began to interest himself in the graphic arts and worked on copper plates which, together with his paintings, led to a magnificent series of landscapes of Provence and Ile de France in thickly applied flat colors. He has illustrated several books, the latest to appear has been the *Georgics* of Virgil.

ERNST, Max

Born in Brühl, near Cologne in 1891. His father, who was a teacher in a school for deaf and dumb, made him continue his studies at the Faculty of Letters of Bonn until 1911. In 1914 in Cologne Max Ernst met Hans Arp, who was one of the founders of the first Dada group in Zurich. Together with Baargeld they created the Dada group of Cologne. Under the sponsorship of André Breton an exhibition of Ernst's works was held in Paris. With Arp he made *collages* called *"fatagaga"* (fabrication of paintings guaranteed to be gazometric) which already announced Surrealism. After the last exhibition of the Cologne group was closed by the police, Ernst left for Paris in 1921 and took part in Surrealist manifestations. At the beginning of the Second World War he left for America and settled down in Arizona, where he constructed a house himself. Dadist, Surrealist, Max Ernst has always enjoyed the thrill of astonishing people, even to creating a scandal. He has employed to a high degree of success the *collage* medium as well as that of rubbing a surface against another *(frottage)*, thus obtaining extraordinary *"matière"* effects. He has published with Paul Eluard (*Répétition* (1900) and *Les Malheurs des Immortels* (1922).

ESTÈVE, Maurice

Born at Culan (Cher) May 2, 1904. His father, who was a shoe repairer, was opposed to the vocation of his son passionately interested in drawing, while his mother, who was a dress designer for *haute couture*, encouraged the young artist. To follow his vocation the young Estève at the age of fifteen left for Paris, where he visited the Louvre, fell in love with Cézanne's work, and continued to draw at the Académie Colarossi. In order to pay for his studies, he worked as a typographer, furniture designer, commercial traveler. In 1923 he directed a drawing atelier in a fabric factory at Barcelona. On his return to Paris he exhibited at the Galerie Yvangot (1930), but it was not till the retrospective exhibition of French art, held at Göteborg, Sweden in 1934 that Estève sold his first painting. From 1931 to 1939 he exhibited at the Salon d'Automne, at the Salon des Surindépendants, and at the Salon des Tuileries. In collaboration with Delaunay, Estève participated in the decoration of the Aviation and Railway Pavillons for the Universal Exposition of 1937. In 1941 he takes part in the "Exhibition of Young Painters of the French Tradition." Influenced first of all by Cézanne and the Fauves, then by Léger and Picasso, Estève's art, which from the beginning was figurative, turns now towards abstract forms which are always strong and rich in color. After having exhibited at the Galerie Louis Carré, he exhibits now at the Galerie Galanis.

ÈVE, Jean

Born at Somai, a small mining village in the North, near Douai, in 1900. Son of a railway worker, he studied at the public school and quite early in life began to draw. As a young apprentice in a mechanical atelier at Thiers, he began to paint purely for his own pleasure. In 1918 he enlisted with the Spahis, and thus had a chance to see the Rhineland, Algeria Tunis and Syria. On his return to civilian life he began as a surveyor-draftsman; he worked in a foundry, in an automobile factory, was employed on the railway and later at the customs, and always never ceasing to paint purely for his own pleasure. He received encouragement from Kisling whom he greatly admired; he received encouragement also from the group called "L'Art Vivant" (Jacques Guenne, Florent Fels, Maximilien Gauthier), and thus is able to work with greater liberty. His first exhibition was held in 1930 at the Galerie Alice Manteau. In 1937 he took part in the exhibition "Maîtres Populaires de la Réalité," which was repeated in 1938 at the Kunsthaus in Zurich and in 1939 at the Museum of Modern Art in New York. Jean Ève is an established artist: he exhibits at the Salon des Indépendants, at the Salon d'Automne without at all giving up his position in the administration. He likes urban landscape: the suburb is his chosen theme as well as churches and cathedrals, which he interprets with a lively poetic sense in an almost photographic resemblance.

FAUTRIER, Jean

Born in Paris May 16, 1898 of Bern origin. His spent his youth in England and it was there at several academies that he received the first elements of his artistic formation. He has always lived a retired and solitary life, far removed from "groups." In 1943 the Galerie Drouin exhibited a series of works entitled "Hostages," inspired by the horrors of war. Fautrier's art is rather difficult to class; we could speak of magic realism, but Fautrier's characteristic is to remain faithful to the impression received, and even when he wishes to retain the appearance of reality, he gives it a poetical transfiguration, where the quantity of pictorial matter, without concern for modeling, depth or opposition of tones, occupies an important place and creates effects of a rare and powerful quality.

FOUGERON, André

Born in Belleville December 1, 1913. He formed his art education alone, taking night courses in 1927-1928. He executed small pieces of sculpture and also lithographs in color, while at the same time he completed large decorations, including one for the Sanatorium for Students at Saint-Hilaire-du-Touvet (Isère). In 1946 he was awarded the Prix National. His searchings in art follow the same lines as those of a Pignon or a Gischia, but at the Salon d'Automne of 1940 he exhibits a painting called *Les Parisiennes au marché*, which leans much more towards realism. This canvas is the point of departure in France for a Neo-Realistic-Socialist school. And it is in this style that Fougeron continues to work.

GILLET, Robert-Edgar

Born in Paris July 10, 1924 of Flemish ancestry. He has been painting since the age of twelve. He spent four years at the Ecole Boulle (1939-1944), studying medal engraving but as he says, "without enthusiasm." He enrolled therefore in the atelier of Brianchon at the Ecole des Arts Décoratifs in order to avoid the S. T. O. (Forced Labor Organization). From 1946 to 1948 he taught at the Académie Julian. His first special exhibition was held at the Galerie Evrard in Lille in April 1953 and in November of the same year at the Galerie Craven in Paris. He exhibited at the Galerie Facchetti (Prix Fénéon) and at the Galerie La Licorne in Brussels in 1954, and since that year he has been showing his work regularly at the Galerie de France. He has exhibited also at the Salon de Mai. He has great admiration for Zurbaran and for Chardin whom he venerates and also for Rembrandt, whose *Saul* and *Portrait of a Woman* from the Hermitage, Moscow, which he had seen at the great Rembrandt exhibition held in Amsterdam in 1956, he admires more than any other. And yet, the human face and all human representation are strangers to him. There was a time when he painted "à la Bonnard," but later he got away from such a formal aspect. What he is seeking is a balance of strong values which are nevertheless discreet. His canvases have a serious quality without being at all austere.

GISCHIA, Léon

Born in Dax (Landes) June 8, 1904. His father was an engineer in a gas factory. Gischia does advanced studies in the field of letters, history of art and archeology. In 1923 he devoted himself to art and becomes a pupil of Othon Friesz and Léger with whom he will teach several years later. He travels in Spain and Italy, and leaves for the United States in 1927, giving up painting: he gives French lessons at the Berlitz School and occupies himself with publicity. He takes up art again in 1936 and is entrusted with decorating the Pavillon des Temps Nouveaux with Léger, Le Corbusier, for the Universal Exposition of 1937. In 1941 he exhibits at the Exposition des Jeunes Peintres de Tradition Française and participates in the foundation of the Salon de Mai in 1944. He exhibits at the Galerie de France. He has also designed numerous stage décors, and has become the chief collaborator in this work for Jean Vilar and his Théatre National Populaire. He is the author of the essays: *Sculpture in France Since Rodin, Primitive Arts.*

GOERG, Edouard

Born in Sidney (New South Wales) of French and Irish parents. He spent a few years in England and come to France when he is seven years old. In 1912 he enrolls at the Académie Ranson. He is a great admirer of Goya, Daumier, Rouault. In 1924 at the Berthe Weill Gallery, he meets Pascin, Gromaire, Per Krogh, but he does not form with them any sort of group; their affinities are rather on a moral plane. Goerg has traveled a great deal—Italy, Belgium, India, Greece, Turkey. He loves youthful nudes and beautiful flowers. He has taught graphic arts at the Ecole des Beaux-Arts and has illustrated several books in which his expressionism is very evident: *Les Fleurs du Mal, The Book of Job, The Apocalypse, The Divine Comedy*, etc. In 1949 he was awarded the Hallmark Prize.

GONDOUIN, Emmanuel (1883-1934)

Born at Versailles January 29, 1883. Started as an apprentice with one of his cousins who was a master glassmaker. He came to Paris to take drawing courses and was excellent in his studies at school. In 1905 he lived in Montparnasse where he became very friendly with Modigliani. In order to earn a living he worked on industrial designs, devoting himself to a series called *"Expressive Heads."* He illustrated *Goha Le Simple* of Albert Adès and painted large landscape having no relationship whatever with reality. During the war Gondouin lived through a period of complete penury before the Gobelins bought one of his paintings in 1920. The following year he had an important exhibition of fifty of his works at the Galerie de la Licorne. He had a house built for him at Cavalaire, he settled down in Sèvres, and a few months later he begins the construction of a large house which he never completes. He undergoes a serious operation at the Necker Hospital. Placed in a convalescent home, he runs away but is transported back and dies a few days later on January 6, 1934. Of his works the Musée National d'Art Moderne has selected his *Negress*, a large painting in which his deep sensual Cubism in full, muted colors, achieves one of its most beautiful expressions.

GROMAIRE, Marcel

Born at Noyelles-sur-Sambre July 24, 1892, his father was French and his mother Belgian. In 1910 he frequents the ateliers of Montparnasse where he meets Matisse's pupils, and receives advice from Le Fauconnier of the Académie de la Palette. He spends a brief time in Belgium, Holland, Germany and England after the war. In 1916 he is wounded fighting along the Somme. After several exhibitions, he begins to exhibit at the Salon d'Automne. he receives the assistance of Dr. Girardin, who brings together a large collection of his works which today is at the Petit Palais. In 1925 he sends a painting called *War* to the Salon des Indépendants, which is one of his most significant works. In 1937 he designs a frieze for the Pavillon de Sèvres at the International Exposition. He paints principally the daily life of peasants and workers and in a rather heavy expressionist style, but to which he adds a constructive accent all his own. On his return from America, Gromaire's colors become richer and fuller. He becomes interested in tapestry and with Lurçat founds the New School of Aubusson; he has also worked considerably in the field of graphic arts. In July 1957 the Maison de la Pensée Française held a large retrospective exhibition of his work.

GRUBER, Francis (1912-1948)

Born in Nancy March 15, 1912, died in Paris December 1, 1948. His father, who was of Alsatian ancestry, was a glass painter and also his brother. His mother was of Polish origin. Of delicate health he suffered from asthma attacks and gave up his studies. He began painting quite early in life and received advice from Bissière and Braque, and in 1928 he enrolled at the Académie Scandinave where Friesz and Dufresne became interested in him. He exhibited at the Salon des Tuileries and at the Salon d'Automne, and in 1930 began to achieve success. In 1935 he exhibited his drawings at the Académie Ranson. In 1936 he executed a mural composition (Homage to Le Nôtre) for the Lycée Lakanal. For a while he taught at the Académie Ranson (1942). In 1947 he was awarded the Prix National. A keen worker he painted up to the very last moment of his life. He exhibited in New York, Buenos Aires, Denmark, Spain, Switzerland. In 1949 the Musée National d'Art Moderne held a retrospective exhibition of his work. Gruber's influence—his tragic expressionism, his "cruel" painting in jagged contours—is still being felt among the young French painters who have remained faithful to reality.

HARTUNG, Hans

Born in Leipzig September 21, 1904. Both his parents were fervent music lovers; his father, who was a doctor, also interested himself in painting. While still young, Hartung became passionately devoted to astronomy. His textbooks from the school in Dresden were covered with drawings. After his baccalauréat, he entered the University of Leipzig to study philosophy and the history of art. He took courses at the Academy of Fine Arts of Leipzig and Dresden, but from 1922 onwards his paintings are abstract. He was one of the first to reject all visible forms and all exterior representation. He visited Italy, Spain, France, Holland, Belgium, the Tyrol and the Scandinavian countries. From 1932 to 1934 he settles down in the Balearic Islands, then returns to Germany. Fleeing the Nazi régime, he settles down in Paris and exhibits at the Salon des Surindépendants until 1938. In 1939 he enlists in the French Foreign Legion, returns to France after the armistice but returns again to North Africa after having been interned in Spain. Seriously wounded in Alsace in 1944 and losing one of his legs, he is awarded French citizenship. He returns then to Paris and begins painting after an interuption of six years. Since 1946 he has taken a regular part in the Salon des Réalités Nouvelles and also in the Salon de Mai. His first one-man show was held at Lydia Conti's in 1947. Afterwards he exhibited at the Galerie Louis Carré and now at the Galerie de France.

HERBIN, Auguste

Born at Quiévy (Nord) April 29, 1882. Began to study drawing in 1901 at the Ecole des Beaux-Arts of Lille. Two years later he settles down in Paris where he begins to paint, influenced by the Impressionists. In 1906 he exhibited at the Salon des Indépendants paintings whose style made one think of Cézanne or van Gogh. Soon afterwards Herbin embarked on his Cubist period, yet without withdrawing himself from reality. In 1909 he was living at the "Bateau-Lavoir." In 1910 Léonce Rosenberg bought all his paintings. Herbin had an important exhibition at Clovis Sagot's. He was one of the first to exhibit a Rosenberg's; when the war had ended, Léonce Rosenberg opened a gallery in the Rue de la Baume with the sign outside "Effort Moderne." Herbin paints large canvases, juxtaposing geometric forms, squares, circles and triangles in violent and contrasting colors, creating a sort of abstract alphabet.

HUMBLOT, Robert

Born at Fontenay-sous-Bois May 13, 1907. Student of Natural Science at the Sorbonne till the age of twenty-four, then enrolls at the Ecole des Beaux-Arts (1931-1934). There he met Georges Rohner. In 1936 he traveled in Italy (Siena, Florence, Rome), and in Northern Spain. He worked at Bandol, in Brittany and in Ile-de-France. He was made prisoner in July 1940, but escaped from Germany in November of 1941. Humbolt was part of an austere group who, united under the name "Forces Nouvelles" in 1935, wanted a "return to drawing, a return to a craft conscientious of tradition, in fervent contact with Nature." In 1946 the Galerie Charpentier organized an exhibition of his Ouessant canvases. Humblot is essentially a landscape painter; Brittany and her ports have never ceased to inspire him.

JANNOT, Henri

Born in Paris January 27, 1905. Pupil of Lucien Simon at the Ecole des Beaux-Arts from 1925 to 1932. During this period he discovers the Fauves and Utrillo, but the influence is short lasting. He meets Rohner, Humblot, then Lasne, who work with him for a year's time. Then new influences—Picasso, Chirico, La Fresnaye, Seurat, Ingres—make themselves felt in the work of the four friends who then formed the group "Forces Nouvelles." Each of the four painters, united under the auspices of Henri Héraut in a common manifestation, has since followed his own personal direction in art. Jannot's work has been influenced as much by realistic painters (exhibition held in 1934—Exposition des Maîtres de la Réalité) as he has been by the works of Masaccio, Piero della Francesca and Uccello (exhibition of 1935). Nevertheless, it has retained its personal accent.

JEANNERET, Edouard
known as LE CORBUSIER.

Born at La Chaux-de-Fonds, Switzerland in 1887. During his entire youth he practises the graphic arts and works at the Ecole des Beaux-Arts of his native city. As architect Le Corbusier has exerted considerable influence through his writings. Most of the conceptions of a modern city stem directly from his ideas. He began to study architecture in 1905 without at all giving up the graphic arts. He was enchanted by early Cubist experiments. In 1920 he launches with Ozenfant an important review called "L'Esprit Nouveau" and becomes the apostle of what he calls "Purism" with the specific intention of having Cubism not fall into the abuse of decoration. For several years Le Corbusier works entirely in the domain of still lifes, and is not till 1929 that he turns to the figure. In this evolution his work has taken on the characteristics of a fresco. He has designed also thirty-six tapestry compositions for Aubusson.

KISLING, Moses (1891-1953)

Born at Cracow January 22, 1891. His father was a Jewish tailor. As a result of a competition, he is admitted at the age of fifteen to the academy of his native city. At that time all painting in this region was entirely dominated by that of Munich. But Kisling's teacher, Josef Pankiewiez, who had been to France and had known the Impressionists, Bonnard and Vuillard, inspires him to go to Paris, where he settles down in 1910 and becomes a well-known figure in Montparnasse. He takes a trip to Brittany, then in 1911-1912, he lives in Céret near Braque, Picasso, Juan Gris and the poet Max Jacob. During this period he paints landscapes inspired by Cézanne, but among the painters of his time it is Derain who impresses him most. Kisling is in Holland when war is declared; he returns to Paris and enlists in the Foreign Legion, thus obtaining his French citizenship. Among his companions in the trenches is the poet Blaise Cendrars. Wounded in 1915 he is invalided out of the service. Until that time he is appreciated only in a very small circle. And it was only as a result of his exhibition at Druet's in 1919 that success finally came to him. During this period he frees himself completely from all influences and acquires a very personal style: gifted with a sense of color and graphic elegance he becomes the portrait painter à la mode. In 1928-1930 he takes a new trip to Holland, and in 1940 he left for the United States. At the end of the war early in January 1945 the Galerie Guénégaud exhibited a collection of his recent paintings. In September 1946 Kisling returned to Paris. He died at Sanary (Var) in 1953.

LABISSE, Félix

Born at Douai March 9, 1905. Influenced by Surrealism. Exhibited in Brussels, then in Paris at Roux-Hentschel in April of 1945. Labisse's canvases are something curiously unexpected. Labisse has designed numerous décors for the theatre, collaborating in particular with Jean-Louis Barrault. He had amused himself in decorating bars. It was he also who, in 1956, organized the Salvador Dali Exhibition held in the casino of Zoute.

LAGRANGE, Jacques

Born of a Parisian family, the son of an architect, July 28, 1917. He went to school at the Lycée Lakanal. Quite young he began to paint, still lifes and landscapes, in an artisan manner which initiates him into the métier. He enrolled at the Ecole des Arts Décoratifs in 1933, at the Ecole des Beaux-Arts to study graphic art and painting in 1938-1939. During his period of captivity in Germany he did merely a few drawings. At the Liberation he traveled in Belgium and Holland. His paintings at that time were influenced by Expressionism. On his return to Paris he sought for a balance of form and color (Still Life with Dishes). His evolution is directed by the spirit of synthesis: he takes leave of Cubism and also of Fauvism. In addition to his other interests he has worked in the field of publicity and has designed décors. But it was only in 1947 that he devoted himself to painting alone, in a deep need to express ideas in a means other than through words. Today color, space, light are the essential elements of his form and design. His art is devoid of extraneous matter but constructed. If he admires Paolo Uccello, Chardin, Velazquez, he finds example in Picasso and Léger as well as in Matisse, not overlooking Mondrian. He first exhibited in 1948 at the Galerie de France and recently (1956) at the Galerie Galanis and regularly at the Salon de Mai. In his tapestries he has known how to free himself from the strong influence of Lurçat, decisive for so many cartoonists.

LANSKOY, André

Born in Moscow March 31, 1902 of an aristocratic family. He began painting in Kiev in 1919. In 1921 he left for Paris and devoted himself entirely to his vocation. He works from Nature: landscapes, still lifes, portraits. In 1924 his work is noticed by Wilhelm Uhde and Roger Dutilleul, and in 1925 the Galerie Bing gives him an exhibition. From 1937 onwards his searchings turn towards non-figurative art. Since 1945 he has been exhibiting regularly at the Galerie Louis Carré. He is equally interested in tapestry.

LA PATELLIÈRE, Amédée, DUBOIS de (1890-1932)

Born at Bois-Benoît (Loire-Atlantique) July 5, 1890. Received a classical education in Nantes and in Vannes, thought of preparing for the

Naval Academy, then for a while took law courses at the Faculty of Nantes. Attracted to painting, he left in 1912 for Paris where he worked with his friend Gérard Cochet at the Académie Julian. Wounded twice during the war of 1914-1918, his health is definitely affected. In 1919 he made a trip to Tunis, then returned to Paris and worked in his atelier in the Rue Visconti; he spent a while in Brittany, then in the Chevreuse Valley at Machery where most of his landscape pictures were painted. He is attracted also by Provence which influenced his work during the years of 1930 and 1931. At that time he was living in Saint-Paul-de-Vence, where he decorated the Hôtel de la Colombe d'Or. He was interested above all in expressing, n a lyrical and expressionist sense, the lives of peasants, animals, people. He has illustrated several books, notably *Colline* of Jean Giono. He died in Paris January 9, 1932 after a very brief illness. The Musée National d'Art Moderne held a large retrospective exhibition of his work in 1945 which was held again in Liège and Brussels.

LAPIQUE, *Charles*

Born at Theizé (Rhône) October 6, 1898 of a university and scientific Lorraine family. He prepared at first for the Ecole Centrale and in 1921 became an engineer, thanks to his drawing. The milieux that he frequented where so different, as the artist himself explained, that it would be quite impossible to enumerate them. As for his beginnings, he refers to them as rather "complicated." Brittany leaves a deep impression on his works, for he was from Paimpol as much as from Paris. Having finished several paintings, he receives a contract from Jeanne Bucher in 1925, then from Pierre Loeb. From 1931 onwards he accelerates the rhythm of his work, becomes friendly with Bazaine, Manessier and Villon. In 1937 he recives a commission for five decorative panels for the Palais de la Découverte. He has exhibited at the Salon des Indépendants, at the Salon d'Automne, at the Salon des Surindépendants. He took part in the exhibition "Jeunes Peintres de Tradition Française" (May 10, 1941) in which his painting *Sainte Catherine de Fierbois* is significant for the trend simultaneously followed by Singier, Le Moal, Bazaine, Estève. Lapicque departs from reality but from it he takes a formula : a network of lines, which imprisons it like a spider's web. Later, he exhibits at the Galerie Louis Carré, then at the Galerie Denise René and finally at the Galerie Galanis. He is influenced by Dufy, then, after a brief stay in Venice, by Tintoretto and Tiepolo, and yet never ceasing to be himself.

LAPOUJADE, *Robert*

Born at Montauban January 3, 1921. He left school at the age of fourteen and several years later became a butcher, then a riveter, then a tile repairer. At the age of twenty he is a teacher in dramatic arts at Arth-sur-Meurthe. Having taken care of young Jews and wishing also to escape from the S.T.O. (Forced Labor Organization), he hides away in 1941 in an obscure part of the Alps. There he spends fifteen months, living in a grotto, where he reads a great deal and completes his education by reading and, at the same time, he makes a careful drawing analysis of trees, branches, even grass. After the Liberation he comes to Paris, and exhibited what he calls "formal" painting at the Galerie Jean Castel in 1947, which is also his first contact with the public. In 1949 at the Galerie Chardin "Fifty Portraits of Writers" (Breton, Claudel, Eluard, Sartre, etc.) made in silver point, a medium which he then appreciated for its precision which allowed no changes whatever. Tired of this formal technique, he covers a canvas one day with green as one would cover a wall, and then afterwards devotes himself to bringing life to the surface by multiplying the number of tones and brushstrokes. Thus 1950 marks the beginning of non-figurative elements in his work. In 1952 he exhibited at the Galerie Arnaud, *Hell and the Mine* without forgetting his *Concentration Camp*, seven large paintings conceived in a non-figurative manner as a reaction against Fougeron's Neo-Realist painting *The Miners* and also to demonstrate that abstract painting is equally capable of social preoccupations. In the summer of 1954 Lapoujade went to Spain. His range source of forms is directly inspired by Nature and, strangely enough, by the old stained walls mentioned by Leonardo da Vinci, whom he cites in his essay *The Mechanisms of Fascination* (Edition du Seuil, 1955). Lapoujade is far from repudiating the subject. But he wants the form of an "allusive ambiguity"; let us first of all be sensitive to the panel painted by Lapoujade himself, to its rhythm, to its color; then read the title of the painting, and we will have found the presence of these things. *The Elephants* (Galerie Pierre) is one of the most striking examples of this; Lapoujade exhibits regularly at the Galerie Pierre. He participates in the Salon de Mai, and teaches drawing and painting at the Ecole Alsacienne.

LE FAUCONNIER, *Henri* (1881-1946)

Born at Hesdin (Pas-de-Calais) in 1881. In 1901 he came to live in Paris and five years later enrolled at the Académie Julian, where Segonzac, Boussingault and La Fresnaye are his atelier comrades. In 1908 and 1909 he is at Ploumanach in Brittany painting rocky landscapes and peasants in colorful costumes and in a well formed style which already announces his coming adherence to Cubism. In 1911 he takes an active part in the presentation of Room 41 of the Salon des Indépendants in which works of the Cubists are on view and where his own work is shown as well. He becomes at the beginning of the following year atelier head of the Académie de la Palette. He is in Holland when war is declared. Unfit for military service he remains in the Low Countries. Having got away from Cubism since 1913, he accentuates his searchings for expression inspired by the Gothic art of the North in which he had become keenly interested before 1914. His expressionism does not go by unnoticed; he has had considerable influence on many a Dutch and Belgian artist. In 1920 Le Fauconnier returns to France, slowly turning his back to an expressionist manner and aiming for austerity, dating from 1925. He whom his friends had dubbed "The Wonderman" was destined to die in January 1946, unjustly forgotten.

LEFRANC, Jules

Born at Laval (Mayenne) May 12, 1887. He has been painting since 1901. But, having kept for a long time the hardware business of his parents, he is for many years merely a Sunday painter. And it was not till 1937 that he was able to devote himself entirely to painting. His art is of a meticulous precision; he uses the T-square and triangle, as Aragon, who admires him, notes; but the minute details of his lines, whether they are of stones or tulips, unite a very strong feeling of mass. His painting in new tones is as brilliant as enamel. His favorite subjects are chateaux, small provincial streets but he likes the sea shore as well as the Eiffel Tower. He exhibited with a group of his works in 1953 at the Galerie de Berri a painting called *"Le Château et son Miroir d'Eau"*: architecturally imposing, with a play of fountains reflected in the water and in the foreground flowers delineated with infinite precision. One of his most characteristic works, it was acquired by the Musée National d'Art Moderne. He has been exhibiting (1956) at the Galerie Lardy.

LEGUEULT, Raymond

Born in Paris May 10, 1898. His mother was a woman of great culture, his father a musician and artist. He grew up a spoiled child. He first studied at the Ecole Commerciale; then, forced to interrupt his studies at the age of sixteen because of illness, he takes advantage of it

as soon as he is well again to enroll at the Ecole des Arts Décoratifs, where he studies till 1917, at which date he leaves for the army. On his return he comes back to the Ecole des Arts Décoratifs where he finds again his comrade Brianchon. Thanks to a grant he leaves for Spain in 1922 and copies Velazquez and Goya. In 1925 he is selected to teach at the Ecole des Arts Décoratifs; he moves in with Brianchon and shares a studio in the Avenue du Maine. And with Brianchon he designs in 1925-1928 the décors for *Griselidis* and *The Birth of the Lyre*. Faithful to his friendships he exhibits last of all in 1956 at the Galerie Romanet with Brianchon, Legueult, Oudot, Planson, etc., under the title "Peintres de la Réalité Poétique" which expresses very well the meaning of their searchings. He now teaches at the Ecole des Beaux-Arts.

LE MOAL, Jean

Born at Authon-du-Perche (Eure-et-Loir) October 30, 1909 of Breton and Ardèche origin. Student at the Ecole des Beaux-Arts (1926-1929), at the Ecole des Arts Décoratifs and at the Académie Ranson in Paris (1934-1938). After having been influenced by Cézanne, Seurat Matisse, he is influenced by Picasso and Cubism, then finally discovers color. He was influenced also by Bissière, teacher at the Académie Ranson. He frequently spent time in Brittany (1935-1938), Spain, Belgium, Holland. His first exhibition took place at the Galerie Breteau in 1938. In 1939 he left France to see the United States; in New York he worked with a team on a ceiling of 1700 sq. yards. He returned to France and in Lyon took part in a group called "Témoignage." For one year his painting is figurative. He returns to Paris. In 1943 he exhibited at the Galerie de France, in 1944 at the Galerie René Drouin, and since 1943 he has been exhibiting at the Salon de Mai. In 1956 a large important exhibition of his work was held at the Galerie de France. In 1953 he was awarded the Prix de la Critique. He has also worked in the designing of stained glass windows in which he excels.

LIMOUSE, Roger

Born at Collo, a department of Constantine October 18, 1894. In 1919 he left Tunis where he was employed by the administration and came to Paris where he spent three years working in the Académie Julian in the atelier of P.-A. Laurens. In 1922 he successfully took the competitive examinations for the teachers of the Paris municipality and also for the lycée teachers. In 1953 he was awarded the Prix des Vikings. He made several trips to Italy, Norway, Holland, Belgium, Spain and

Morocco. After an Impressionist period and the influence of Bonnard, he aims—following the example of Matisse and that of the children he is teaching—at a plastic synthesis of object which he achieves by means of extreme simplicity and intensity of colors. His canvases becoming rich in surface thickness. He also exhibited at the Galerie Romanet in 1956 with the group who called themselves "Peintres de la Réalité Poétique."

LORJOU, Bernard

Born at Blois (Loir-et-Cher) September 9, 1908. His father was a newspaper vendor. Lorjou formed his artistic education by himself. His first painting is a portrait of his parents, at that time he was fourteen years old. In 1931 he made a trip to Spain which aroused his enthusiasm; he was impressed by El Greco, Velazquez and Goya. After World War II he contributed to the renaissance of a realistic and popular movement. He exhibited at the Salon d'Automne and at the Salon des Indépendants and, in 1954, at the Galerie Charpentier, as well as in New York, under the auspices of Madame Walter. A recent exhibition of his work was held in 1957 in one of the booths of an itinerant fair which took place at the Esplanade of the Invalides. Critics were summoned by telegram.

LURÇAT, Jean

Born at Bruyères (Vosges) July 1, 1892 of a family of Spanish ancestry. He began painting in Nancy in the atelier of Victor Prouvé. He came to Paris at the age of eighteen and studied under Bernard Naudin. Mobilised in 1914 he wrote anti-militarist poems and articles, and for this he is sent to prison. After the war he travels a great deal; the Spanish countryside (1919), the Sahara Desert (1924) have a considerable influence on his work. Already inspired by Surrealism, Lurçat paints large landscapes with a feeling for space and dreams, often cut by the vertical of a dismantled fence. In 1930, fascinated by the beauty of a shipyard construction, he introduces in his painting several maritime elements. Lurçat has never given up painting, nevertheless his most significant and important work is in the field of tapestry. 1915 dates his interest in this mural art, and it is to him that we are indebted for this veritable renewal of twentieth-century French tapestry art. Lurçat excels also in ceramics.

MANESSIER, Alfred

Born at Saint-Ouen (Somme) December 5, 1911. His family is of Picardy ancestry; his father was a wine dealer; one grandfather was a stone carver, the other shoe repairer. After first having studied at the Ecole des Beaux-Arts of Amiens, Manessier comes to Paris to take courses in architecture, but he studies painting instead, copying the Old Masters in the Louvre (Rembrandt, Tintoretto, Renoir). "The world of the Beaux-Arts School frightened me," he wrote. So he worked in the Montparnasse academies and followed the advice of Bissière at the Académie Ranson. He becomes friendly with Le Moal and Bertholle. He exhibits first of all at the Salon des Indépendants of 1933, then at the Salon d'Automne and at the Salon des Tuileries. May 10, 1941 he took part in the exhibition called "Jeunes Peintres de Tradition Française." In 1943 he spends a few months at La Trappe and is left with a very profound impression. An exhibition of an ensemble of his works was held in Paris in 1949, in Brussels in 1951. He was awarded the Prix de Peinture at the Biennale of São Paulo of 1953. Manessier collaborated on the decoration of the Aviation and Railway Pavillons for the Universal Exposition of 1937. He has also designed theatre décors and costumes (1945), and in the field of art sacré he has designed many stained glass windows (churches of Bréseux, Doubs, la Toussaint at Basle; that of Saint-Pierre-de-Trinquetaille of Arles, etc.).

MARCHAND, André

Born at Aix-en Provence February 10, 1907. His mother was from Provence, his father of Flemish ancestry and teacher of mathematics. Marchand studied at Aix-en-Provence, while at the same time he frequented the drawing courses held in the evening. His early admiration goes from Egyptian and Primitive art to Cézanne. When he comes to Paris, in order to earn a living, he sells Le Monde at the subway exit. He becomes friendly with Tal Coat and Gruber; four years later he meets Darius Milhaud, who introduces him to Pierre Colle. He exhibits for the first time at the Salon d'Automne of 1930, at the Salon des Indépendants of 1931, then finally with the group which calls itself "Forces Nouvelles" yet without becoming a part of it. He made several trips in France: Provence and Bourgogne, and spent seven months at Biskra, returning to Paris with a group of canvases which he exhibits in 1934. In the following year he visits Vienna, Warsaw, even traveling as far as Moscow. In 1937 he is awarded the Prix Paul Guillaume. He was mobilised and served in the war. In 1942 he was Fontainebleau, then afterwards at Saulieu. In 1945 he exhibited at the Salon de Mai. In 1947 the Galerie Maeght organized a special and important exhibition of his works. In 1945 he returned to southern France, dividing his time between Aix-en-Provence and Paris. His artistic evolution continued, leading to a less figurative conception of creative forms (Exhibition at the Galerie Drouant-David and at the Galerie Visconti 1956).

MASSON, André

Born at Balagny (Oise) January 4, 1896. Formed his artistic education by himself. The first paintings—landscapes—that he exhibits in 1922 show the influence of Derain; then, from 1922 to 1924, his works remind one of the Cubists (*The Card Players*, 1923). From 1924 to 1928 he exhibits with the Surrealist group, but never taking on their almost photographic technique. Masson has traveled a great deal, especially in Spain, where the civil war inspired him to paint scenes of terrible slaughter, often transformed in an erotic way. In 1947 he settled down in Aix-en-Provence, and the setting has greatly influenced his recent work, giving to his compositions the aspect of a mad rush of colored commas. He has illustrated the writings of many of his Surrealist friends, such as Michel Leiris, Gertrude Stein, Robert Desnos, André Malraux. He has made large mural decorations and has designed décor-models for the theatre.

MATHIEU, Georges

Born at Boulogne-sur-Mer (Pas-de-Calais) in 1921. Studied law and philosophy and received a degree in English. He began to paint in 1942 and established himself in Paris in 1947. He exhibited at the Salon des Réalités Nouvelles and at the Salon des Surindépendants. He organized, with Bryen and several others, different exhibitions of abstract art which are meant to be "lyrical" and "psychic," and are presented "in a reactionary spirit against the formalism of abstract art." He feels a definite analogy in ideas with the Neo-Expressionist American painters. For Mathieu the graphic quality has given way to *Tachism* (drippings and spots of paint in both liquid and solid form). He is fond of giving his paintings pseudo-historical titles such as "the Entelechy of the Capets," "The Battle of Bouvines," "No Escape from Capets."

An important exhibition of his work was held in 1950 at the Galerie Drouin, at the Kootz Gallery in New York in 1954, and at the Galerie Rive Droite in 1954 and 1956.

MICHAUX, Henri

Poet and painter Henri Michaux was born in Namur, Belgium in 1899. His pictorial compositions are like plastic commentaries of his Surrealist writings. "I would like to draw the effluvium which circulates between people,

"he said," and also: "Will power, death of art." Henri Michaux has published *Peintures et Dessins avec un avant-propos et des légendes extraites de l'œuvre poétique de l'auteur*. (Edit. Point du Jour, 1946).

MINAUX, André

Born in Paris September 5, 1923. His father, who was a dealer in fabrics, was also a decorator. He was already painting during the time he was finishing his secondary studies; he paints in a lyrical spirit, almost romantic, without any transposition. His art is noticed at the Ecole des Arts Décoratifs by Brianchon, who appreciates his talent. At the La Patellière exhibition held in 1943 at the Musée National d'Art Moderne, he realizes that his own searchings are analogous to those of his famous elder, and he reacts accordingly in order to express himself in a more personal manner. Minaux's art, properly speaking, lies at the edge of Neo-Realism and an extended Expressionism. He has exhibited at the Salon d'Automne since 1944, at the Salon de Mai and at the Salon des Indépendants since 1948. Exhibitions of his work have been held at the Galerie Saint-Placide since 1948.

MIRÓ, Jean

Born at Montroig, Spain (near Tarragona) April 20, 1893. He has often returned to this family domain which has given him with the theme for several paintings among which is *The Farm*. At the age of fourteen he entered the School of Fine Arts of Barcelona, left it three years later, and worked in a store. In 1912 he returned to painting and at the Gali Academy studied Baroque architecture which played a great role in his artistic formation. In 1915 he decided to work alone; he became influenced by Fauvism and by the paintings of van Gogh. In 1918 he exhibited for the first time at the Dalmau Gallery in Barcelona. The following year he left to conquer Paris. Under Picasso's protection he exhibited at the gallery called "La Licorne." In 1924 Miró's work evolved towards Surrealism. After a special exhibition at the Galerie Pierre, under the patronage of André Breton, he took part in this same gallery in the first Surrealist manifestation. From then on Miró was an important figure in the art world. He exhibited at the Valentine Gallery in New York and at the Galerie Goemans *(papiers collés)*; he designed ballet décors and costumes. On several occasions the Galerie Maeght has exhibited his work, not only paintings, but also tapestries, ceramics, polychrome wood-sculpture. Miró was awarded the Graphic Arts Prize at the 1956 Venice Biennale.

MOREAU, *Luc-Albert* (1882-1948)

Born in Paris December 9, 1882. He meets Segonzac in the Atelier Jean-Paul Laurens at the Académie Julian, where he is taking courses while studying at the Ecole des Langues Orientales. Afterwards he goes to the Académie de la Palette. In 1907 he spent a short time at Saint-Tropez in the company of Segonzac and Boussingault in a villa that the three artists had rented from Signac. In 1909 he made a trip to the Balearic Islands and lived there in complete isolation, until he was noticed by Octave Mirbeau. Towards 1911 he is carried away with the enthusiasm which attracts artists to Cubism. In 1914 his art becomes more realistic. Seriously wounded in 1918, Luc-Albert Moreau does not return to painting until 1920, and devotes himself at that time to a series of war paintings which still have all the signs of Cubism. But it is to lithography that he owes his definite getting away from this influence. At the beginning of 1925 he returns to live in Saint-Tropez; he paints still lifes, portraits (especially those of women), interiors, landscapes, and many paintings inspired by boxing. After keeping to a rather dark range of color in a paint laid on very thickly, his painting during the last years of his life, had a tendency to become clearer and lighter. In the spring of 1948 Luc-Albert Moreau suddenly died. In addition to his paintings, Luc-Albert Moreau has done very important work in the field of drawing and lithography.

NALLARD, *Louis*

Born at Algiers in 1918 where he went to school. He began quite young to exhibit his paintings in the city of his birth; his first non-figurative exhibition was in 1945. In 1947 he came to Paris. He traveled in Holland and in Spain. Exhibited at the Galerie Jeanne Bucher in 1953; took part regularly in the Salon de Mai. He has often exhibited with his wife, the painter Maria Manton. His delicate colors which nevertheless are of a rather violently limited range are often restrained to ochres and browns.

OUDOT, *Roland*

Born in Paris July 23, 1897. His paternal grandmother and his father both were painters. In 1912 he entered the Ecole des Arts Décoratifs for four years of study and later taught there. Afterwards he collaborated with Léon Bakst on the décors for the Ballets Russes, and worked with him till his death in 1923. Oudot worked also for the decorators Sue and Marc, and furnished fabric and furniture designs. He has been very much influenced first by Cézanne, then by Bonnard. Towards 1921 his production

undergoes a short realistic period. But his true personality did not distinguish itself till 1923. He exhibited for the first time at the Salon d'Automne beside Legueult and Brianchon; and he exhibited with them again at the Galerie Romanet in 1956; then regularly at the Salon d'Automne and at the Salon des Tuileries. He has interested himself in all subjects: portraits, still life, and especially landscape; he is a painter of land, earth, seeing the desolate, static, solitary aspect of Nature.

OZENFANT, *Amédée*

Born at Saint-Quentin (Aisne), April 15, 1886. He began to study drawing at the Ecole Quentin-de-la-Tour in his native city. Shortly afterwards he frequented the Académie de la Palette, where he was the pupil of Charles Cottet, Jacques-Emile Blanche and Georges Desvallières. In 1908 he exhibited at the Salon de la Nationale and in 1910 at the Salon d'Automne, and in the following year at the Salon des Indépendants. He traveled across the Low Countries, in Italy, and spent three years in Russia. Theorist as well as artist, he launched in 1915 the review *L'Elan*, published three years later *Après le Cubisme*, then with Le Corbusier in 1920 the review *L'Esprit Nouveau*, which appeared until 1925. Ozenfant made himself the apostle of "Purism" and as result returned to less strict formulas. At that time he was painting, in addition to other things, large monumental compositions. In 1930 he founded the Académie Ozenfant and began to lecture around the world. During a period of seven years he worked on a vast composition including more than one hundred figures which is now in the Musée National d'Art Moderne. From 1935 to 1938 he stayed in London, where he opened a school; in 1939 he published his journal entitled *Journey Through Life* describing the years 1931 to 1934. He established himself in 1938 in New York, where he opened the Ozenfant School of Fine Arts. He has lately returned to Paris. His painting today differs greatly from the Purism he formerly advocated and tends to be treated in a more romantic manner.

PASCIN, *Julius* (1885-1930)

Pascin is from his real name Pincas. He was born in Vidin (Bulgaria) March 31, 1885 of a Spanish Jewish father and of a mother of Italian origin born in Serbia. Pascin was destined to become a sort of contemporary international type. At the age of fourteen, in Munich to finish his studies, he is noticed by the writer Gustave Meyrink who makes it possible for him to work as a regular collaborator on the satirical paper *Simplicissimus* on *Judge*, and on *Lustige Blätter*. In 1905 he came to Paris; already famous, he collaborated on several Parisian publications. Before the war he took a trip to Algeria and Tunis. He had hardly spent two months in England when the First World War broke out; in September of the same year he sailed for the United States where after many years he was finally awarded American citizenship. He lived in New York, but he took trips to Cuba, Texas, Florida, Louisaina, South Carolina. In 1918 in New York he married Hermine David, who was also a painter and who accompanied him on his travels. In October of 1920 he returned to Paris and rented an atelier in Montparnasse where he made many portraits of his writer friends, notably André Salmon, Pierre Mac Orlan, Marcel Sauvage, and also painted several large compositions, many of which were inspired by the Bible. Afterwards he leads an itinerant life; returning to Paris in 1930, he meets Lucie Krogh again, the wife of the painter Per Krogh, whom he had met in 1910. Their mutual attachment, hindered by circumstances, brings about in Pascin a state of depression aggravated by the torments and uneasiness of his artistic conscience, all of which leads him to seek forgetfulness in alcohol. On June 2, 1930, the very day of the opening of his exhibition, held at Georges Petit's, he committed suicide.

PATRIX, *Michel*

Born at Cabourg (Calvados) May 25, 1917. His father was an engineer, dealer in wood, very musical, as was also his mother, passionately interested in everything that was art "except," as Patric tell us, "what concerned my career." When he was twelve years of age he painted water colors from Nature, with the aid of his teacher. After passing his *baccalauréat* in philosophy at the Lycée of Castelsarrazin (Tarn-et-Garonne), a subject he would very much have liked to continue, and having frequented during his study years the Cloister of Moissac, the museums of Toulouse, Albi and Montauban, where he copies the drawings of Ingres, he finally had to break with his family in order to follow his vocation as a painter. He worked at all kinds of jobs: dockhand, factory hand, salesman. Demobilised in 1941 he came to Paris where he frequented the academies, while always practising other vocations, especially that of decorator which he worked at for a long time. He studied with André Lhote, then with Othon Friesz together with his friends Busse, Cortot, Calmettes and others who later formed the group "L'Echelle." Patrix said: "I think that one should leave the domain of the non-figurative to music otherwise one may fall into a symbolism that is rather out of date." He also remarked: "The deeper I go into painting, the more interested I become in the painting and less in the painter himself, and in the painting sometimes I am seized with a detail, with everything that expresses the things said, right down to the means themselves." Patrix exhibited in 1945 with the group known as "L'Echelle"; he exhibited also at the Paul Rosenberg Gallery in New York in 1948 and 1949, and at the Galerie Drouant-David in 1950 and 1954.

PEYRONNET, *Dominique* (1872-1943)

Born at Talence, a suburb of Bordeaux, in 1872, died in Paris in 1943. Peyronnet was a printer and did not begin painting till the age of fifty, bringing to this new métier the same scruples and consciousness that he brought to the printing profession. His favorite theme is the sea, and he sincerely thought that no one represented it better than he did. His naïve pride is touching. If he lacks the imagination of a Rousseau, the fine expression of a Vivin and prefers to paint in a rather careful, detailed way, he avoids in his work, none the less, an unpleasant dryness.

PIAUBERT, *Jean*

Born in Bordeaux January 27, 1900. Until he was twenty years of age he studied at the Ecole des Beaux-Arts of Bordeaux, then went to Paris where he settled down and worked in collaboration with the famous couturier Paul Poiret. He traveled in Spain in 1928; in Italy (Venice), England, Belgium in 1929. His first exhibition was held in 1932 at the Galerie Zak. During a period of ten years (1936-1946) he did not exhibit at all. Instead, he designed and worked for the typographers Draeger *Frères*. In 1946 he showed his work at the Galerie Greuze, then at the Galerie Denise René from 1947 to 1950, taking part in the Salon de Mai from 1948 onwards plus numerous exhibitions abroad. He took part in the first Salon des Réalités Nouvelles held in 1956. Starting as a realistic painter, he came to abstraction in 1943. After having painted "the wild noise of gun fire" (Pierre Descargues) in large panels, he arrived at a profound need to reduce everything to essentials, turning to austere geometric forms translated into paintings in a strict scheme of black, white and gray. His first venture into the art of lithography was in 1947 when he illustrated the poems of Noël Burreau, then later the *Thirty Three Sonnets* of Jean Cassou, which was an occasion for the artist to express his many experiences.

PICHETTE, James

Born at Châteauroux August 1, 1920, of a Canadian father of Normand ancestry and of a Nîmes mother. He spends part of his youth in Marseille. As result of the war he is compelled to spend a prolonged period of time in the mountains. And it is there he begins to paint in 1943—paintings which are entirely figurative and which he shows for the first time at the Salon des Surindépendants of 1947. In 1948 he spent a short time in Rome. Thanks to a government grant he is able to go to Holland where he lived at the Maison Descartes in Amsterdam, profiting by the occasion to visit at his leisure the many museums and study the Dutch Masters. His first abstract compositions of 1948 are characteristically more circled and less clear than his recent ones. His stay in Holland influenced, once again, for a certain time, his palette; his colors became darker. But his deep affection for the south of France brings about a change in his colors, they become more alive, more vivid, like the splash of multicolored feathers. He professes to be non-figurative; and even more, he rediscovers with liveliness the world of Nature with its multiple harmonies of red: *Les Voiles Folles* (Italy, 1956), *Joie Méditerranéenne* (1957) or *Le Rouge Fou* (1956). His first important exhibition was held in 1949 at the Galerie Morihien in Paris. Afterwards, he exhibited regularly each year at the Galerie Henri Bénézit in Paris and at the Galerie Lesperut in Marseille.

PIGNON, Edouard

Born at Marle-les-Mines (Pas-de-Calais) February 12, 1905. He worked in the mines, then afterwards on building construction. He spent his military service in Syria, then settled down in Paris. He did all kinds of jobs: packer in a chocolate factory, walk-on in Charles Dullin's famous theatre L'Atelier, machine manager at the Citroën automobile plant, laboratory clerk, photograph retoucher. He takes evening courses and studies first with Auclair, then with Wlérick and Arnold. He begins painting in 1934, encouraged by Picasso. But it is not till 1943 that he is able to devote himself entirely to his art. In 1932 he began to send his paintings to the Salon des Indépendants, to the Salon des Surindépendants and to the Salon des Tuileries. In 1941 he took part in the exhibition called "Jeunes Peintres de Tradition Française." In 1946 an important exhibition of his work was held at the Galerie de France. The following year, and in the same gallery, he exhibited a large ensemble of his works all inspired by the sea: masts, nets, ropes, sails—themes which he brought back from his stay at Ostend. About 1950 he returns to a more tragic theme, such as *The Dead Miner*, 1952. Like all painters of his generation, Pignon has been influenced by Matisse's chromatism and by the work of the Cubists—intensity of color, concern for rare tones, a searching for the most expressive lines of a given situation and movement, and a recognition that certain sacrifices are necessary.

PLANSON, André

Born at La Ferté-sous-Jouarre (Seine-et-Marne) April 10, 1898. His parents were vine-growers. He spent a short time at the Académie Ranson; was awarded in 1932 the Blumenthal Prize. In 1954 the Galerie Durand-Ruel held a large exhibition of his work. Planson's painting is closely allied with the earth; colorful, rich and solid, full of good-heartedness and alacrity. A great admirer of Delacroix, he brings Courbet to life with a sharpness of Fauvism.

POLIAKOFF, Serge

Born in Moscow January 8, 1906, emigrates to Paris in 1924, then to London, where he remains till 1937. During this period he painted nudes in a Velazquez style. His return to Paris in 1938 coincides with his beginnings in the field of abstract art. He met Kandinsky and Delaunay, but did not at all become influenced by their work. He created for himself an expressive style which was entirely original. He employed simple forms with absolutely no concern for reality, overlapping one against the other, which take on a spatial organization in a mobility and a mineral silence. The colors create a subtle and rich ensemble; often red and yellow predominate in compositions with their harmonies discreetly broken. Unnoticed for a long period of time, Poliakoff was obliged, in order to earn a living, to play the guitar in many Paris night clubs. His veritable fame dates from his exhibition at the Brussels Palais des Beaux-Arts in 1953.

RAVEL, Daniel

Born in Aix-en-Provence March 3, 1915, of Provençal origin. His father was a French teacher in the province of Dauphiné. After finishing his studies, Ravel entered the Ecole des Arts Décoratifs of Grenoble where he studied lithography. Afterwards he entered the Ecole des Arts Décoratifs of Paris (1934-1937). But until that time he did nothing but draw. He had the greatest admiration for Daumier. On his arrival in Paris he began to paint, but always he had the intention to become a painter. His admiration for Cézanne and van Gogh, which attracts him to color, soon united with this interest in drawing and subsequently draws him to the enthusiastic discovery of Cubism. He admits being influenced by La Fresnaye, Delaunay, Paul Klee and Jacques Villon "However," writes Jacques Busse, "he very freely thinks back to all that Villon had taught him. Ther are color range of Daniel Ravel, an orchestration of the most incisive yellow and oranges, is in every way comparable to that of his inspired example." In his still lifes the numerous and diverse objects, "are arranged according to strictly plastic laws, transposed in structure and by their high tone to the limits of abstraction." Ravel exhibited at the Salon des Indépendants from 945 to 1950, at the Salon de Mai since 1946, and a few years at the Salon d'Automne. An exhibition of his work was held at the Galerie Lucien Durand in 1956. Since 1957 he has been exhibiting his paintings at the Galerie Jacques Massol.

REBEYROLLE, Paul

Born at Eymoutiers (Haute-Vienne) November 3, 1926. Fascinated by drawing since his childhood, he came to Paris in 1945 to devote himself to painting. He is soon noticed for the vigorousness of his abilities. He soon turns towards a violent realism in which he finds his taste once again for the Spanish painters. Rude peasant figures of his native land, dead animals, a dog or a goat with an enormous belly—these are his familiar themes. In 1950 Rebeyrolle was awarded the Prix de la Jeune Peinture and in 1951 the Prix Fénéon. He exhibited at the Salon d'Automne, at the Salon des Indépendants, and at the Salon des Tuileries. Jury member for the Salon des Jeunes Peintres, he is appointed for the committee of the Salon de Mai in 1957. In 1956 the Maison de la Pensée Française organized a large exhibition of his work. Today Rebeyrolle is one of the spearheads of the new realistic reaction.

RIMBERT, René

Born in Paris September 19, 1896. His father, a master framemaker, allowed him quite early in life to see painting and took him to many salons and museums. Self-taught in everything. At the age of thirteen he entered the postal service and was retired in 1956. Demobilized in 1919 he exhibited at the Salon des Indépendants of 1920: he admired Gromaire who encouraged him. In 1924 he made the acquaintance of Max Jacob, who in 1927 wrote the preface for his first exhibition which was held at the Galerie Percier. Afterwards he met Wilhelm Uhde. Conscientious, working minutely, he painted very slowly (time for him meant nothing), finishing only six or seven paintings a year. From 1931 to 1945 he interrupted all work. Having been retired a short period before he profits by his free time to paint more. Above all he is a landscape painter; for a while he devotes his interest to views of the quarter of Saint-Germain-des-Prés, but more often his city and country landscapes are purely imaginary. He felt the need to express his "deepest desires: harmony, serenity, peace and the habitual silence arising from the presence of the mysterious." His work was shown for the first time at the Salon des Indépendants of 1920, where he exhibited until 1928, sending his work one year, 1924, to the Salon d'Automne. In 1956 the Galerie Montmorency exhibited an ensemble of more than twenty of his canvases.

ROHNER, Georges

Born in Paris July 20, 1913 of Swiss family origin. He is the student of Lucien Simon at the Ecole des Beaux-Arts (1929-1933). At the beginning of his career as a painter he undergoes the influence of Picasso, Derain, La Fresnaye, Ingres, Seurat, then that of the seventeenth-century French painters, as result of the exhibition held in 1934. He shares his experiences with his friends Humblot, Jannot, Lasne, Despierre whom he had known at the Ecole des Beaux-Arts, and with a few others whom he met elsewhere, such as Gruber. Until 1934 he worked in Provence. From 1934 to 1935 he spent his military service in the West Indies and during that time he decorated the Hotel de Ville of Basse-Terre and the bank of Guadeloupe at Pointe-à-Pitre with a series of seven large paintings. In the interval in 1935 he became part of the movement called "Forces Nouvelles"; and in this group his work is the strictest and the most stripped away of essentials. Under the auspices of Henri Hérault he exhibited with the group in 1935. On his return to the West Indies he exhibited at the Musée de la France d'Outre-Mer in 1937. He spent a short time in 1938 in Bourgogne and also traveled in Holland. In 1938 he exhibited at the Galerie de Berri. The war stops all work; he is taken prisoner, and he is interned at Trêves. In 1941 he paints a panel for the chapel of Stalag XII D (which he has kept in his atelier) *Christ and the Prisoners.* Shortly afterwards he is able to continue his work whose direction is unchanged. If *The Drowned Man* of 1939 shows in Rohner a tendency towards expressionism which is confirmed by certain large canvases, such as *The Forty-first Day,* his permanent taste, however, is for still life, always powerfully constructed in very strong dark modeling, whose general order he likes to render more subtle by the curved lines of musical instruments or brighten it by the folds of material. He exhibits at the Galerie Framont; he also occupies an important place in the field of tapestry design (Aubusson).

ROUSSEAU, *Henri*, known as *Le Douanier* (1844-1910)

Born at Laval May 21, 1844, died in Paris September 2, 1910. Son of a tin-worker, he hardly studied at all. He enters the army at the age of eighteen, and was assigned to the 52nd Infantry Regimental Band. After leaving the army in 1869 he marries. His first marriage results in the birth of a daughter who is taken away from him after the death of his first wife, as people considered him too strange in his ways to take care of a child. After having taken part in the war of 1870, Rousseau enters the customs service as second-class clerk. He has made allusions to having taken part in the Mexican campaign, but the facts seem rather unlikely. It is impossible to know exactly what it was that attracted him to painting; he devotes himself to it seriously when he was about forty years old, after having received his retirement from the customs service. He lived by giving all sorts of lessons (painting, diction, harmony) and by painting portraits of neighboring shopkeepers. He was also sales inspector for the *Petit Parisien*. In his room he held artistic soirées during which he showed his own work as well as that of his pupils. Introduced by Signac in 1886 at the Salon des Artistes Indépendants, where he regularly sent his work until 1888, then from 1901 to 1910. From 1905 on he exhibited also at the Salon d'Automne. In 1899 he wrote a drama in five acts called "The Revenge of the Russian Orphan," which was given without any success whatever at the Théâtre du Châtelet. He remarried and later lost his second wife in 1903. In 1907 he met Wilhem Uhde, who wrote the first monograph on him. In 1908 he was "given a start" in the art world, thanks to Guillaume Apollinaire, Alfred Jarry and André Salmon. It was at this time that the famous banquet was held in Rousseau's honor in Picasso's atelier of the "Bateau-Lavoir." One has sometimes considered this banquet rather as a joke, but according to Uhde the reason for it was quite serious. But Rousseau's naïve and confident character forced his friends to introduce comic elements. In 1910 he exhibited his painting *The Dream* at the Salon des Indépendants. Shortly before his death, he courted a young girl who worked in a department store; she treated him as a joke, but he sent declarations of his love right up till the last moment of his life. He died at the Necker Hospital. His tomb is in the Bagneux cemetery with an epitaph by Guillaume Apolli-naire. He has painted Paris scenes, historical scenes, large exotic pictures, group portraits, and allegorical paintings as well.

ROY, *Pierre* (1880-1950)

Born in Nantes August 10, 1880, died in Milan September 26, 1950. He wanted to be a sailor but gives up the idea and begins studying architecture. He comes to Paris in 1904, enters the Ecole des Beaux-Arts, then the Académie Julian and later the Ecole des Arts Décoratifs. He traveled in England, Holland, Germany and Italy. In 1910 he developed a relationship with the Fauves and becomes friendly with André Salmon, Max Jacob, Guillaume Apollinaire. He created a series of typographical ornaments for the Peignot foundry. After having exhibited at the Salon de la Société Nationale and at the Salon des Indépendants, he joined in 1920 the future Surrealist group and took part in the first two exhibitions at the Galerie Pierre in 1925 and at the Galerie Surréaliste in 1935. He is considered one of the precursors of the Surrealist movement. His technique which has every sign of certainty allows him to represent faithfully the most ordinary everyday objects which he puts together arbitrarily, creating a feeling of mystery and strangeness. He was jury member for the Carnegie Exhibition in Pittsburg in 1930, took part in the exhibition in New York in 1932 and also that in San Francisco in 1938. In 1939 he went to the Hawaian Islands for publicity purposes because he had been asked to paint pineapples "on the spot." He has designed theatre décors for the Swedish Ballet for Henri Ghéon, Leonide Massine, Igor Stravinsky. On his way to Bergamo where he was to take part in an exhibition of his work he died suddenly in Milan.

SCHNEIDER, *Gérard*

Born at Sainte-Croix, Switzerland, April 28, 1896 in the canton of Vaud. After his studies at the College de Neuchâtel, he came to Paris in 1916 and entered the Ecole des Arts Décoratifs and later at the Ecole des Beaux-Arts. In 1922 he became a picture restorer, a métier which, he admitted, contributed greatly to the development of his artistic culture. At first Post-Impressionist, Cubist, Surrealist, then Expressionist, Schneider has tried to assimilate all modern efforts and aims before throwing himself into abstract art (1944) which was the logical evolution of his painting. He rejected completely and utterly all exterior influence, he wanted to express what he found in himself, without the aid of any natural form. Working directly in thickly laid on colors, Schneider creates on the canvas a series of lyrical harmonies

170

in a scientifically orchestrated composition. His painting has much in common with music. He himself is a passionate admirer of Beethoven, Bach, Mozart. He took part in the Salon d'Automne of 1926, in the Salon des Surindépendants from 1935 to 1940, in the Salon des Réalités Nouvelles from 1947 to 1949 and since 1949 he has been exhibiting at the Salon de Mai. He exhibits quite often in Paris and in other countries, in a one-man show or with a group. He received his French citizenship in 1948.

SÉRAPHINE (1864-1942)

Séraphine Louis, known as Séraphine de Senlis, was born at Assy (Oise) September 2, 1864. She spent her childhood watching over animals, then worked in Senlis as a housekeeper. It was there that Wilhelm Uhde discovered her talent and encouraged her to continue. Later on Uhde returned to live in Senlis and saw her work in an exhibition of regional paintings held at the Hôtel de Ville of Senlis. He went to see his former housekeeper and supplied her with canvases and paint, but without ever having succeeded in seeing her paint. Séraphine's mind gave way about 1930; she began to spend money wildly and at the same time began to predict the end of the world. She faded away December 11, 1942 in an asylum at Clermont. She painted only flowers and strange fruits, with no relationship whatever with reality.

SINGIER, Gustave

Born at Warneton, Western Flanders, in Belgium, February 11, 1909. His father was a cabinetmaker, his mother a weaver. He took out French citizenship papers, and has been living in Paris since 1919. About the age of fourteen he discovered the Cubists and began to paint from Nature. For three years (1925-1927) he took courses at the Ecole Boule. He worked as a draftsman in the arangement of shops. During this period he frequented evening courses, the academies of Montmartre and worked alone in the Louvre. He exhibited at the Salon des Indépendants of 1937, at the Salon d'Automne of 1937, etc., and since 1943 he has been exhibiting at the Salon de Mai. In 1936 he received encouragement from Charles Walch. In 1943 he designed the décors and costumes for "Abisag" which was given at the Comédie des Champs-Elysées and forbidden by the Germans. In 1945 he executed a large decorative painting for the Dominican Convent in the Rue de la Glacière. He has executed also stained glass windows (The Dominican Convent of Villefranche-de-Rouergue), tapestries (French Institute of New York), and has also worked in graphic art.

Several exhibitions of his works have been held at the Galerie de France. One of them was seen in many German cities in 1956.

SOULAGES, Pierre

Born at Rodez (Aveyron) December 24, 1919 of peasant ancestry. His father died when he was five years old, he studied in his native city where he passed his *baccalauréat*. From the age of fourteen he began to paint without any formation whatever than that of his lycée teachers; his subject matter was the local landscape. He knew nothing about painting: he knew Corot by name only and was ignorant of the Impressionists. These early landscapes while he was still a young boy, he likes to point out, already were cut vertically by a dark brown area of trees. Shortly afterwards he follows van Gogh in new spontaneous efforts and aims in the field of landscape painting. 1938 dates his first visit to Paris, telling his family that he was going to seek a teaching position in drawing. He stays away from the Ecole des Beaux-Arts but visits the Louvre where he sketches a good deal. To escape from the S.T.O., he returns to his native country which does not help his vocation as a painter. But his true beginning in the world of painting takes place in 1946 when he returns to Paris. At the age of eighteen he discovers Romanesque painting from reproductions before going to the places themselves and losing himself in ardent enthusiasm before the magnificent frescoes. He claims from an early age this influence of Romanesque art (the abbey of Conques) and the engraved standing stones in the Rodez museum. However, an entirely traditional formation quickly brought him, from 1946, to the form of expression that is his today. He is in love with Romanesque architecture as much as ever which has given him a feeling for monumental verticals. He prefers suggestive color rather than color in its extreme tonal intensity as used by the Fauves. All the same he prefers a restrained dynamism to a movement that is evident. His first contact with the public was in 1947 at the Salon des Surindépendants. After having exhibited at the Galerie Louis Carré, he exhibits regularly now at the Kootz Galery in New York and in the Galerie de France in Paris. In June 1957 he receives the Prix International of the Ministry of National Education in Tokio, and at the same time the Prix Windsor which enables him to spend some time in the United States.

SOUTINE, Chaïm (1894-1943)

Born in Smilovitch, near Minsk (Lithuania) in 1894, died in Paris August 9, 1943. He was the tenth of a family of eleven children. His father was a tailor and did not succeed in providing for his family. At the age of four, he stole one of his mother's kitchen utensils to buy a colored pencil; he was nearly driven out of the village because he draws the portrait of his school teacher, since Jewish law prohibited drawing the human face. At the age of thirteen, to avoid becoming a shoe repairer, as his parents wished, he runs away from home and arrives at Minsk where he takes his first drawing lessons. Then he goes to Vilna, takes courses in the Fine Arts Academy, at the same time working as a camera operator. Drawn by Krémègne's reputation, and helped by a doctor who lends him a little money, he comes to Paris in 1911, enrolls in the Atelier Cormon, then in 1916 hires an atelier at La Ruche, where Chagall, Lipchitz, Blaise Cendrars, and Krémègne already live. He lives in extreme penury, and as soon as he has some money he drinks it away. Modigliani, who had painted his portrait in 1917, and whose intimate friend he was, influences Zborowski to help him. Zborowski sends Soutine to Céret in 1919 but considering execrable the canvases which Soutine bring back to him, casts them aside and they are not discovered till 1923 by Dr. Alfred H. Barnes; the famous art lover is highly enthusiastic, buys a hundred canvases and installs Soutine in a villa near the Parc Montsouris, where Braque, Lurçat, Foujita and Chana Orloff already live. The painter then lives in Cannes for a while. On his return to Paris in 1926 he begins to paint carcasses; he even procures a flayed ox in the slaughter houses which he sets up in his atelier (Pl. p. 41). At Chatel-Guyon in 1929 he makes the acquaintance of Castaing who offers him a home in the chateau of Lèves near Chartres. Henceforth he lives there during the summer and comes to Paris in the winter. Now there are terrible periods of depression and sometimes he tears or destroys his paintings. From 1933 to his death he hardly produces anything more. In 1935 his first important exhibition takes place at the Fine Arts Club in Chicago. Moreover he hates exhibiting and only does so once more at the Salon de l'Art Indépendant in 1937. At the beginning of the war he wants to join up but is not accepted. He refuses to flee to the United States in 1940 but takes refuge at Champigny-sur-Veude in Touraine to escape the menace of a concentration camp. Striken by an intestinal rupture in 1943, brought too late to hospital, he dies after the operation. He is buried in the cemetery of Montparnasse. The Salon d'Automne in 1944 held a restrospective exhibition of his work; the Galerie de France exhibited in January 1945 forty of his canvases; the Maison de la Pensée Française held an important retrospective exhibition of his work

in 1956 as did the Museum of Modern Art in New York.

STAËL, Nicolas de (1914-1955)

Born in St. Petersburg January 5, 1914 (December 23, 1913 following the Russian calendar). Nicholas de Staël committed suicide March 16, 1955 at Antibes. Son of Baron Vladimir Ivanovitch de Staël-Hoslein related to the family of Madame de Staël and of Lioubov Berenikoff, a woman passionately interested in painting and music. In 1919 to escape the Revolution, the de Staël family emigrate to Poland. Some time after (1922) his parents being dead, Nicholas de Staël is sent to Belgium, where he receives a solid classical education. He enters the Royal Academy of Fine Arts in 1932 and is awarded the first prize of the competition. He sets out for Holland, discovering Rembrandt, Vermeer, Hercules Seghers, then comes to Paris, where he is greatly impressed by the work of Cézanne, Matisse, Braque and Soutine. Then de Staël lives for a while in Spain for nearly a year and afterwards visits Italy, Morocco and Algeria. In 1939 he joins the French Foreign Legion, in 1942 back in France again he discovers his true personality as a painter. Henceforth he dedicates himself entirely to his art. He leans towards abstraction but will always keep an element of realism in his work. He is inspired, for example, in an entire series of paintings, by a football match played at night which he had seen in the Parc des Princes (Pl. p. 131). First of all he paints in dark tones, then his palette becomes more luminous, long white bands of color brighten his canvases. He likes large-size canvases; makes reds, blues and powerful yellow contrast with delicate grays. He draws astonishing effects from a thickly painted surface laid on with a palette knife. Nevertheless his last canvases painted in his atelier in Antibes which faced the sea, are much more fluid in color, almost without coating. Before reaching the fame which the great retrospective exhibition of the Musée National d'Art Moderne confirms on him (March 1956), Nicolas de Staël is first of all appreciated in the United States. His first exhibition took place in the Galerie L'Esquisse (1944), then at Jeanne Bucher's (1945), and finally at Jacques Dubourg's who remains interested in him up to the time of his death.

SURVAGE, Léopold

Born in Moscow July 31, 1879 in the Gregorian calendar, the son of a Finnish father and a Danish mother. Destined to become an architect, Survage enters the Moscow Fine Arts Academy. There he meets Lorionov, Falk,

Soudekin and turns his attention towards painting. In 1908, he leaves for Paris and takes part in Cubist experiments. He exhibits with them in 1911 at the Salon des Indépendants; in 1913 with Gleizes and Archipenko, he reorganizes the Salon de la Section d'Or. In 1920, 1921, 1922, Léonce Rosenberg devotes private exhibitions to his work. Survage, now given a start, exhibits in New York and Chicago. He paints four large compositions for the Railway Pavilion of the Universal Exposition of 1937. Influenced by Cubism, Survage's art is above all symbolic. For him the painter is a *"voyant"* who must translate the deep reality of things into a particular rhythm by means of a extremely refined surface technique (he rediscovers the ancient method of casein painting).

TAL-COAT, *Pierre*

Born at Clohars-Caoët, Finistère of a peasant family December 12, 1905. When still a boy he draws, paints and works in sculpture. From 1924 to 1926 he lives in Paris during the period of his military service, then moves to Doélan near Pouldu. Already his strong personality asserts itself and many art lovers are interested in his work. Back again in Paris in 1931, he takes part in the activities of the group "Forces Nouvelles." In 1936 the Spanish Civil War influences his art. It is the period of those "Massacres" in violent colors with sharp and tortured forms. In 1940 he settles down in Aix-en-Provence, then in Château-Noir in 1943. Untiringly and without any concession to public taste, he continues his experiments in the field of light, movement and the elements (this is the period of paintings called "Fishes"). From 1947 onwards his painting becomes more and more essential and undergoes the influence of Chinese art. He is absorbed by lichen, by a rock, seeking always to penetrate the mystery of matter and of Nature. The Galerie Maeght devotes several exhibitions to his work.

TANGUY, *Yves*

Born in Paris January 5, 1900 of Breton parents. He was attracted to the merchant marine. He travels in England, Portugal, Spain, Africa and South America. He meets Jacques Prévert during his military service in Avignon. At the age of twenty-four the chance glimpse of a painting by Chirico is enough to decide his vocation as a painter and he immediately gets down to work. He joins the Surrealist group and exhibits with them in France and in other countries, as well as at the Salon des Surindépendants. He paints very little and speedily his art stagnates. With an involved technique he tackles the problem of representing photographically a dream world inhabited by a flora and fauna composed of nearly inorganic larvae. He contributes to many Surrealist publications and signs all their manifestos. In 1939 Tanguy leaves France for the United States, lives in California and then in Canada; in 1942 he buys a farm in Connecticut and becomes a naturalised American citizen in 1948.

UBAC, *Raoul*

Born at Malmedy August 31, 1910. His father was a conciliation magistrate, his mother's parents tanners. Ill success at school made him give up his ideas of entering as a candidate for the Forest and Water Service. After his *baccalauréat* in 1929 he came to Paris. He soon deserted the Sorbonne for the academies of Montparnasse. He traveled in Belgium, Germany, Austria, Yugoslavia and Italy. From 1932 and under the influence of the *collages* of Max Ernst and the work of Man Ray, he devoted himself entirely to photography of Surrealist expression. About 1934 he joined the group of the "Minotaure" and collaborated regularly with them. In addition he took active part in the great Surrealist exhibition of 1937. The war, however, was to separate him quite definitely from this movement. In 1934 he exhibited at the Librairie Dasté, Rue de Tournon, a series of pen drawings all of different inspiration. From this moment on he gave up photography completely in order to devote himself exclusively to drawing and painting; he came to painting rather slowly by way of gouache and India ink. He exhibited his first gouaches in 1946 at the Redfern Gallery in London and at the Galerie Lou Cosyn in Brussels, and in 1949 at the Hanover Gallery in London. The first exhibition of an ensemble of his work was held in December 1950 at the Galerie Maeght: along with his gouaches he exhibited canvases of a brownochre, mouse-gray color, evoking his native forest of the Ardennes, and also carved and engraved slates.

VASARELY, *Victor*

Born in Pécs, Hungary April 9, 1908. He studied medicine in Budapest in 1926. In 1929 he entered the Bauhaus of Budapest, the *"Muhely"* of Bortnyik. He attended the lectures of Moholy-Nagy and became acquainted with the works of Malevitch, Mondrian, Gropius, Kandinsky, Jeanneret. He came to Paris in 1930, and became part of the group of the Galerie Denise René from its foundation in 1944 and there exhibited regularly. He exhibited also at the Salon de Mai, the Salon des Surindépendants, the Salon des Réalités Nouvelles. From 1930 to 1933 he exhibited in Budapest, in Copenhagen in 1950, in Stockholm in 1952, in Brussels in 1954. His work is made up of strict geometrical lines and is largely indebted to the emphasis of construction which marked the work of his early teachers, to which he has added movement. Vassarély has made abstract films and tapestries in addition to lithographs: *Bangor*, printed by Mourlot, *Xingou*, by Desjobert.

VENARD, Claude

Born March 21, 1913 in Paris of shopkeeping parents of Burgundian origin. His artistic formation can be summed up in his night courses in applied arts during the years 1928 to 1933 and two days at the Ecole des Beaux-Arts in 1934. Then followed travels in Morocco and Algeria, in Belgium, Holland and Germany and short stays at Pont-Croix in Brittany gives Venard the opportunity of expanding his artistic horizons, and of feeding him with ideas and experiences. If Venard for whom painting is the only reason for living, belonged for a certain time to the group called "Forces Nouvelles," and found there sincere friends, this only goes to show that he has been constantly haunted by the idea of perfection. But his rich Burgundian nature could not but soar beyond this slightly austerebackground. We notice disparities in his work which are nothing more than the successive stages of a gifted temperament always evolving and always seeking new modes of expression.

VIEIRA DA SILVA, Maria-Helena

Born in Lisbon in 1908, naturalised French citizen in 1906. Quite young she begins to draw. Arrived in Paris in 1928 she puts herself under the tutelage of Bourdelle and of Friesz; Hayter teaches her the technique of graphic art. Her real beginnings date from 1936 with curious paintings in which colored spots form a pattern on a neutral background. Very soon she finds her own personal style, a construction of a world, of a new space formed of lines which are intentionally vertical and in which there are no figures and where the spectator travels and loses himself in the infinite. Married to a Hungarian Arpad Szenes, she spends the duration of the war with him in Brazil. Back again in Paris she exhibits at the Galerie Pierre and in numerous galleries abroad. (Stockholm, Copenhagen, Berlin, Vienna, London, etc.)

VIVIN, Louis (1861-1936)

Born in Hadol (Vosges) July 27, 1861, died in Paris May 28, 1926. After studying in the college of Epinal, he entered the postal service in 1881 as a supernumary. First employed in the distribution department, then inspector, he was decorated with academic palms. From his childhood he painted, influenced by Corot and Courbet. In 1889 he exhibited at the Salon des Employés de Poste a painting entitled "The Flemish Rose." Living in Montmartre in the Rue Caulaincourt, he exhibited from time to time at the Foire aux Croûtes, near the Sacré-Cœur. In 1925 he was discovered by Wilhelm Uhde. At the age of sixty-two he retires from the postal service and thus was enabled to paint at leisure; but stricken by paralysis he had to give up his art during the last years of his life. First he painted everyday scenes, hunting scenes and floral subjects, then Paris scenes in a very personal style in which a stone gray color dominates.

WALCH, Charles (1898-1948)

Born at Thann (Haut-Rhin) August 4, 1898, died suddenly in Paris December 12, 1948. Belongs to an old peasant family. In 1918 he receives a State scholarship to study in Paris and takes courses in the Ecole des Arts Décoratifs until 1922. From 1925 onwards he exhibits at the Salon d'Automne, at the Salon des Indépendants and at the Salon des Tuileries. Towards 1927 to 1932 a time of penance follows and this born colorist turning away from a multicolored palette in favor of experiments in the field of construction and balance in painting, then paints in a monochromatic manner. In 1932 Georges Besson notices his work as does also Bonnard who appreciates his sense of Intimism. And he is noticed by Albert Marquet too. Walch is awarded the Gold Medal of the Universal Exposition of 1937. Scrupulous and retiring, he did not want to see a display of his work. It is not till the age of forty that he decides to organize an exhibition of his work which was held in 1938. He receives the Legion of Honor in 1948, the year of his death. A retrospective exhibition of his work was held November 1949 in the Musée National d'Art Moderne. Stricken with polio at the age of two he is forced to do all his painting, sculpture and graphic art with his left hand, without being afraid to work directly on the stone.

WAROQUIER, Henry de

Born in Paris January 8, 1881, takes courses in architecture given by Charles Génuys. By frequenting assiduously from 1895 to 1900 the galleries of the Rue Laffitte (Vollard, Durand-Ruel, Bing), his taste and desire to paint are formed. Waroquier begins to paint under the influence of the Impressionists who are in turn superseded by the influence of Far Eastern art. He draws and paints the land of Brittany which he visits regularly from 1901 to 1910 (l'Ile-aux-Moines, Belle-Isle-en-Mer) with a stylization in every way the same as that of Japanese art. In the year 1912 comes the revelation of Italy. From 1917 in reaction to his "white" manner and inspired by the Italian frescoes, he begins to paint imaginary landscapes in ranges of very dark tones. But soon leaving the landscape of fantasy for Nature he tends more and more towards easel-picture painting. This return to Nature is plainly visible in the landscapes which he paints in Italy in 1920 and above all in his Spanish paintings of 1921. The realm of his inspiration grows larger; he ceases being exclusively a landscape painter, turns to still life painting and human figure which even tend to predominate in his landscapes. For several years tortured by the desire for greatness, he enters into an Expressionist period which is deeply marked by a tragic fury. *The Tragedy* for the Palais de Chaillot Theatre in 1937; *Afflicted Spain* at the Salon des Tuileries 1938. A retrospective exhibition of his work was held in Zurich in May 1946 and presented an important ensemble of canvases selected from those which from 1917 to our day express most vividly conflict and sorrow.

WOLS (1913-1951)

His real name was Otto-Alfred Schultze-Battemann. Born in Berlin in 1913, died in 1951 in Paris, where since the age of nineteen he had definitely settled down and established himself. He met Miró, Max Ernst, Tzara and Calder. In 1933 he traveled in Spain. To earn his living he took all kinds of photographs which led to an exhibition of his work in 1937. Since he was a German subject, he spent a year of internment. Liberated he painted in the south of France before returning to Paris. He became friendly with Jean-Paul Sartre who encouraged him. An exhibition of his work was held in 1947 at the Galerie Drouin and at the Hugo Gallery in New York in 1950. "When Wols' art," writes Michel Seuphor, "goes beyond literary allusion (his series of *Cities*) and lasciviousness (drawings of Expressionist and Surrealist remembrances) and reaches pure abstraction, his art sometimes achieves a real depth of nervous force and unleashes an extraordinary magnetism. His large paintings made up of an incalculable number of small things, forming an entire mass both changing and homogeneous, are perhaps among the most powerful and the rarest works in the domain of abstract art." Wols has also written poems: his natural anarchism finds a favorable climate in the world of Chinese mysticism. He has illustrated the writings of Kafka, Artaud, Paulham, Sartre.

ZACK, Léon

Born at Nijni-Novgorod, Russia July 12, 1892. His father was a druggist. He began to draw while still a child and at the age of ten decided to become a painter. He studied at the Faculty of Letters of Moscow and frequented the ateliers of painters. Several years after his arrival in Paris, about 1925-1927, he is a figurative painter with a tendency to the geometric. Afterwards he undergoes a Neo-Humanist period which arrives at a form of expression tending more and more towards abstraction. He exhibited at the Salon d'Automne, at the Salon des Surindépendants, at the Salon de Mai. His first exhibition was held in 1927 at the Galerie Percier. Afterwards he exhibited at the Galerie Bonjean in 1930, at the Galerie Wildenstein in 1936. His recent exhibitions have been at the Galerie Kleber (1955 and 1957).

ZAO WOU KI

Born in Peking February 13, 1920, came to Paris in 1948 and took out French citizenship papers. At the age of fifteen he entered the National School of Fine Arts of Hangchow and taught there from 1941 to 1947. The painter Ling Fong Mien advised him to go to Paris where he arrived in 1948. He discovered Europe, traveled in Italy, Belgium, the Low Countries, England, Spain. His first exhibition was held at the Galerie Greuze in 1949 with a preface to his work written by Bernard Dorival. He exhibited at the Galerie La Hune and at the Galerie Pierre from 1949 to 1956 with a recent showing at the Galerie de France. Rarely has such a perfect harmony been achieved between the poetical and subtle graphic elements of Far Eastern art and the modern European conceptions of painted work.

The biographical notes in this volume have been compiled under the editor's direction.

BRIEF BIBLIOGRAPHY

We are indicating here only those works which are the most important or the most recent. Those whose date is not preceded by any indication of place are published in Paris. We have excluded from this bibliography articles published in revues. The reader may consult them principally in the following revues : *Art d'Aujourd'hui, Cahiers d'Art, Cimaise, XXᵉ siècle.*

GENERAL WORKS

Consult the brief bibliography in the first volume *Twentieth Century Painters; Nabis, Fauves, Cubists.*

THE ADVANCEMENT OF NAIVE PAINTING

1) GENERAL WORKS

CATALOGUE OF THE EXHIBITION *Les Maîtres populaires de la Réalité*, 1937.

JAKOVSKY, Anatole
   La Peinture naïve, 1949.
   Les Peintres naïfs, 1956.

UHDE, Wilhelm
   Cinq maîtres primitifs, 1949.

2) MONOGRAPHS

BODMER-BING, H.
   Camille Bombois, 1951.

CATTON-RICH, Daniel
   Henri Rousseau, New York, 1942 (2nd edition, 1946).

GAUTHIER, Maximilien
   André Bauchant, 1943.

JAKOVSKY, Anatole
   Louis Vivin, 1953.

PERRUCHOT, Henri
   Le Douanier Rousseau, 1957.

THE REALISTIC REACTION
AND ITS CONSEQUENCES

1) GENERAL WORKS

ASSAILLY, Gisèle d'
   Avec les peintres de la réalité poétique, 1949.

2) MONOGRAPHS

ALAZARD, Jean
   Céria, 1930.
   Christian Caillard, 1948.

ALLARD, Roger
   Luc-Albert Moreau, 1920.

AUBERTY, Jacqueline, and ADHÉMAR, Jean
   Henri de Waroquier, 1951.

CARCO, Francis
   Asselin et son œuvre, 1924.

CHAMPIGNEULLE, Bernard
   Chapelain-Midy, 1944.

DESCARGUES, Pierre
   Jean Aujame, 1949.

DUNOYER DE SEGONZAC, André
   Boussingault, 1944.

FARGUE, Léon-Paul
   Vingt dessins de nus de Henri de Waroquier, 1946.

FELS, Florent
   Jules Cavaillès, 1943.

GAUTHIER, Maximilien
   Constantin Terechkovitch, 1948.

GRANOFF, Katia
   Bouche, 1956.

HEYD, Richard
   Brianchon, Neuchâtel, 1954.

JAMOT, Paul
   Dunoyer de Segonzac, 1929 (2nd edition, 1941).

LAPRADE, Jacques de
   Roger Limouse, 1943.

MAC-ORLAN, Pierre
   André Planson, Geneva, 1954.

RENÉ-JEAN
   Raymond Legueult, 1943.

REY, Robert
   Paul-Elie Gernez, 1947.

ROGER-MARX, Claude
   Dunoyer de Segonzac, 1951.
   Roland Oudot, Geneva, 1952.

ZAHAR, Marcel
   Maurice Brianchon, Geneva, 1949.
   Jacques Despierre, 1950.

THE REACTION OF IRRATIONAL FORCES
THE PAINTERS OF ANGUISH

ALAZARD, Jean
Amédée de La Patellière, Geneva, 1953.

ALLARD, Roger
Yves Alix et son œuvre, 1944.

BESSON, Georges
Charles Walch, Souillac-Mulhouse, 1947.

BOURET, Jean
François Desnoyer, 1944.

BRABANT, G.-P.
André Marchand, 1954.

DIEHL, Gaston
Edouard Gœrg, 1947.

DORIVAL, Bernard
François Desnoyer, 1943.

GAY, Paul
Notre ami Charles Walch, Saint-Jeoire-en-Fau-cigny, 1949.

GROMAIRE, François
Marcel Gromaire, 1949.

REY, Robert
Robert Humblot, 1957.
Georges Rohner, 1957.

SZITTYA, Émile
Soutine et son temps, 1955.

WHEELER, Monroe
Soutine, New York, 1950.

THE REACTION OF IRRATIONAL FORCES
PAINTERS OF THE FANTASTIC

1) GENERAL WORKS
BARR, Alfred H. Jr.
Fantastic Art, Dada, Surrealism, New York, 1936 (3rd edition, 1947).

2) On CHAGALL
LASSAIGNE, Jacques
Chagall, 1957.

SWEENEY, James John
Marc Chagall, New York, 1946.

VENTURI, Lionello
Chagall, Geneva, 1956.

3) On CHIRICO
FALDI, G.
Giorgi di Chirico, Venice, 1949.

SOBY, James Thrall
Giorgio di Chirico, New York.

4) On DADA
HUGNET, Georges
L'Aventure Dada, 1957.

5) On SURREALISM
BOUQUET, Joë, and TAPIÉ, Michel
Max Ernst, 1950.

BRETON, André
Manifeste du Surréalisme, Poisson soluble, 1924.
Le Surréalisme et la Peinture, 1928.
Second manifeste du Surréalisme, 1930.

BRETON, André, and DUCHAMP, Marcel
Le Surréalisme en 1947, 1947.

DICTIONNAIRE ABRÉGÉ DU SURRÉALISME, 1938.

GREENBERG, C.
Miró, New York, 1948.

LEIRIS, Michel, and LIMBOUR, Georges
André Masson et son univers, Geneva, 1947.

NADEAU, Maurice
Histoire du Surréalisme, 1945.

PRÉVERT, Jacques, and RIBEMONT-DESSAIGNES, Georges
Joan Miró, 1956.

SOBY, James Thrall
Salvador Dali, New York, 1946.
Yves Tanguy, New York, 1955.

WYSS, D.
Der Surrealismus, Heidelberg, 1950.

THE CONTINUATION OF PURE PAINTING

1) On PURISM
OZENFANT, Amédée, and JEANNERET, Ch.-E.
Après le Cubisme, 1918.

2) On HERBIN
HERBIN, Auguste
L'Art non figuratif, non objectif, 1949.

MASSAT, René
Auguste Herbin, 1953.

3) On BISSIÈRE
FOUCHET, Max-Pol
Bissière, 1955.

THE AWAKENING OF AVANT-GARDE PAINTING

1) GENERAL WORKS
COURTHION, Pierre
Peintres d'Aujourd'hui, Geneva, 1952.

LEBEL, Robert
Premier bilan de l'art actuel, 1937-1953, 1953.

2) MONOGRAPHS
BAZAINE, Jean
Notes sur la peinture d'Aujourd'hui (2nd edition, 1953.)

CAYROL, Jean
  Manessier, 1955.
FRANCASTEL, Pierre
  Estève, 1956.
LEFÈVRE, Henri
  Pignon, 1956.
LESCURE, Jean
  Lapicque, 1956.
MAEGHT, Aimé
  Bazaine, 1954.

THE FIGURATIVE REACTION

1) GENERAL WORKS
LEBEL, Robert
  Premier bilan de l'art actuel, 1937-1953, 1953.

2) MONOGRAPHS
BOURET, Jean
  Vinay, 1952.
BOURET, Jean
  Joseph Pressmane, 1952.
BOURET, Jean, DEVOLUY, John, and AUDUT,
  Jean-Pierre
  Bernard Lorjou, 1950.
CHEVALIER, Denys
  Clavé, 1951.
  André Minaux, 1949.
DESCARGUES, Pierre
  Rebeyrolle, 1951.
  Bernard Buffet, 1952.
  Paul Aizpiri, 1952.
LIMBOUR, Georges
  L'Art brut de Jean Dubuffet, 1953.
PAULHAN, Jean
  Fautrier, l'enragé, 1949.
RAGON, Michel
  Fautrier, 1957.

THE ABSTRACT REACTION

1) SOURCES
ESTIENNE, Charles
  L'Art abstrait est-il un académisme ? 1950.
VAN GINDERTAEL, Roger, and ALVARD, Julien
  Témoignages pour l'art abstrait, 1951.
LAPOUJADE, Robert
  Les Mécanismes de la fascination, 1955.
RAGON, Michel
  Expression et non-figuration, 1951.
REY, Robert
  Contre l'Art abstrait, 1957.

ROGER-MARX, Claude
  Avant la destruction d'un monde, 1947.
TAPIÉ, Michel
  Un Art autre, 1952.
ZAHAR, Marcel
  Le Désordre dans l'art contemporain, 1950.
WATELIN, J.
  La Peinture moderne en délire, 1957.

2) GENERAL WORKS
BOURET, Jean
  L'Art abstrait, 1957.
BRION, Marcel
  L'Art abstrait, 1956.
JUIN, Hubert
  Seize peintres de la jeune école de Paris, 1956.
LEBEL, Robert
  Premier bilan de l'art actuel, 1937-1953, 1953.
RAGON, Michel
  L'Aventure de l'art abstrait, 1956.
SEUPHOR, Michel
  *L'Art abstrait, ses origines, ses premiers
  maîtres*, 1949.
  Dictionnaire de la peinture abstraite, 1957.

3) MONOGRAPHS
DESCARGUES, Pierre
  Piaubert, 1952.
  Jean Dewasne, 1952.
DEWASNE, Jean
  Vasarély, 1952.
DUTHUIT, Georges
  Nicolas de Staël, 1950.
VAN GINDERTAEL, Roger
  Nicolas de Staël, 1951.
JEANSON, Francis
  Lapoujade, Brussels, *no date*.
LECUIRE, Pierre
  Voir Nicolas de Staël, 1953.
LOEB, Pierre
  Kallos, Brussels, *no date*.
RAGON, Michel
  Poliakoff, 1956.
ROUSSEAU, Madeleine, SWEENEY, James John,
  DOMNICK, Ottomar
  Hans Hartung, Stuttgart, *no date*.
ROY, Claude
  Zao Wou Ki, 1957.
SOLIER, René de
  Vieira da Silva, 1956.
  Bernard Dufour, Brussels, *no date*.
VERDET, André
  Atlan, 1956.

ALPHABETICAL INDEX

179

180

TABLE OF CONTENTS